Dancing Shadows of Bali

T0347288

Dancing Shadows
of Bali

Theatre and Myth

Angela Hobart

Routledge
Taylor & Francis Group

LONDON AND NEW YORK

First published in 1987 by
Kegan Paul International

This edition first published in 2010 by
Routledge
2 Park Square, Milton Park, Abingdon, Oxon, OX14 4RN

Simultaneously published in the USA and Canada
by Routledge
711 Third Avenue, New York, NY 10017

Routledge is an imprint of the Taylor & Francis Group, an informa business

British Library Cataloguing in Publication Data
A catalogue record for this book is available from the British Library

ISBN 13: 978-0-7103-0108-6 (hbk)
ISBN13: 978-0-415-86525-8 (pbk)

Publisher's Note
The publisher has gone to great lengths to ensure the quality of this reprint
but points out that some imperfections in the original copies may be
apparent. The publisher has made every effort to contact original copyright
holders and would welcome correspondence from those they have been
unable to trace.

To the Balinese

Contents

Preface

This book began in Bali during 1970–72, when I was there doing research for my Ph.D. on the shadow theatre for the School of Oriental and African Studies in London. However, two subsequent trips to Bali in 1980 and 1984, when I studied other forms of dance-drama and ritual, greatly contributed to the work. The first and longer of these trips in 1980 was financed by a grant from the British Academy. This support is gratefully acknowledged.

My fieldwork took place in south Bali. During my stay there I lived in a village, Tegallalang, in Gianyar, which lies somewhat inland from the commercial, and increasingly also tourist, routes towards the coast. At first I conducted my research in Indonesian, but later in Balinese which I initially learnt with Dr Hooykaas. During my times on the island, I witnessed numerous dance-drama performances in Gianyar, Badung, Klungkung and Bangli, and my study focuses on these regencies, in particular that of Gianyar. These reputedly belong to the heartland of Balinese culture which was exposed to Indo-Javanese culture in the past. Perhaps it is because of this that theatre in the area reached a high degree of sophistication and aesthetic competence. There are also frequent performances of the different theatre genres in the bigger villages.

The shadow theatre is a magnificent field of study as the Balinese hold it in high esteem and enjoy talking about it. Even the humblest of villagers is aware of the rich symbolic content of the puppets' iconography and the people, in daily life, often refer to the characters in the plays or episodes in the stories. The theatre has also profoundly affected the other arts. One needs only to enter a temple or palace to see statues or reliefs based on puppet imagery. Yet there are few works on the subject in Bali, perhaps because of the complexity of the language spoken during the performance. Important works worth citing are by Sugriwa (1963) on its philosophical aspects, McPhee (1966 and 1970) on the music, Hooykaas (1973b) on its religious background, and Hinzler (1981) on the *Bima Swarga* story in the shadow theatre. Hinzler requires special mention. Her fieldwork is rather more recent than mine, and her first short introductory book (1975) and her subsequent work includes observations on the different puppet styles and performances in various parts of the island, including the north. Here, in an area comprising about 17 per cent of the population, there seems to be a distinct variant form of the shadow play. At times Hinzler's information differs from mine, but this would seem likely when a dramatic art has been largely transmitted orally from one generation to the next.

So many people helped me during the course of my fieldwork and afterwards that there are too many for all to be mentioned individually. I thank them all. Outside of Bali I would like to express my special gratitude to the late Dr Hooykaas whose cultural and linguistic knowledge was invaluable and who taught me so much on Bali. I also thank Anthony Christie for his help during various stages of the Ph.D. and for his patience as I was beginning my studies. I am also grateful to Professor John Middleton for his penetrating comments on parts of my thesis. I thank Mark Hobart for the photographs that he took in the field, a number of which appear in the book, and for his assistance during the first research trip. Later, after my thesis was completed, I still benefitted considerably academically from two years of anthropological study at the London School of Economics and Political Science. Here I owe a particular intellectual debt to Alfred Gell and Jonathan Parry.

However, my greatest thanks must go to my Balinese friends and research assistants, who include a number of specialists in the field of dance-drama. A special place is reserved for the late Cokorda Gedé Agung Sukawati for his unfailing kindness and hospitality. I am also grateful to the now deceased I Gusti Bagus Sugriwa, who attempted to improve my Balinese and who explained aspects of the shadow theatre, and to I Gusti Ngurah Bagus, the head of the Anthropology Department at the Universitas Udayana, for his warm friendship and support during the past years. I thank I Wayan Raos, who was a puppeteer, *dalang* – though he rarely performed – and an exceptionally good puppet craftsman, for producing the beautiful drawings of the iconographic parts of the puppets on the medium of paper which to him was unusual. These give an idea of the richness of the icono-graphic tradition. Copies of these are included in the book.

My special thanks though go to three Balinese without whom this book could not have been written: I Ewer, Anak Agung Oka and I Ketut Kacir. *Dalang* I Ewer is one of the most learned *dalangs* left on the island. He started chanting sessions of texts (*mekakawin*) in my hamlet which the elders in the community were always eager to attend. During these he read and translated the *Adiparwa*, the first volume of the *Mahabharata*, which he insisted was a requisite background for anyone wishing to do research on the shadow theatre. This, together with his comments on the characters and episodes in the epic, gave me an invaluable framework through which to understand the subject. With him I watched my first shadow play performances which were sometimes given in remote villages in the mountains. I remember walking carefully along winding paths together with his musicians and assistants to the place where he intended to perform. Gathered in rhythms of silence, we wandered through dark rice fields and across narrow bamboo bridges, under which streams leapt over ferns and rocks, with the starlit sky above, and fireflies dancing in front of us. In the past Anak Agung Oka had frequently acted in operetta, the masked dance and contemporary drama. He was also one of the operetta teachers of greatest repute in my area. His favourite role had been that of *wijil* in operetta, the younger servant, known for his verbal fluency and insight into other characters and situations on the stage. He was delightful to work with as he was a fountain of local wisdom, while he could not desist from cracking continual jokes during the discussions. Finally, I thank I Ketut Kacir, my *juru raos*, my spokesman and mediator, as he aptly called himself, who accompanied me to dance-drama specialists and performances, which he helped tape-record and transcribe. With lucidity, humour and patience he taught me about Balinese society and culture.

A note on Balinese language and spelling

The spelling of Balinese follows the official Indonesian system intro-duced in 1972. Pronunciation is straightforward apart from 'c', which is 'ch' as 'chair'. It is also convenient to distinguish 'è' and 'é', as in French, from 'e' the central vowel.

Where possible I have translated indigenous terms by their rough English equivalents. As will emerge, the shadow theatre is far more than a simple puppet play. Hence it is appropriate to keep two terms in the vernacular: *dalang*, puppeteer or shadow play performer; and *wayang*, puppet, or dramatic performance.

The Balinese language is complicated by the existence of a number of speech levels (Kersten, 1970, pp. 13–25). Where relevant the different levels are distinguished, but otherwise the forms given are those appropriate for the subject. In my area of research, in south Bali, the main distinction is between the high language, *basa alus*, which is refined speech and is used for that which is pure and elevated; ordinary Balinese, *basa biasa*, which is used to inferiors and between common villagers. Below this there is coarse speech, *basa kasar*, which is polluting and used for animals or deliberate insults. Refinement also connotes distance and so the ordinary speech may indicate familiarity in a high-caste family.

1

Introduction and setting

In this book the shadow theatre in Bali is described and its place in the society and culture explored. It is so called, as during the night performance puppets cast vibrant shadows against a white cotton screen which is illuminated by a flickering coconut-oil lamp. The lamp hangs over a cross-legged puppeteer, or *dalang*, who is sitting in an enclosed, raised booth, facing the screen and at arm's length from it (see p. 129). The *dalang* is also one of the consecrated priests in the community. He manipulates the puppets while narrating a story from the sacred classical literature, so bringing to life mythic beings of both the natural and supernatural worlds. Musicians, who sit behind him in the booth, accompany the story with the clear, sweet tones of a small percussion orchestra. Through the rhythms of the shadows, the spectators on the other side of the screen from the puppeteer are drawn into other ways of seeing, or comprehending reality.

The shadow theatre exists, or has existed in the past, in a fairly defined strip of territory extending from China in the east, to Turkey and western Europe in the west. The island of Bali in Indonesia is unique in this context as it, more than any other area outside India, has retained strong ties with its Hindu heritage, yet extraneous influences – including ones from Chinese, Islamic and, more recently, European sources – have been subtly blended with an indigenous tradition to form a distinctive culture. The shadow theatre is deeply embedded in the social and religious life of the people and is among the most important and evocative vehicles of this culture which it reflects and helps create.

The study concentrates on four main aspects of the theatre: the mythology, the iconography, the performance and its social and cultural significance. Chapter 1 gives a background description of Balinese society and culture, which includes an introduction to the puppeteer, the *dalang*, then, in Chapter 2 the mythology which forms the basis of the plots is examined. Most of the characters are derived from the great Hindu epics, the *Mahabharata* and *Ramayana*. Mention is here also made to the servants who appear in the oral literature and are not found in the epics. While numerous individuals flit across the screen during a performance, the four main male servants are in some ways the most important actors on the stage.

Chapter 3 is an account of the puppets, their craftsmanship and symbolism. The puppets are flat cut-outs of hide, delicately chiselled and painted according to precise traditional regulations. While, in general, the puppets represent characters from the epics, they also form a self-contained symbolic system which sustains a select pattern of meanings relating to the villagers' daily life.

The symbolic system, however, only gains efficacy in the performance for it is only here that the actors, the puppets, 'wake up' and 'dance' (Chapter 4). Each play takes place in a ritual setting and is a contrivance of great complexity combining varied dramatic stimuli of light, movement, voice, speech and music which are ingeniously woven together by the *dalang* to produce a rich and intricate theatrical fabric. At the same time, the screen acts like a threshold across which the gods are said to communicate to men.

There is, in fact, another type of performance, which has hardly been touched on by scholars. It is usually given during the day with the same flat puppets, but without a screen. Because it engenders little dramatic interest few spectators watch it. It takes place as one of a complex of rites in an area marked off spatially from everyday life in a household or temple. Chapter 4 also describes this type of performance.

Finally, in Chapter 5, the significance of both types of performance, the one dramatized at night and the other given during the day, is analysed. Both types of performance can be viewed as a unit which asserts a link, among other things, to the world as a cosmic unity and the sense of change and stillness in life. The religious nature of the theatre and its connection with morality emerge in this chapter. Here the relationship of the theatre to the other arts is also discussed as it has profoundly affected them. It is the most esteemed and conservative theatre form and hence its dramatic and aesthetic principles link it to the other dance-dramas, statues, reliefs and traditional painting. Of these the shadow play is regarded as the original form. Through these various manifestations the villager is able to probe and analyse his assumptions of self, in a world which is increasingly affected by modern trends, while retaining his human dignity.

Numerous works have appeared on myth, symbolism and ritual. Durkheim, who was one of the earliest scholars to study myth and ritual, which he saw as two sides of the same coin, wrote in 1915 on the traditional mythology of a society:

> .... the mythology of a group is the system of beliefs common to this group. The traditions whose memory it perpetuates express the way in which society represents man and the world; it is a moral system and a cosmology as well as a history. (1976, p. 375)

For the scholar, both ritual and myth were part of the religious system and had the same function: to express and maintain social solidarity. Rarely, though, have the issues of myth and symbolism been discussed as linked components in theatre set within a ritual context where they acquire special force, giving meaning to experience, both collective and individual. While a number of detailed works specifically on the shadow theatre in South East Asia and India exist, these tend to concentrate on its literary, historical, philosophical or artistic aspects. The focus has also tended to be on Java where it is often associated with the court.

The shadow theatre in Bali, in contrast to its counterpart on Java, belongs predominantly to the folk tradition and expresses values which are essentially a product of the community as a whole. It is interesting that the people initially take an almost Durkheimian stance when describing the genre, drawing attention to the ethical values dramatized by the stories. In this role it is also seen as offering the spectators an integrated scheme for living and a design for selfhood and personal identity. However, the night performance is clearly more than just a didactic vehicle. Each show, if skilfully performed, is a work of art with aesthetic appeal which stimulates and entertains a crowd of villagers. At the same time, the shadow theatre possesses something of the sacred seriousness of classical Greek theatre. Like the performers of antiquity, the *dalang* is believed to be divinely inspired while on the stage, and so empowered to reveal a transcendental world or higher truth.

A number of scholars have influenced my approach in the book. Apart from Durkheim, Lévi-Strauss, Victor Turner, and Susanne Langer deserve singling out. However, above all I have been guided by the Balinese themselves. They are primarily interested in the individual performance as an event, brought to life by a particular *dalang*. This applies especially to the night performance; less so to the one given during the day as it does not set out to communicate to humans. The villagers, who watch the former type of performance, are highly critical of the *dalang*'s technique in moving the puppets, his voice, his ability in creating and recreating the narrative, and his expertise in co-ordinating all the dramatic elements. In fact I witnessed one night performance where the villagers walked off in disgust after half an hour and the show petered to an unsuccessful end, the *dalang* returning home shamefaced. He had tried to mingle episodes from both the *Mahabharata* and *Ramayana*, but had failed to produce a coherent story which entertained. The villagers, moreover, pointed out that it was inappropriate to mix incidents derived from both epics in a single play. The audience also found fault with his voice which was harsh and rasping. That *dalang* has never again, to my knowledge, been asked to perform in that village.

An outsider's interpretation, taking in both the structuralist and semiotic perspectives, as well as the performance, is still necessary. I tend, however, to stress the latter aspect. Only by adopting such an approach can the wealth of data and indigenous information on the subject of dance-drama, and the shadow theatre in particular, be analysed. It then emerges that the shadow play is a unique vehicle for disseminating the Indian epics, although these are ingeniously modified and adapted to fit the Balinese context. Further the principles underlying the shadow theatre can then be explored and their similarities or differences to those of the other art forms investigated. Ultimately, it is essential to see the shadow theatre in the light of the whole society, as part of the fabric of the life of the villagers, rather than as a separate and isolated activity.

Balinese society and culture

Bali is a small, fertile island, covering about 5,620 square kilometres. It lies just south of the Equator, to the east of Java and to the west of Lombok, but separated from them by dangerous waters (Map 1). As such it is one of the many islands comprising the Indonesian Archipelago. Because of its ecological affinities with Java, it is generally included within the tropical rain forest of central South East Asia. The backbone of the island consists of a chain of volcanoes, the highest of which is Gunung Agung to the east, rising over 3,000 metres. Set within the volcanoes are large crater lakes which are the

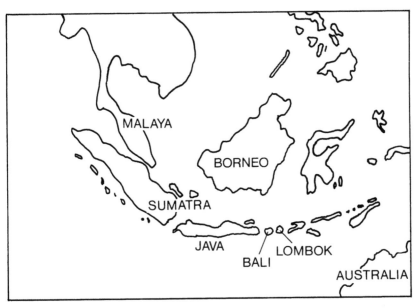

Map 1.1   South East Asia

Map 1.2   Bali

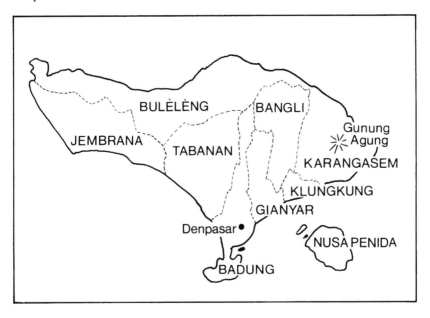

main source of water for the island. Over two million people live in Bali, the bulk of whom are concentrated on the gently sloping plains of the southern part of the island. This region with its rich soils is intersected by numerous streams and rivers which flow down the mountains, cutting deep into the soft volcanic rock. The tightly clustered villages or hamlets (*banjar*) are often perched on top of ridges, surrounded by terraced rice-fields. They are linked to one another by paths or roads which more or less follow the courses of the streams from the interior to the coast, cross-cut by others from east to west, which are breached at regular intervals by gorges fanning out from the mountains.

Traditionally Bali contained some eight kingdoms. The most eastern of these, Karangasem, had strong links with Lombok, where Balinese immigrants colonized the indigenous Sasak people. The kingdoms were governed by aristocratic families under the titular overlordship of a king, *raja*. Regions within the kingdoms were ruled over by princes or aristocrats who often lived in elegant courts, *puri*, possessed extensive agricultural estates and kept many retainers. After the conquest of south Bali by the Dutch in 1908, the power of the indigenous rulers was gradually curtailed, first by the establishment of the colonial administration and then by the Indonesian Reform Laws in 1960. Since 1970, however, there have been further changes in the structure of the administration and the island now forms one province of the state of Indonesia government and the former kingdoms have become regencies or local administrative centres (*kebupatèn*) (Map 2). The capital of the island is Denpasar.

According to tradition the heartland of Balinese culture is in the south – in Gianyar, Bangli and Klungkung. This was the region most exposed to early Indo-Javanese influences, and it is here that the old court capitals flourished: first Pèjèng, then Gelgel and Klungkung. The ruler of Klungkung, the Déwa Agung (literally the Supreme King), was nominally the sovereign of the whole island until its colonization by the Dutch. Even today, the precedence of the regent of Klungkung over the other princes is reflected in his title.

Balinese social structure is complex. It is noted for its stratification into ranked descent groups, or *wangsa* (peoples): Brahmanas, Satriyas, Wèsyas and Sudras, according to an ideology similar to the Indian caste system, with spiritual and temporal power being distinguished between the Brahmanas and Satriyas respectively. While Wèsyas in India are often merchants, in Bali they are subsumed effectively under the Satriyas. Further, while the castes above and below them are relatively stable, the Wèsyas are involved in intense competition to achieve upward mobility. The three high castes are said to be descended from aristocrats who came over from the great Hindu Javanese kingdom of Majapahit when it fell at the end of the fifteenth century AD to the onslaught of Islamized coastal sultanates. The Sudras, or *jaba*, literally outsiders to the court, as they are commonly called, in contrast to the *jèro*, the insiders, or princes, comprise 90 per cent of the population and are for the most part peasants (Plate 1).

At the same time, the Balinese possess a complementary system which cuts across the hierarchical structure and which emphasizes the equality of men. This is apparent in the hamlet council (*balé banjar*), a partly autonomous unit in the government's administration, which organizes most collective work in the community, such as rice harvesting, rituals in specified temples or the renovation of public buildings. The people also participate on an equal basis in the field of art. Today, actors and spectators of all castes mingle with ease at performances.

The Balinese have a peasant economy based on irrigated rice culti-vation where water is adequate. Elsewhere they may depend on dry crops and small-scale husbandry of pigs and cattle. The island is predominantly rural. Settlements vary from isolated hamlets to large residential complexes comprising a number of hamlets, with popu-lations ranging from two hundred to several thousand inhabitants. The hamlets are formally ruled by princes who claim the status of Satriya. To most Balinese their hamlet is their most important com-munity, apart from kinsmen, and it is where the majority of peasants live and die.

A standard hamlet consists of family compounds (*kuren*) arranged around a central square at the intersection of the two main avenues, running from north to south (or from 'mountain' to 'sea') and east to west. Each compound is made up of a number of pavilions and the entire plot of land on which each compound stands is enclosed by a white-washed mud or brick wall in order to make a sharp distinction between private and public life. Most communal activities, such as the meeting of the hamlet council, the market, cockfights and dance-drama shows, take place at the central square which is also the main area where villagers congregate in the evening to discuss daily matters or to gossip.

Each compound is made up of one or more households who all share the same kitchen and worship at the same household temple dedicated to the gods and paternally related ancestors. Residence in the compound is based on a type of patrilineal descent (or 'patrifiliation' as dyadic and not linear connections are emphasized; Geertz, 1975, p. 47). So a son inherits property and position in his father's patriline. Marriages are verilocal, with women marrying into the compound. Although polygamy is practised, it is rare nowadays, except in some wealthy or high-caste families.

Religion

The Balinese are a Malayo-Polynesian people, practising a variant form of Hinduism. Indian culture and Hinduism seem to have infiltrated the island from Java after the eleventh century. Events before then are unclear. Apart from the Hindu trinity of Brahma, Wisnu and Siwa, a great number of gods belong to the Balinese pantheon of gods. On a more abstract level they are seen as manifestations of a higher truth, a transcendental spiritual unity or world order, now generally called Sang Hyang Widi (*sang* and *hyang* designate the divine, the more-than-human, while *widi*, from the Sanskrit *widhi*, means order, law; see Swellengrebel, 1960, p. 52). As well as the gods, the deified ancestors, or *leluhur*, are worshipped. Conceptually they are placed in the same sublime category as the gods, so it is not surprising that the Hindu god Siwa and the common progenitor may both be referred to as Batara Guru, literally Lord Teacher.

There are many kinds of ritual practitioners in the society. The most high-ranking are Brahmana priests, *padanda*. There are two kinds of these *padanda*: Siwaite (*padanda* Siwa) and Buddhist priests (*padanda* Boda), with the former in the majority. They largely differ in their ritual practices although they officiate in the same temples and both offer daily devotion to Siwa in his aspect as sun god Surya, whereby union is sought with him (Hooykaas, 1973a, p. 14). These rites are of little concern to the Sudras, the low castes, who mainly rely on the Brahmana priests for the holy water, *tirta*, that they prepare. In fact, as purification by holy water is so important in Balinese religion, the people have been known to call it *agama tirta*, the religion of holy water (*ibid.*, p. 11). Lower-ranking ritual practitioners include the village priest, the *jèro mangku*, who is non-Brahmana, the indigenous medical practitioner, the *balian*, a type of exorcist priest, the *sengguhu*, and the puppeteer, or *dalang*.

Balinese folk religion is communal, ritualistic and aesthetic. Rituals, which occur frequently throughout the island, are colourful, elaborate and involve lengthy preparation of strictly prescribed offerings to the gods as well as the demons, or *buta*. The most common occasion for a grand religious festival is the anniversary of a temple, *odalan*, which takes place every two hundred and ten days of the Hindu Balinese *wuku* calendar.[1] As there are over 20,000 temples on the island (Plate 2), such festivals are frequent. Ideally, every local religious community (*désa adat* – a community which has residual rights over traditional residential land and which is internally divided into several hamlets)[2] has at least three great temples, collectively called *kahyangan tiga*. They include the village origin-temple, *pura pusèh* (*pura* means temple; *pusèh* navel) dedicated to the depersonalized ancestors of the present inhabitants of the community; *pura balé agung* (which is sometimes part of the *pura pusèh*), the temple of the great assembly hall, which is well suited for village meetings; and *pura dalem*, usually translated in the literature as temple of the dead, located near the cremation grounds. In addition, there are temples of irrigation, descent group temples, temples for specific geographical sites and the six great temples, *sadkahyangan*, to which the mother temple of Bali, Besakih belongs. Besakih, with its steep, simple terraces and dark wooden shrines (*méru*) with sober pagoda-like roofs, is situated on the sacred volcano Gunung Agung, which is figuratively at the centre of the island. During the anniversary of a temple, both the Brahmana priest and the village priest sprinkle the congregation with holy water in order to 'cleanse' them spiritually. Purification through sanctified water occurs during all rituals and is considered by the villagers to be a crucial aspect of their religion.

During these temple festivals dances and dramas are performed and gamelan orchestras play. Of these the shadow theatre is the most venerated because of its deep religious significance. The plays serve as a source of distinctive conceptions about man's relationships to his fellow beings and to the natural and cultural world.

Background to the shadow theatre

An historical perspective

Indonesia has a rich and complex dance-drama tradition. While its roots probably go back to prehistoric times, before the Christian era, the classical forms of the shadow theatre, *wayang kulit*, the masked dance, *topèng*, and dance drama, *wayang wong*, only developed during the period that Hindu culture penetrated the islands from about AD 200 to AD 1000. *Wayang kulit* is probably the most refined and complex of these. In Bali *wayang kulit* refers to two types of performance given with puppets: the night *wayang* and the day *wayang*. The term *wayang* means 'shadow' and refers to either the puppets or, in a wider sense, to a dramatic performance (whether with puppets or human actors) and will be used as such here; *kulit* is leather or hide and indicates the flat puppets cut out of hide.

It is not my aim to explore the origin of *wayang kulit* in Indonesia (for a summary of the arguments, see Holt, 1967, pp. 129-131). Scholars have basically three opinions on its origin: that it derives from India, China or is an indigenous invention. The first view is perhaps the most widely held. It should be noted in this context that, while it is generally conceded that other areas in South East Asia owe their shadow theatre to Java (*ibid.*, p. 130), they too have at some time in their history been under the influence of Indian culture.

It is of interest here to observe that the Balinese, like the Javanese, ultimately see the play as stemming from the gods. The myth of its origin is told in the palm-leaf manuscripts, *Siwagama*, and is summed up as follows:

> The god Siwa and his wife, Uma, were cursed and sent to earth in the form of demons. Uma became Durga and bore numerous demon children by Siwa, all of whom were misshapen. In order to placate the demons and restore Siwa and Uma to their previous forms, the gods Brahma, Wisnu and Iswara decided to give a *wayang kulit* performance on earth. Iswara became the puppeteer, or *dalang*, Brahma the lamp and Wisnu the musical instruments. Offerings were also made for the demons. Initially the three gods had no success in their mission. They then repeated the performance and also gave a masked dance. Finally, Siwa and Uma heeded the message imparted by the shows and were restored to their former beauty.[3]

The earliest reference to what may be *wayang kulit* in Indonesia is to a performance called *wayang* from a stone inscription in central Java, dated 906 (*ibid.*, p. 128). In Bali in the eleventh century, the royal inscription, *Prasasti Anak Wungçu* mentions *topèng*, a masked dance, and *wayang*, i.e. a *wayang* performance, being given for the king. Although it is not definite that the term refers to *wayang kulit*, the possibility exists.[4] It seems that some time between the eleventh and fourteenth centuries AD *wayang kulit* came from Java to Bali. Dynastic marriages first linked the islands in the eleventh century (Stutterheim, 1935, p. 14). Indo-Javanese influences later reached Bali through a series of conquests; after the fall of the east Javanese kingdom of Majapahit, scholars, priests and aristocrats fled to Bali to find refuge there, bringing with them their classical literary manuscripts (Swellengrebel, 1960, pp. 21-23; Hall, 1966, p. 82). The Balinese in general say that *wayang kulit* came over during the period of Majapahit (*c.* thirteenth to fifteenth centuries AD).

While Balinese and Javanese shadow theatres are related, it is clear that they have developed separately and so almost no reference is made to Java in the subsequent chapters. Javanese puppets evolved into their extremely stylized forms during the last three centuries, perhaps as a result of the Islamic proscription of image-making (Holt, 1967, p. 135; Brandon, 1970, pp. 6–7). It is, however, largely during the eighteenth and twentieth centuries that *wayang kulit* developed in Java under court patronage into a sophisticated theatre genre which came to have a special meaning for the élite, *prijaji* (Geertz, 1960, pp. 269–78), that was not accessible to the common man. This, for example, is evident in the story of *Bima Suci* (*Bima Purified*) which is still performed on certain occasions. As the late Sultan Mangkunagara VII of Surakarta (1895–1944) pointed out, prince Bima in this myth searches for the 'waters of immortality', i.e. his 'spiritual self' in the depth of the ocean, 'the world filled with light and no shadows' (1957, p. 18). The sultan further explained that the aim of such stories is 'to dare to lift a small tip of the veil to show how in *wayang* performance, lies hidden the secret knowledge concerning the deepest significance of life' (*ibid.*, p. 1). The élite used these stories in order to elaborate salvation doctrines which helped them to escape from the mundane world through *semadi*, meditation, and become one with the Absolute.

Wayang stories dramatized in Bali do not seek to illustrate salvation doctrines for the high castes (see *Bima Suci*, p. 32–3). The style of the puppets also reflects the rustic nature of this theatre genre. The puppets have a lingering affinity with figures on reliefs of east Javanese temples dating from between the thirteenth and fourteenth centuries, i.e. Jago or Panataran (Kats 1923, pp. 2–3; Holt 1967, p. 135), being sturdier and more naturalistic than the stylized, often ornate Javanese puppets.

The first outsider who described the Balinese *wayang kulit* at some length was Chinkah, a Siamese master of a junk which landed in Bali in 1846 (trans. Charnit, 1969, pp. 83–122). The king of Klungkung gave a performance for him. This royal gesture can be seen within an historical context for the aristocrats were the traditional patrons of the arts and they undoubtedly stimulated their development. They were also instrumental in linking the arts to the village sphere (Stutterheim, 1935, p. 7; Geertz, 1970, p. 103). However, over the years the classical tradition, stemming from the royal courts, and the little or folk tradition have intertwined to form a distinctive, colourful culture which is Balinese.

Occasions of a *wayang* performance

The occasions when *wayang kulit* is performed emphasizes how intimately it is bound up with the religious life of the villagers. This close link between religion and theatre also occurred in the ancient world and is reflected in the Greek word drama: as Harrison (1912) pointed out it is derived from *dromenon*, religious ritual, literally 'things done'. It is only relatively recently in the West that a dramatic performance has become predominantly a secular event given primarily as entertainment to an urban élite.

Before describing the occasions when *wayang* is performed it is essential to distinguish between two types of performance: *wayang peteng*, the night performance (*peteng*, night and dark) and *wayang lemah*, the day performance (*lemah*, day and light), as they are usually called.[5] When considered together, they also highlight the proximity which exists on the island between theatre and ritual.

The night and day *wayang* are related by the fact that in both a *dalang* moves puppets and narrates a story from the sacred classical literature. However, their orientation is entirely different. The former, while it entails ritual elements, is clearly a form of theatre which provides entertainment for the villagers. The term 'theatre' is from the Greek *theasthai* meaning 'to view' or 'to see', i.e. implying a show that is given with the intent of communicating to an audience, most of whom in the night *wayang* watch the shadows of puppets projected on to a screen for a period of about three to five hours. The day *wayang*, which is enacted without a screen, is dramatically unexciting. Yet it has a much higher status than the night *wayang*. While it is terminologically and conceptually performed during the day, the play may also take place at dusk or even night. It is essentially one of a complex of rites given in a household or temple to an audience, but in this case an invisible one, i.e. the gods and not men. So, unlike the night *wayang*, the human audience is unimportant in the day *wayang*. Despite controversy as to its meaning, I am defining rite or ritual here (following Lewis, 1976, p. 130; Turner, 1982, p. 79) as prescribed formal actions, which have reference to invisible beings or powers in whose efficacy the people believe, as this definition corresponds to how the Balinese interpret their ritual behaviour.

A standard night performance, *wayang peteng*, is given voluntarily either on behalf of a community or a household. It is usually chosen by a *dalang*, in consultation with a priest, to fall on an auspicious day of the year.

The most frequent occasion for a performance is during the anniversary, *odalan*, of a temple every two hundred and ten days, when it is paid for by the temple congregation. Throughout the island it is customary to have a form of entertainment on each of the three final days of an anniversary. These range from dance-drama without masks, masked dance, operetta, pure dance and contemporary drama to the shadow theatre. *Wayang kulit* is often chosen for one of the nights as it is cheaper than the other theatre genres which require a troupe of actors or dancers. Moreover, the plays are thought fitting as they have moral and religious content, and so are in accordance with a festival in which the gods are entreated to descend to reside in the temple for a few days.

The night *wayang* may also be performed in conjunction with a 'thanksgiving' or a 'vow', *mesangi*. On this occasion a sponsor, in fulfilment of a vow, shows his gratitude to the gods for granting him a request by giving a performance. Typical requests include having one's child restored to health, recovering a valuable lost object, or having a good harvest after a drought.

A performance may also take place during the celebration of a domestic event such as marriage or birth in a high-caste or well-to-do Sudra household. The sponsor, who then of course finances the *wayang*, hires a *dalang* to give a show, partly for its own sake, but also because it enhances his own prestige in the eyes of the community since it indicates respect and awareness of traditional culture, as well as being a display of wealth.

There are two further instances of night *wayang* which require special mention. The first is a *wayang*, dramatizing the myth of the witch Calon Arang. Although very rare, it is said sometimes to be performed in order to test the supernatural power, *kesaktian*, of the *dalang* (a process known as *uji dalang*). In passing, it is worth pointing out that *wayang Calon Arang* can be viewed as part of the system of social control, because during the play the witches in the area, or *léyak*, are said to be exposed on the stage to the public and so rendered harmless.[6]

The other type, *wayang sudamala*, has a more prominent role in society. *Sudamala* connotes the destruction of physical ailments or deformities (Hooykaas, 1973b, p. 158). The main occasion for a *wayang sudamala* (also called *wayang Sapuh Lègèr*) is for a child born during the week of Tumpek Wayang, which occurs every thirty weeks in the Hindu-Balinese year.[7] Such a child is believed to be prone to illness or injury from the demon-god, Kala, and demons. In order to protect him

25

from their influence the *dalang* first narrates a special myth about Kala (see p. 39) and then, with the help of certain high-ranking puppets, carries out the *sudamala* rite during which he makes purificatory water, *toya penglukatan* (see pp. 135–37).[8] This is given to the child to drink with the aim of purifying him so that no danger can beset him.

The *sudamala* rite, together with a *wayang* (irrespective of whether it is the night or day *wayang*), is also essential for a person who died unnaturally, i.e. by accident (*salah patih*). A *dalang* may perform the same rite for cremation or to ensure the health of a family member – but the dramatic performance is then optional. Attention has already been drawn to the importance the Balinese place on spiritual 'cleansing' through holy water, and the *sudamala* rite exemplifies the purificatory power the puppets may possess.

The day performance, *wayang lemah*, is more closely tied to the religious life of the people than the night *wayang*. Hence it plays an integral part in the five ritual cycles, *panca-yadnya* (Hooykaas, 1975, pp. 246–259), and must be seen in connection with them. They comprise life-cycle rites, *manusa-yadnya*; rites for the dead, *pitra-yadnya*; rites for gods, *déwa-yadnya*; rites for demons, *buta-yadnya*; and a somewhat obscure cycle of rites for priests, *resi-yadnya*. My informants considered the day *wayang* obligatory for certain of these ritual occasions (this tallies with my own experience; cf. Hinzler, 1981, p. 22, who points out that *wayang* is only compulsory for a child born in Tumpek Wayang and for an unnatural death, although it is still the preferred choice on other occasions). It is always performed at the same time that a Brahmana priest recites his litany.

Rites of passage take place within the sphere of the family. They mark basic turning points in life involving changes in the social status of individuals. The day *wayang* usually takes place on the following occasions in the courts or the houses of Brahmanas: the ritual performed on the 105th day after the birth of a child (*tigang odalan*), upon which it attains a normal state and may enter temples, or for subsequent birthdays (*oton jumu* or *oton*); tooth-filing (*mepandas*); and marriage (*mekerab*). The performance is rarely given in a Sudra family. It is not required and would merely add to the cost of the event.

Rites for the dead are numerous and complex, involving both burial and cremation. The aim is to purify the soul of the dead person so that it can become a deified ancestor worshipped in the household shrine. In a high-caste family the day *wayang* is performed for cremation (*pelebon*) and possibly for additional occasions of purification (*ngasti, meligya* and *ngeluwèr*). It is also performed for village burials (*ngabèn*), held about once every ten years.

The rites associated with the anniversary of a temple are splendidly decorative. A day *wayang* is one of a complex series of rites carried out in all temples for the anniversary.

Once a year the ritual *nyepi* is given to the demons in order to chase them away from the island. This takes place on the main crossroads in local village communities. A day *wayang* is performed on this occasion. Sometimes a loud orchestra accompanies the *wayang* which is supposed to frighten away the demons.

Apart from the above cycle of rites, the day *wayang* is often performed during the ceremony of consecration of a new temple or after extensive repairs (*melaspasin*). The day *wayang* is also performed after the birth of twins of the opposite sex (*anak kembar buncing*) to a Sudra family. Such an event, while an auspicious sign in a high-caste family, is a great misfortune for Sudras; as a result, the entire hamlet becomes impure. Purificatory rites, including the day *wayang*, have then to be carried out.

A final point worth noting in regard to the day *wayang* is that the stories enacted always fit the occasion for reasons which will be discussed in Chapters 2 and 5.

The dalang

The *dalang* is the central figure behind every play (plate 3). He is its director, creator and sole narrator, and manipulates all the puppets. In folk etymology *dalang* is derived from *galang*, bright or clear (van Eck, 1876), the implication being that the *dalang* is a man who makes clear the sacred classical literature. In his role as *dalang* – as a man of knowledge and a recognized ritual practitioner – he has an honoured place in the community. Hence he is also given the honorary title of *jèro*,[9] (insider) if low caste, and *amangku*[10] (associated with *mangku* or *pamangku* implying a priestly role), if high caste.

Dalangs are always male. Table 1 gives an idea of the distribution of *dalangs* in relation to the population in four of the seven subdistricts (*kecamatan*) in the regency of Gianyar (in 1972); it also shows their caste and the type of performance they give. (Hinzler, 1981, pp. 45–6, in her overall, but less detailed survey of *dalangs* in Bali, estimates that there are 11 *dalangs* in Gianyar and 108 *dalangs* altogether on the island, out of which 72 are Sudras.) Although it is deemed fitting that *dalangs* are Brahmanas, as traditionally literary and religious matters are their prerogative, it is clear from surveys that the majority of *dalangs* are Sudras. For example, the best *dalangs* are said to come from

Table 1.1 Subdistricts in Gianyar where *dalangs* are known

Subdistrict:	Approx. pop. in 1972*	No. of *dalangs*	No. of persons per *dalang*	No. of *dalangs* performing w.l. only	No. of *dalangs* performing w.l. & w.p.	Castes		
						Brah.	S/W	Sudra
Tegallalang	29,006	15	1,934	4	11		1	14
Tampaksiring	26,657	10	2,666	2	8	2	4	4
Ubud	31,414	7	4,496	3	4	2		5
Sukawati	40,827	13	3,141	2	11	1	1	11
					Total	5	6	34

Notes

w.l.: *wayang lemah* (day performance)
w.p.: *wayang peteng* (night performance)
Brah.: Brahmana
S.: Satriya
W.: Wesya

* The population figures were obtained from the local administrative offices of the respective subdistricts.

Sukawati. At the time of my research, there were thirteen *dalangs* of repute in this village. Out of these eleven were Sudras and only two high caste.

Dalangs, by the time that they actively perform, are either married or widowers. This is in line with the importance attached to being married and having offspring in Bali. In fact in myths those without descendants are severely punished by ogres in the hereafter. Often they are hung upside down from a tree and then harshly beaten. In view of the above it is appropriate that only married people are allowed to participate in the village council. Wives of *dalangs* help make offerings for the rites associated with the night or day *wayang*. Otherwise they are not involved in this genre of theatre which essentially belongs to the sphere of the men (see p. 126, 185).

Dalangs may be very mobile – well-known ones travel great distances to perform the night *wayang*. Yet *dalangs* in southern Bali can rarely live off their art. Even the most popular *dalang* is not likely to give more than five to twelve night *wayangs* in a month. In 1972 the fee for a performance was between 7,000 and 20,000 Rp., depending on his reputation.[11] In 1984 a performance could cost up to about 50,000 Rp. The fee is divided between the *dalang*, the musicians and his assistants. The *dalang* receives the largest share – about 50 per cent, the musicians 40 per cent and the assistants 10 per cent. A *dalang* can of course earn substantially more if he performs for tourists, yet there are very few performances for them. (The main tourist dances are the masked dance, *topèng*, the monkey dance, *kècak*, and the dance between the witch Rangda and the mythical lion, *barong*.) Day *wayangs* take place more often than ones at night as they are necessary for domestic and temple rituals, but the financial reward, from between 2,000–6,000 Rp., is minimal. The primary occupation of most *dalangs* is rice cultivation.

While in theory anyone may become a *dalang*, the rôle commonly descends within the patriline. Sometimes two sons become *dalangs*. They then share the puppet-chest between them. A puppet-chest is a necessity for a *dalang* and is a family heirloom (*pusaka*). It is difficult and expensive to obtain otherwise. Most young *dalangs*, however, do not feel courageous enough to perform until the older member of the family has died or has granted them permission to do so. It is thought disrespectful to give a *wayang* if a member of the senior generation is still able and willing to perform.

Apart from becoming a *dalang* because the art is hereditary, other motives stimulate an individual to assume this role. It is an outlet for someone with a creative urge and dramatic sense. It is also a means of obtaining knowledge of the classical literature. This was especially important in the past, before the arrival of the Dutch, when there was little formal education. To become a *dalang* is. also a way of gaining respect from the villagers – although this may fluctuate and depends on the *dalang*'s skill, his learning and his general standing in the community. *Dalangs* themselves say that an individual can only become a good *dalang* if the gods so wish it.

There is no special school in Bali for *dalangs*, although nowadays classes on the subject of *wayang kulit* are held at the conservatory in Denpasar. The main teachers of an aspiring *dalang* are his older relatives. It is rare, though, that a *dalang* learns everything from one source. A novice may join an ensemble of musicians or be accepted as a pupil of a *dalang* of repute. As a teacher receives no fixed payment, a pupil gives him occasional presents and assists him generally. A novice also learns from observing different *dalangs* or even famous actors in dance-dramas. From them he may pick up jokes, witty sayings or songs, which he can intersperse with the lines of his play.

One eminent *dalang* listed for me the following requirements of an accomplished *dalang*:

1 *uning Dharma Pawayangan* (to know the *Dharma Pawayangan*): to have an understanding of the mystic treatise, the *Dharma Pawayangan* or 'Laws of the *wayang*'. This contains the philosophical background of *wayang kulit*, religious incantations for the puppets and for the different performances (excluding the day *wayang*) and rules for the conduct of a *dalang*.

2 *uning satua* (to know myths): these stem from the classical literature and form the basis of the plots.

3 *uning mebasa* (to know the language): mastery of the different speech levels appropriate to the status of each figure (see preface on language).

4 *uning megamel* (to know how to play the musical instruments, in particular the *gendèr*): to obtain knowledge of the music. This is important as in the performance the music and narration must be co-ordinated to create a rhythmic, melodic background to the play.

5 *uning sesolahan wayang* (to know the dance of the puppets): to know how to move the puppets elegantly and gracefully.

6 *uning raos wayang* (to know the voices of the puppets): to know how to vary pitch and vocal quality in order to express the characters in the play and to indicate their sentiments towards others.

7 *nyusup pikayunan ring wayang* (to project thoughts into the puppets): to identify completely with the characters and so bring them to life.

8 *mesikang pemineh* (to unify the thought): to concentrate exclusively on the myth and so unfold it in an appealing way.

9 *mangda kereng raos* (to have a strong voice): to have stamina to talk for several hours.

10 *uning mekakawin* (to know how to chant the classical texts): implying knowledge of Old Javanese, or *kawi*, and the different metrical forms.

11 *uning ngeletekan keropak* (to know when to tap the puppet-chest): to know how to tap correctly with the gavel which is held between the toes of the right foot, and punctuate the speeches (*raos angsel*). Energetic tapping always accompanies battle scenes.

12 *uning mekarya penyelah* (to know how to embellish). This occurs mainly in the sub-plots and includes:
   a. *sebet ngai-ngai*: to work up sadness in the audience.
   b. *nyasin satua*: to ornament the myth by describing the characters and situations eloquently, with lyricism and charm.
   c. *mekarya bebanyolan*: to make jokes and humorous puns.
   d. *uning sesohangan*: to know proverbs.

13 *uning indik kesaktian* (to understand supernatural power): behind this statement is the implication of having contact with supernatural power, *kesaktian*, which can be obtained from the gods, in particular the goddess Durga (p. 47). It is important to have contact with this power as major characters in the plays are said to manifest it when in battle.

Dalangs vary considerably in the standard of scholarship they attain, largely due to the fact that the training is highly individual. *Dalangs*, however, point out that the most essential aspect of their learning is to gain an understanding of the *Dharma Pawayangan* (Hooykaas, 1973b). All are acquainted with the religious incantations, or *mantras*, in the treatise, even if in a garbled version.

Essentially there are two types of *dalang*. There are those who are primarily skilled performers and whose dramas the predominantly low-caste audience enjoys. *Dalangs* of the second type, while they may also be able performers, are mainly renowned as scholars. They have a deep understanding of the philosophical background of *wayang kulit*, are well versed in the classical literature and know Old Javanese. Courts often establish close connections with these *dalangs* and, irrespective of their caste, become their patrons. Such *dalangs* then attend

31

study clubs at the court, or sometimes their own homes, where the classical literature is chanted and interpreted (see p. 37).

However, during a play, all *dalangs*, regardless of their literary knowledge, improvise extensively on the outline of a plot derived from the classics. One such outline is included here. The myth is called *Bima Suci* (*Bima Purified*), mentioned earlier in the context of Java where it may be dramatized for the elite as a doctrine of salvation. This story is also popular in Bali, but here it retains a rustic, down-to-earth flavour, befitting an art form which essentially belongs to the village domain. Although there are different versions of the myth, this particular one entails all the elements the villagers consider necessary for the idiom of *wayang*: it is interesting, exciting and possesses religious and ethical elements that can be creatively expanded during the actual drama.

Bima Suci (as narrated by the late *dalang* I Badra, from Tegallalang, Gianyar)

The Brahmana priest, Drona, requested the prince, Bima, the tempestuous second Pandawa brother, to go into the forest in order to fetch the holy water, *tirta kemandalu*[12] known for its great purificatory powers. Drona deliberately lied to Bima as to the whereabouts of the holy water as he hoped that the mighty prince would be killed by ogres in the forest.

Once in the forest, Bima was indeed attacked by a fierce ogre, but he slit its throat with his long thumb-nails, *waspenek*. As the soul of the ogre departed from earth, it took on the form of the god Indra. Indra paid homage to the prince and asked his forgiveness for having attacked him. Bima, though, pointed out that it was not proper for a god to ask forgiveness from a mortal. Bima then brought the ogre's head back to the horrified priest who told him the true whereabouts of the holy water – in the middle of the ocean.

When Bima arrived at the shore of the ocean where the holy water was to be found, large snakes approached him intending to eat him, but he cut off their heads. As he continued into the waters he met his death. The heavens became dark and swayed in sorrow for the brave prince. The supreme god, Tunggal, had compassion on Bima, whom he dearly loved because of his honesty and brought him back to life. He then told Bima that if he wished to obtain the holy water he would have to enter his (the god's) body as it was kept there. Bima was amazed as in front of him he saw a tiny figure who was a replica of himself.

The prince first asked the god several questions. Why did man have to die? Why did man dream? What was the purest thing in the world? The god Tunggal replied as follows. Death takes place at a certain stage in man's life when the gods have left the body. When man dreams his soul leaves the

Plate 1 Ploughing the rice fields

Plate 2 Pura Tanah Lot, temple off the coast of Tabanan

Plate 3 *Dalang* I Ewer in his household temple,
dressed up ready to perform

Plate 4 Narada

Plate 5 Tunggal

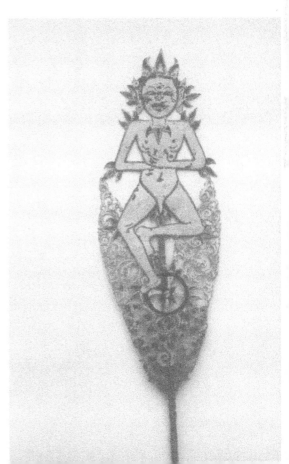

Plate 6 Wisnumurti

Plate 7   Bima

body and wanders around. Nothing on earth is perfect. Apart from the god of love, Semara, all the gods are still impure. Even the flowers used for worshipping are not completely pure.

Having answered Bima's questions, Tunggal spread apart his legs and told the prince to enter his body through the phallus. When Bima entered he found himself in heaven and the holy water was stored there in a gold casket in a five-tiered shrine. He took the casket and returned home.

His family rejoiced when they saw Bima as they thought he had been killed. Bima then offered the casket to Drona, who, though, did not believe it contained holy water and flung it away. At that moment Tunggal entered Bima's body and Bima cursed Drona who became seriously ill. The priest cried bitterly and begged Bima's forgiveness for his actions. Bima did not think it fitting that his former teacher should ask his pardon and forgave him.

It is of interest that, consonant with Balinese religion, this myth emphasizes the importance of holy water. It also highlights the *dalang*'s role as teacher and priest. In the first, he illuminates through his narration ethical values characteristic of his culture; for example in *Bima Suci*, the focus is on Prince Bima's strength, bravery, single-mindedness and above all honesty – all qualities admired especially by adult males in the society. In his second role he directs the attention of the villagers to the sphere of the gods.

As one of the ritual practitioners in the community (p. 20), the *dalang* must be consecrated. This ritual is necessary for everyone who has a religious rôle on the island. It is optional for sculptors, painters, dancers and musicians. There are two forms of rite: the lesser is consecration with flowers, *mewinten bunga*, and the greater, which is the standard form, *mewinten ageng*, or great consecration. A village priest or even just a specialist in the making of offerings (*tukang banten*) suffices for the first, while a Brahmana priest is required for the second. Most *dalangs* and all village priests undergo the larger consecration. It is preferred because it is believed to confer greater purity on the candidate. A *dalang* is consecrated either in the priest's household temple or his own.

A *dalang* can also be consecrated together with his puppet chest. A Brahmana priest carries out this rite, appropriately called *mesakapan*, meaning 'to marry'. This is performed after a chest is bought or taken over from a member of the mother's family, a distant relative in the patriline, or from someone who is not a member of the family. It may also be performed when a *dalang* wishes to give *wayang sudamala* or *wayang Calon Arang*, when he needs to have special command over supernatural power (cf. Hinzler, 1981, p. 43).

The *dalang*'s priestly role is clearly stated in a passage from the treatise *Dharma Pawayangan* (Hooykaas, 1973b, p. 19):

> The Enlightened *Dalang* incorporates the earth, ogres and the Gods.
>
> His other name is 'Leader' for he is Siwa, Sada-Siwa, Parama-Siwa (manifestations of the supreme god)[13] and the Unfathomable God.
>
> For 'Tintya' ('he who cannot be imagined' in Sanskrit) is the unification of all worlds; empowered he chooses his position.
>
> Thus is the origin of Him who is called *dalang*; he is empowered to command speech.

However, the *dalang*'s role as teacher is as important as that of priest. Accordingly, he may sometimes be referred to as *siwan dalangé*, 'one who functions as a teacher' (van der Tuuk, 1897). Formerly there were three types of recognized teachers, or *gurus*. The father, or teacher of origin, *guru réka*, who is responsible for instructing and supervising his child so that he becomes an upright member of the community; the moral guardian and ruler, *guru wisésa*, whose job it is to guide his subjects; and finally the pedagogue, *guru pengajian*, who teaches the classical literature. The last group comprises both the Brahmana priest and the *dalang*. As already shown in the myth of *Bima Suci*, the *dalang* takes select moral precepts contained in the texts, which he then illustrates and elaborates in the performance. This emerges vividly in the night *wayang* when the myths are adapted to fit the social context of the villagers. It is then that the stories are also sprinkled with bawdy jokes and spicy sayings in order to entertain young and old alike.

Conclusion

In passing it is of interest to look for a moment at the resemblance which exists between the *dalang* and the shaman. The *dalang*, like the shaman, is considered an inspired priest while performing, who has knowledge of the three realms of sky, earth and underworld, and is able to mediate between them. Although he may not actually experience a state of altered consciousness or be a 'technician of ecstasy', as Mircea Eliade (1964, p. 4) has termed this religious specialist, he, too, is a 'master of the spirits' in the sense that he can become at will a mouthpiece of the gods during his narration. This is expressed by Balinese *dalangs* in the following words: if an individual is not 'inspired by the gods', *metaksu*, (which is derived from *taksu*, the shrine in a *dalang*'s household temple dedicated to his special god, Iswara, who is said to act as an interpreter for the other gods), he cannot become a *dalang*. In his role as *dalang*, as will emerge more clearly later, he contributes to the spiritual and moral welfare of the community; at the same time he provides entertainment for the villagers. It is important, though, to realize that he combines most of his roles as priest, visionary, poet, teacher, performer and entertainer while on the stage. On infrequent occasions he may also act as healer. This comes to the fore when he makes special holy water which is given to children born in the week of Tumpek Wayang in order to purify them so that the demon-god Kala can no longer threaten them. During daily life, the *dalang* is generally treated like any other peasant who usually works in the fields for his living; this is of course especially true if, like most *dalangs*, he is a Sudra.

However, unlike the majority of shamans, a *dalang* does not dance. He is remote and, for all intents and purposes, invisible to most of the audience (when in his booth during the night *wayang*) who watch the puppets 'dance'. It is they who bring to life the mythic world of *wayang* for contemplation by others.

Notes

1 There are two main ways of reckoning the year in Bali: the *wuku* year, based on the numerical computation of a set of current weeks (*wuku*) ranging in length from 1 to 10 days, in which the three most important weeks of 5, 6 and 7 days define a 210-day cycle; and the Hindu system of 12 solar-lunar months (Goris, 1960, p. 116).

2 The Balinese social system is best considered as a complex pattern of cross-cutting, but not territorially discrete, social groupings. Of these the *désa adat* and its congregation is the most important religious grouping. Other groupings include the hamlet, irrigation associations, patrilineal descent groups and voluntary organizations (Geertz, 1975).

3 This myth is derived from the manuscript *Siwagama* (Hinzler, 1975, pp. 11–2). A similar myth can be found in the *Tantu Panggelaran*, written between 1500 and 1635 (Holt, 1967, p. 287).

4 This was personally communicated by Doctor Atmojo Sukarto.

5 The night and day *wayang* are sometimes also referred to as *wayang wengi* (*wengi*, night) and *wayang gedog* (*gedog*, chest) respectively.

6 *Wayang Calon Arang* is outside the scope of this book; nor did I witness it. It is sufficient to note here that women marrying into the compounds of related males may be accused of being witches and are often held responsible for illness or trouble in the family.

7   Special days in the *wuku* year are devoted to certain things which play an important part in daily life, such as coconut palms, domestic animals, keris, musical instruments and so forth. The Tumpek week is the last of the 7-day weeks in the year.

8   Purificatory water is also made by Brahmana priests and village priests, but it must be the *dalang* who makes this water for a child born during the Tumpek week.

9   *Jèro* is a title of respect. It is also used to refer to a village priest, *jèro mangku*, or a low-caste woman who has married a high-caste man.

10 According to Hooykaas (1973a, p. 14) only a *dalang* who makes purificatory water and performs the day *wayang* is given the honorary title of *amangku dalang*. This is also the formal title of the *dalang* in the treatise *Dharma Pawayangan* 1973b (p. 6). Hinzler (1975 p. 29) points out that *jèro* and *mangku* are mainly used in the north. This does not correspond to my experience: high-caste *dalangs* were only addressed as *mangku* or *amangku*.

11 In 1972 the currency value was: £1 = Rp. 1,000 (Rupiah); $1 = Rp. 420 (Rupiah).

12 *Tirta kemandalu* is one of the holy waters a Brahmana priest prepáres. It is needed for the death ritual (Hooykaas, 1973a, p. 10). *Dalangs* equate it with *amerta*, the elixir of immortality.

13 According to the doctrine of *Siwasiddanta*, the supreme god manifests himself in gradations. He comes from the sphere of the inconceivable and immaterial to the sphere of the material via an intermediary stage that partakes of both. The forms in which he reveals himself are Parama-Siwa, Sada-Siwa and Siwa. In his most earthly manifestation as Siwa he is one of the Hindu trinity. This doctrine took root in Bali, but it is rarely referred to by the villagers (Swellengrebel, 1960, p. 62; Pott, 1966, p. 125).

2

The literary basis of the shadow theatre

In the shadow theatre a large number of myths are disseminated and perpetuated. Most of these are derived from the Hindu-Javanese classical literature which flourished at the courts of East Java from between the tenth and the fifteenth centuries. Indigenous non-Hindu texts, composed in subsequent centuries in Bali, may also be drawn on, but these are rarely, if at all, enacted nowadays.

These myths are written down in palm-leaf manuscripts, *lontar*, in *kawi* (Old Javanese). Most such manuscripts are kept in the homes of Brahmanas (*geriya*) or at the courts of Satriyas. The classical literature is highly esteemed in Bali as it is thought to preserve in the sacred language of the gods (*kawi*) eternally valid truths over time and space. While the texts are essentially an inheritance of the past, they still play an active role in the society. They are studied in so-called *bebasan* clubs, which comprise about ten male members who meet once or twice a week (Robson, 1972, pp. 309–29). Here one man recites the text and another paraphrases it (*mekakawin*) while the others listen. *Dalangs* often participate in such clubs, especially if in their neighbourhood.

Although *dalangs*, as already mentioned, vary considerably in their knowledge of the texts, these provide a mythological framework to the performance. This is of course reinforced by the puppets, most of which represent mythic characters from the classical literature. O'Flaherty, in discussing Indian myths, eloquently writes that they

> force us to speculate not only about the relationships between our mental perception of the world and its mental perception of us but about the relationship between our dreams of God and God's dream of us (1984, p. 304).

In the context of Balinese *wayang*, it is myths pertaining to the *Mahabharata* in particular which allow such speculation to arise, as well as alluding to intricate moral, political and social issues which have repercussions in this world and the next. It is therefore unsurprising'that these myths are the most popular on the island and frequently performed. Because of this, the focus in this chapter and subsequent ones is on the *Mahabharata* and characters who derive from it, although other important ones are included. First, however, there is a survey of the different repertoires into which *wayang* is divided.

The repertoire

The Balinese divide *wayang* into different repertoires which are based on the subject-matter of the plays.

Wayang parwa

The repertoire is primarily drawn from the *Mahabharata*. Until recently only eight of the eighteen volumes or *parwas*, of this epic were known in Indonesia (see summaries in Zoetmulder, 1974, pp. 68–100). Lately one more has been added (Hinzler, 1981, p. 29)[1]. The earliest surviving versions of the *parwas* are in Old Javanese prose, but they show their proximity to the Sanskrit by direct Sanskrit quotations scattered through the text (Zoetmulder, 1974, p. 68). The four earliest *parwas*, which include the important first volume of the epic, the *Adiparwa*, were composed around the tenth century (*ibid.*, p. 96).

The central theme of the *parwas* is the tragic conflict between two families of the Kuru clan, the Pandawas and Korawas. The quarrel culminates in the great war, the Bratayuda (Bharatayuddha), in which the five Pandawa brothers confront their first cousins, the one hundred Korawa brothers. After eighteen days of terrible fighting, in which thousands of men are killed, the Pandawas emerge as victors and the eldest Pandawa brother, Yudistira, succeeds as heir to the throne of Nastina. The heroes of most of the myths are one or more of the Pandawa brothers – the gentle Yudistira, the strong and brave Bima, the noble and comely Arjuna, and their younger twins, Nakula and Sahadéwa.

There are a number of other Old Javanese poems which are reckoned to belong to the *parwa* cycle. The best known of these are

Cantakaparwa, Bima Swarga, Sutasoma (a story of Buddhist origin), *Sudamala* and its sequel *Sri Tanjung, Arjunawiwaha, Bima Suci* (also called *Déwaruci* or *Nawaruci*), *Bomantaka* and *Bratayuda* (for *Cantakaparwa*, see Ensink, 1967; for *Bima Swarga*, see Stutterheim, 1956, and Hinzler, 1981; the other poems are summarized in Zoetmulder, 1974).

Most of these poems are indirectly linked to the *parwas* as they recount adventures which relate to the same characters. Plays drawn from this cycle are by far the most numerous in Bali.

Wayang Ramayana

This repertoire is drawn from Old Javanese and Balinese versions of the *Ramayana* and *Uttarakanda* which resembles in language and style the *Mahabharata*, although it is considered the last part of the former epic (for summaries, see *ibid.*, pp. 83–7 and 217–26). The *Ramayana*, dating from the early part of the tenth century, is perhaps the oldest poem composed in central Java. It is based on a derivative form of the Sanskrit epic ascribed to Walmiki (*ibid.*, p. 231).

The myths tell of the abduction of the beautiful Sita by the demon-king, Rawana. Her husband, Rama, finally retrieves her with the help of monkey armies led by the monkey god, Hanuman.

Plays based on this cycle are infrequently dramatized. The myths are less complex than those from the *parwa* cycle and less popular, focusing mainly on the battles between the monkeys and Rawana's supporters. Moreover, few puppet collections include the puppets needed for *wayang Ramayana* (i.e. all the requisite monkeys) and only few *dalangs* specialize in the repertoire. The plays are also expensive as the orchestra requires about ten men, whereas plays from *wayang parwa* have at the most four musicians.

Wayang sudamala (or Wayang Sapuh Lègèr)

The plays are based on the prose text *Kala Purana* (or *Japa Kala*; in Balinese *Capa Kala*) or the Balinese poem *Sapuh Lègèr* (Hooykaas, 1973b, pp. 159–315).

The myth tells of the demon-god Kala (a wrathful emanation of Siwa) who threatens to devour the twin brothers born in the week of Tumpek Wayang. The *dalang* Empu Lègèr conquers Kala by staging a *wayang* performance and carrying out a rite of exorcism afterwards.

The myth is only dramatized for children born in the week of Tumpek Wayang in Bali and the *sudamala* rite always follows, thereby spiritually purifying the child.

Wayang Calon Arang

The plays are derived from the myth of Calon Arang, the widow (Rangda) from Girah. Old Javanese and Balinese versions of the myth exist in both prose and poetry (Zoetmulder, 1974, p. 436).

Calon Arang is a powerful witch. Because of her evil reputation her daughter, Ratna Manggali, is unable to find a husband, as men are terrified of her mother. In fury, Calon Arang sends plague and destruction throughout the land, before a holy man, Mpu Barada, manages to convert her to good.

This myth is rarely dramatized because during the play dangerous supernatural powers are said to be released which may harm the *dalang*. Special puppets representing witches are used during the play in addition to the standard ones.

Wayang Cupak

The myth, which originated in Bali (Pigeaud, 1967, p. 211), tells of two brothers, the coarse, gluttonous Cupak and the refined Grantang, who vie with each other in the quest to retrieve the stolen Javanese princess, Radèn Galuh. After numerous adventures, it is Grantang who succeeds in marrying the princess, not his elder brother.

The story used to be popular in the south, but is no longer performed.

Wayang gambuh

The myths belonging to this cycle are derived from the Javanese-Balinese Panji romances composed in Old Javanese and Balinese. They tell of the east Javanese prince, Panji, and his many adventures while searching for his beloved princess.

A special set of puppets resembling the stylized Javanese puppets, is required for *wayang gambuh*. Myths from this cycle seem no longer to be performed (Hinzler, 1981, p. 30; and confirmed by my informants).

Wayang Sasak

The repertoire is based on *Serat Menak*, an Islamic tale from east Java, which tells of the prince Jayengrana and his battle against hostile rulers.

The cycle is only known in Lombok and in the east of Bali, Karangasem (*ibid.*, p. 32).

The *Adiparwa* in relation to the shadow theatre

The *Adiparwa* is the first book and prelude to the *Mahabharata*. *Dalangs* agree that it is the core of the epic. It is generally considered the most sacred text of the classical literature and so *dalangs* often draw on it when narrating in the day *wayang* which has a higher standing than the night *wayang* (p. 24). In the Javanese and Balinese versions, the *Adiparwa* contains numerous myths, many of which are concerned with the creation of the world and the gods of the Hindu pantheon and their counterparts, the demons and ogres, the *détia, buta* and *raksasa*. The book also recounts the origin of the Pandawas and how the Pandawas and their cousins, the Korawas, are raised together at the court of Nastina. In it the seeds are sown for the bitter feud between the cousins which culminates in the great war.

The following myths[2] are given in some detail as they provide essential information to the subsequent discursive variations produced in the performances. This is especially true of the myths telling of the origin of the Pandawa brothers and the circumstances surrounding their birth and those of their cousins, the Korawas, as at least one of these princes appears in most *wayang parwa* plays. These myths are rarely, if ever, dramatized in the night *wayang* (although they may be narrated in the day *wayang*), for they are not so much concerned with the pursuits of humans as with explaining the circumstances relating to the ancestry of main aristocrats and priests (see also kinship diagrams, p. 58–61). Comments by *dalangs* on the myths are added if relevant to the general understanding of the shadow theatre in Bali.

The origin of the Pandawa brothers and Drupadi

This is perhaps one of the most important myths in the *Adiparwa*, setting the scene for later developments concerning the Pandawas and Korawas. It recounts the story of the tournament held at the court of King Drupada for his daughter Drupadi. Although all five Pandawa brothers enter the contest in disguise, it is the regal third brother, Arjuna, who wins her hand. To the king's consternation, the brothers tell him they intend to share the princess between them, i.e. to make a polyandrous marriage. The sage Biasa then comes forward and leads Drupada to a deserted spot where he explains the circumstances regarding her birth and that it had already been decreed in heaven that she should become the wife of the five Pandawa brothers.

The events take place some time ago while the god Yama is making a sacrifice in the forest Naimisa in heaven. Earth is similar to heaven. There is peace and men do not become ill and die. The gods, however, are displeased as no difference is apparent between heaven and earth. Indra confronts Brahma and asks him why men do not suffer. Brahma tells him not to worry; once Yama finishes his sacrifice, men will grow old and die. The gods are happy to hear this and return with their consorts to their respective homes.

The god Indra is wandering along the river Ganges. Suddenly he sees golden lotuses drifting in the water. These suprise him and he follows them to their source. They lead him to a weeping girl. It is her tears, as they drop into the river, which become lotuses. Indra asks her to whom she is married and why she is weeping. She replies that she is the rice goddess, Sri, the wife of Wisnu. She is miserable as she has seen a couple on the peak of a mountain making love to one another and she is jealous of them. Sri asks Indra to have pity on her and to strike the couple with his weapon, the thunderbolt. Indra agrees to help her and accompanies her to the mountain.

The couple are Siwa and his wife, Uma, who have taken on human form. The moment that Indra tries to strike them, he is unable to move. He then becomes one with the mountain which divides into five parts, *panca-indera*. Each part emits the same amount of light. Siwa then orders each part to incarnate into a human; each is to be married on earth to Drupadi, who is an incarnation of Sri. In this way Siwa sentences Indra and Sri for their misconduct.

Having received his sentence, Indra goes to Wisnu and asks him to accompany him to earth so that he should have a friend there. It is because of these events that Kresna (an incarnation of Wisnu) and Baladéwa (an incarnation of Brahma) are born as brothers in the Yadu family. At the same time the *panca-indera* are incarnated as the five Pandawa brothers, whose genitors are the gods Darma, Bayu, Indra and the Aswins; and Sri is incarnated as Drupadi.

(cf. Widyatmanta *Adiparwa* II, 1958, pp. 88–90.)

Drupada, on hearing Biasa's words, is satisfied to have his daughter wed the five Pandawa brothers.

The birth of the Pandawa brothers

This myth tells how it came about that the genitors of the Pandawas are gods.

The king, Pandu, goes hunting in the forest with his two wives, Kunti and Madrim. There he sees a beautiful, small, white deer being courted by another deer. This is in fact the Brahmana Kindama who has become so enchanted with the small deer that he changes his appearance to follow her.

Pandu shoots at the two deer with his arrow. The Brahmana then reverts back to his human form and curses Pandu, saying that he has not the proper affection for animals, especially those in the process of courting. As a result the king will die if he has sexual intercourse.

(cf. *ibid.*, pp. 10–11.)

In great distress Pandu and his wives decide to remain in the forest to meditate. As the years pass, Pandu begins to long for children. Kunti then explains that she possesses a religious incantation, *mantra*, which enables her to summon the gods and bear children from them. The *mantra* was a gift from a Brahmana in return for food which she prepared for him. This way she bears three sons, Yudistira, Bima and Arjuna by the god of righteousness, Darma, the god of wind, Bayu, and the king of the gods, Indra. Kunti then presents the *mantra* to Pandu's second wife, Madrim, who summons the god, the Aswins, and in due course she gives birth to twin sons. After each birth a heavenly voice is heard saying the following about the boys:

> The eldest son is to be called Yudistira. He will have knowledge of the way of *darma* (duty and virtue). The second will be very *sakti*, supernaturally powerful. Indeed, just after he is born, a tiger approaches Kunti who rushes off, dropping the infant from her lap. The stones on which he falls break. Pandu, in admiration for his strong son, names him Bimaséna (implying he who is stronger than stone).
> The third child is to be called Arjuna as he will be as skilled in warfare as Arjuna Sahasrabahu (who kills the demon-king Dasamuka, see p. 49). He will possess a magical arrow (*pasopati*) and will be able to defeat all his enemies. Flowers rain down from the heavens and gamelan music is heard as the gods and celestial sages rejoice at Arjuna's birth.
> The twins, Nakula and Sahadéwa, will be wise and talented.

(cf. *ibid.*, pp. 16–19.)

Pandu dies soon afterwards as he transgresses the imposition laid down by the Brahmana and couples with his wife Madrim.

This myth should be taken in conjunction with the myth telling of the birth of the Korawas.

The birth of the Korawas

Gandari, the mother of the one hundred Korawas, is the wife of King Dastarastra, who rules the kingdom of Nastina jointly with his younger brother Pandu. Both brothers are in some way disabled:

Dastarastra is blind and Pandu is unable to have children. The following events lead to the birth of the Korawas.

> The Brahmana Biasa, having completed his period of meditation, goes to Queen Gandari in order to ask her for food. He is so pleased with the food that she prepares for him that he agrees to grant her any request. The queen asks for one hundred children.
>
> Gandari soon becomes pregnant, but remains so for two years. In the meantime Kunti gives birth to Yudistira. In grief at hearing this news, Gandari hits her stomach and out pours blood and she gives birth to one hundred pieces of flesh. Biasa, in fright at seeing this, instructs Gandari to mix the pieces of flesh with milk in a pot and to recite *mantras*. After ten months one hundred healthy sons emerge from the pot. Gandari then gives birth to one daughter. The birth of the eldest son, Duryodana, coincides with that of the second Pandawa boy, Bima, and hence they take a particularly violent dislike to one another.
>
> Although Yudistira is the first born of the Kuru clan Dastarastra points out that his own son Duryodana should be heir to the throne. At this point, the howling of dogs is heard from north, east, south and west. Widura, the younger brother of Dastarastra and Pandu, explains to Dastarastra that the howling is an omen indicating disaster and war were Duryodana to become king of Nastina. Dastarastra refuses to listen as he loves his children.
> (cf. *ibid.*, pp. 7–10.)

The birth of the priest Drona

Drona is one of the most important Brahmana priests in *parwa* plays. Yet events relating to his birth are inauspicious and indicate that eventually he will side with the Korawas in the great war.

> A beautiful heavenly nymph called Gertawira is playing at the same place where the sage Baradwaja is meditating. Suddenly a strong gust of wind blows open her dress which she tries quickly to secure. This is seen by the sage who has an ejaculation. His sperm settles in the rolled leaf of a corn plant. After some time has elapsed a child is born who is given the name of Drona.
> (cf. *ibid.*, p. 24)

The birth of the priest Krépa

Like Drona, the Brahmana priest Krépa eventually sides with the Korawas. His origin is also impure.

> The sage Gotama had one son called Saraduan who is born with a bow and arrow. One day Saraduan goes to meditate. Because of his steadfastness,

the god Indra becomes worried and decides to disrupt his meditation by subjecting him to temptation. So the goddess Yanapadi is sent to him. When Saraduan sees her bathing he is filled with longing for her. His semen enters the bow and eventually twins are born from it.

The king Santanu comes across the babies while hunting and he takes them to his court. The boy is called Krépa and the girl Krépi.

(cf. *ibid.*, p. 23)

In due course Krépi marries Drona.

Not all *dalangs* know the *Adiparwa* in great detail. Simple *dalangs* from isolated hamlets, may have limited knowledge of the texts and be unacquainted with the myths telling of the origin of the Pandawa brothers and Drupadi or of the events relating to the birth of Drona or Krépa. Yet all *dalangs* seem familiar with the myths describing the birth of the Pandawas and Korawas. *Dalangs* point out that the unnatural circumstances surrounding their birth are indicative of their superhuman qualities. Kunti bears sons by gods, and as a result they have noble and heroic characteristics and may also possess magical attributes or weapons. The very fact that Pandu has been cursed by a Brahmana for his lack of respect and affection for animals who are courting one another leaves the way open for Kunti to summon the gods. On the other hand, in line with Gandari's difficult pregnancy and the violent events connected with their birth, the Korawas are disruptive to harmony in the universe.

In Bali polyandry is frowned upon. Yet *dalangs* say that in Drupadi's case it was decreed by heaven and so human ethics do not apply. It is also of interest to note that some *dalangs* identify the *panca-indera* with the five senses, *panca-indriya*, hearing, feeling, sight, taste and smell. So the struggle between the Pandawas and Korawas may be given certain psychological overtones on the stage (p. 176).

A final point should be made about these myths. *Dalangs* may draw attention to the disabilities of the fathers of the Pandawas and Korawas as they point out that these have a bearing on the characters of the boys, irrespective of the fact that Pandu is only the social father of his sons. Dastarastra is born blind while Pandu, though unable to beget children, can see. Hence Dastarastra is born with a so-called dark body (referred to as *pawakan gelap*: *pawakan* is body; *gelap* is dark in Indonesian) or with the body of an ogre (*pawakan raksasa*). As a result his sons are associated with night or darkness and are all unenlightened. Pandu's sons, in contrast, are associated with daylight and virtue. So the Pandawas and Korawas signify respectively the two divisions of the cosmos, daylight (*lemah*) and darkness (*peteng*).

The interpretation given by *dalangs* of Pandu's and Dastarastra's defects shows the importance of the sense of sight in Bali. The full significance of this is discussed later (p. 183–84) as the implication of sight versus blindness can only be understood in the context of Balinese culture – it is not elaborated on in the texts.

Although only a few myths from the *Adiparwa* are included here, they provide relevant background information on the main protagonists in *wayang parwa*, before they actually appear on the stage. The *Adiparwa* continues to narrate events relating to the early lives of the Pandawas and Korawas and the ever-increasing animosity between them as they grow up at the court of Nastina. Bima , for example, often seizes the Korawas and throws them into the river. Duryodana, seeking his revenge on Bima, tries to make him drunk on *tuak*, rice wine, then ties a rope around him and flings him into the river. Duryodana also tries unsuccessfully to poison Bima. This increasingly bitter conflict leads to the great war, the Bratayuda, which is described in the *Bismaparwa* (which includes the *Bagawadgita*) and the poem *Bratayuda* (Zoetmulder, 1974, pp. 77–9, and pp. 256–63).

Main characters in the shadow theatre

This section briefly describes some of the main characters (Plates 4–18) represented by the puppets in a standard collection, which in the case of most *dalangs* is based on the *parwa* cycle. The focus is on the characters' dominant qualities and kinship ties (see p. 58–61). Although a collection can portray up to ninety individuals, minor ones with small rôles or ones not referred to later are not included in the survey. In a few instances *parwa* puppets can represent more than one important character (for reasons outlined in Chapter 3, p. 82–3). These may derive from texts other than the *Mahabharata*, such as the poems *Sutasoma* or *Ramayana*. Some of the more prominent of these individuals are also described here.

The synopses are largely based on the classical literature, although the indigenous tradition is referred to when relevant. The latter is especially important in the case of the servants who do not even enter the epics. A variety of sources are drawn on for the synopses. When the authoritative work on Old Javanese literature by Zoetmulder, *Kalangwan* (1974), is used, the text only is cited in brackets; other sources are given in full.[3] For the sake of clarity the characters are ordered alphabetically and according to their social category. In this way an overall picture can be gained of the wide range of characters embraced by a standard *parwa* collection. The implication of their kin emerges in the subsequent discussion.

The puppets illustrated here were originally owned by the ruler of the court of Peliatan. The court still safeguards the collection for the puppets are well over one hundred years old and in excellent condition.

Heavenly beings

Antaboga Snake god who lives in the seventh layer under the earth. His daughter Nagagini, marries Bima and their son is called Antaséna (Hardjowirogo, 1968, p. 29).

Bayu God of wind. He is the progenitor of Bima (*Adiparwa*).

Brahma God of fire who in Bali is associated with the unfavourable direction 'to the sea', *kelod*, and with the south in the nine-fold division of the cosmos, *nawa-sanga* (on directions see p. 105–6, 108). Although an important god, he rarely appears in plays.

Durga Wife of Siwa in her dread aspect. In Bali she is associated with the temple of the dead, more appropriately referred to as 'The Temple of Majesty' (whom one is afraid to call by name, i.e. Durga or Yama; Hooykaas, 1978, p. 937). She is able to grant supernatural power, *kesaktian* (see p. 119), to humans (cf. Weck, 1937, pp. 189–202). Durga has an important rôle in the poem *Sutasoma* when she teaches the prince Sutasoma how to destroy hostile forces (*Sutasoma*).

Gana Elephant god, son of Siwa and Uma. He defeats the demon Nilarudraka who is threatening heaven (*Smaradahana*). He is usually identified with Ganésa in Bali.

Narada (Plate 4) Heavenly sage (*resi*) who admonishes Duryodana into making peace with the Pandawas (*Udyogaparwa*). He meets Yudistira on his way to heaven after his reign on earth (*Swargarohanaparwa*).

Siwa Commonly also called Batara Guru, Lord Teacher, in Bali. He has a prominent place in Hindu-Balinese religion. In the five-fold and nine-fold division of the cosmos he takes the central position (see p. 105–6, 108). Homage is paid to him and his consort, Uma, in the beginning of the *Adiparwa*. He gives the magic arrow *pasopati* to Arjuna (*Arjunawiwaha*). His role in other plays tends to be small.

47

Supraba Heavenly nymph who tries to seduce Arjuna while he is meditating. Later she helps him kill the demon Niwatakawaca. She is one of the seven nymphs with whom Arjuna enjoys marital bliss in heaven (*Arjunawiwaha*).

Tunggal (Plate 5) Tunggal (unity in Balinese; also called Acintya, he who cannot be imagined, in Sanskrit) is the supreme god in *wayang*. Ensink (1961, pp. 423–4) suggests that although his name Acintya is Sanskrit, he stands apart from the Hindu pantheon of gods and may be a god of pre-Hindu Balinese religion. He never talks in the plays and, except in major rites, is only fleetingly seen.

Wisnu Wisnu is the god of water in Bali who is associated with the propitious direction 'to the mountains', *kaja*, and north in the nine-fold division of the cosmos (pp. 105–6, 108). Kresna and Rama are both incarnations, *avatara*, of the god (*Bismaparwa* and *Ramayana* respectively).

Wisnumurti (Plate 6) Also called Butasiyu *tengawan*, the thousand-fold ogre of the right or the greater *pamurtian* (McPhee, 1970, p. 192) who represents the transcendental state of anger of a god. Kresna takes on this shape after hearing of Duryodana's conspiracy to kill him (*Udyogaparwa*) and when confronting Boma (*Bomantaka*).

Yama Lord of the Dead. In the *Bima Swarga*, Bima enters Yama's kingdom in order to liberate his father's soul from hell (Stutterheim, 1956, p. 121).

The Triwangsa (the high castes)

Abimanyu Beloved son of Arjuna and Sumbadra, sister of Kresna. He marries Utari, daughter of Matsyapati, king of Wirata (*Adiparwa*). In the Bratayuda he is killed by the Korawas (*Bratayuda*).

Arjuna (Plate 8) Third son of Kunti and Pandu, but his genitor is Indra (*Adiparwa*). He is an unequalled warrior and so handsome that women are easily attracted to him. Because of his ability at archery he wins Drupadi at the tournament held for her hand. She becomes the wife of the five Pandawa brothers. Owing to a breach of the rule between them concerning their intercourse with her, Arjuna goes into exile for twelve years. During this time he elopes with Sumbadra, Kresna's sister (*Adiparwa*). During the Bratayuda he kills his half-brother, Karna (*Bratayuda*). He attains great spiritual power while meditating on Mount Indrakila where Siwa presents him with the magical arrow, *pasopati* (*Arjunawiwaha*).

Arjuna Sahasrabahu i.e. Arjuna with the thousand arms. He imprisons the demon king Dasamuka who is threatening the gods, but spares his life (*Arjunawiwaha*).

Aswatama Son of Drona. In the Bratayuda he avenges the death of his father by slaying Drupadi's five sons while they are sleeping during the night (*Bratayuda*).

Baladéwa Son of Basudéwa, brother of Kunti, and hence first cousin to the Pandawa brothers. He is an incarnation of the god Brahma and the king of Madura. He remains neutral during the war (*Udyogaparwa*), but his actions show that his loyalties are split between the Pandawas and Korawas (*Gatotkacasraya*).

Banowati Daughter of Salya who marries Duryodana, but is secretly in love with Arjuna. In the war she is killed by Aswatama, who is infuriated by her lack of loyalty to the king (Hardjowirogo, 1968, p. 188).

Basudéwa Son of Kuntiboja, king of Madura, and elder brother of Kunti. He is the father of Baladéwa, Kresna and Sumbadra (*Mosalaparwa*).

Biasa An ascetic, *bagawan*, who is the son of Durgandini by Palasara, former king of Nastina. He is the father of Dastarastra, Pandu and Widura and hence the grandfather of the Pandawas and Korawas (*Adiparwa*). It is told that he composed the *Mahabharata* (*Adiparwa*).

Bima (Plate 7) Second son of Kunti and Pandu, but his genitor is the wind god, Bayu (*Adiparwa*). He is the strongest and most impulsive of the Pandawa brothers. After Yudistira lost Drupadi at dice against the Korawas, he swears that he will avenge her cruel treatment at the hands of Dursasana and drink his blood. Among the opponents whom Bima slays in the Bratayuda are Duryodana, Dursasana and Sakuni (*Bratayuda*). He is a mystic figure who in the *Bima Swarga* liberates his father from the underworld (Stutterheim, 1956, p. 121). He also meets the god Déwa Ruci, who is a tiny replica of himself, on his way to fetch the waters of immortality (*Bima Suci* or *Nawaruci*).

Bisma Son of goddess Gangga by Santana. Although a Satriya, he vows to remain celibate (*brahmacari*). He teaches the Pandawas and Korawas when young (*Adiparwa*). During the Bratayuda, he is made commander of the Korawa forces, but is struck down by Arjuna under cover from Sikandi (*Bratayuda*).[4]

Buriserawa Son of Salya. He is deeply in love with Sumbadra, Arjuna's wife (Hardjowirogo, 1968, p. 183). In the Bratayuda he fights on the side of the Korawas. Arjuna shoots off his arm and later he is killed (*Bratayuda*).

Cédi He tries to obtain Rukmini's hand, but fails as she becomes Kresna's wife (*Hariwangsa*). He fights on the side of the demon king Boma (*Bomantaka*).

Dastarastra Son of Ambika by Biasa. He is born blind as his mother, on seeing Biasa who came to sleep with her, closed her eyes as she was frightened by his straggly red moustache and piercing eyes. Because of his defect, Dastarastra rules Nastina with his younger brother, Pandu (Widyatmanta, *Adiparwa* I, 1958, pp. 144–5). Dastarastra marries Gandari who bears him one hundred sons and one daughter who are commonly known as the Korawas – descendants of Kuru (*Adiparwa*).

Drestajumena Son of Drupada. In the Bratayuda he succeeds in cutting off Drona's head (*Bratayuda*).

Drona Son of a heavenly nymph by a Brahmana ascetic. He has one son, Aswatama. Bitter enmity exists between him and Drupada.[5] He becomes the teacher of the Pandawas and Korawas while they are young (Widyatmanta, *Adiparwa* II, 1958, pp. 23–31). He is shrewd and crafty. In the Bratayuda he is made commander of the Korawa forces, but is killed by Drestajumena after hearing that his son, Aswatama, has been slain. This was in fact a ruse suggested by Kresna to Yudistira, for only an elephant called Aswatama had been killed (*Bratayuda*).

Drupada King of Pancala and father of Sikandi and the twins Drupadi and Drestajumena. He is a firm ally of the Pandawas (Widyatmanta, *Adiparwa* II, 1958, pp. 78–9).

Drupadi Daughter of Drupada and incarnation of the rice goddess, Sri (*ibid.*, pp. 88–90). She becomes the wife of the five Pandawa brothers (*Adiparwa*). She adds fuel to the feud between the Pandawas and Korawas. After the dice game in which Yudistira loses, Dursasana mistreats her and she swears she will not rest before she has washed her hair in his blood (Hardjowirogo, 1968, p. 124).

Dursasana (Plate 9) Second Korawa brother. He is violent and brutal. After Yudistira loses the game of dice he tears open Drupadi's gown at the thigh and pulls loose her bound hair (*ibid.*, p. 124). In the Bratayuda he is killed by Bima who drinks his blood to avenge Drupadi (*Bratayuda*).

Duryodana (Plate 10) Eldest of the hundred Korawa brothers and king of Nastina. In the Bratayuda his kingdom falls and he is slain by

Bima who, on Kresna's bidding, unfairly strikes his thigh (*Bratayuda*).

Gandari Daughter of king Basubala. She marries Dastarastra and gives birth to one hundred pieces of flesh which become the hundred Korawa brothers (Widyatmanta, *Adiparwa* II, 1958, p. 8).

Gatotkaca Son of the ogre, Dimbi, by Bima. As he is partly an ogre he is a powerful and dangerous opponent. In the Bratayuda Karna kills him (*Bratayuda*).

Irawan Son of Ulupuy by Arjuna. He is killed in the Bratayuda (Hardjowirogo, 1968, p. 154).

Karna Illegitimate son of Kunti by the sun god, Surya. Ashamed of him, Kunti abandons him on the river where he is found by a charioteer and his wife who adopt him (*Adiparwa*). Kresna tries to persuade him to join the Pandawas (*Udyogaparwa*), but he remains loyal to Duryodana who has befriended him and given him the kingdom of Awangga. He is the only opponent of the Pandawas considered Arjuna's equal in nobility and skill. Because of Salya's treachery in the war, Arjuna is able to kill him by shooting an arrow into his neck (*Bratayuda*).

Krépa He is the former teacher of the Pandawas and Korawas. He points out that the Pandawas will emerge as victors in the war (*Bismaparwa*).

Kresna (Fig. 3.10) Son of Basudéwa and younger brother of Baladéwa. He is an incarnation of Wisnu and the king of Dwarawati. He tries to reach a peaceful solution to the conflict between the Pandawas and Korawas, but without avail. In fury at Duryodana's conspiracy to kill him, he then assumes his divine shape as the god Wisnu in his terrifying aspect (*Udyogaparwa*). At the outbreak of war he explains to Arjuna, who hesitates to fight against kin and teachers, that the sacred duty (*darma*) of a Satriya is combat (*Bismaparwa*). In the war Kresna is Arjuna's charioteer (*Bismaparwa* and *Bratayuda*). He is a great lover and is accredited also with a thousand wives (*Hariwangsa*). His actions show that he is brilliant, but amoral (see Drona, Duryodana and Yudistira).

Kunti Daughter of Kuntiboja, king of Madura, and the sister of Baladéwa. She marries Pandu. She has four sons by gods: Karna by the sun god, Surya; Yudistira by the god Darma; Bima by the wind god, Bayu; and Arjuna by the god Indra (*Adiparwa*).

Laksmana Son of Dasarata and devoted younger brother of Rama. He helps Rama retrieve Sita from Rawana (*Ramayana*).

Laksanakumara Son of Banowati by Duryodana. He loves Siti Sundari.

She, however, loves Abimanyu who takes her for his wife (*Gatot-kacasraya*).

Matsyapati King of Widura and father of Séta, Utara, Sangka and Utari (Hardjowirogo, 1968, p. 65). The five Pandawa brothers find refuge at his court after Yudistira loses at dice to the Korawas (*Wirataparwa*).

Nakula Son of Madrim and Pandu, but the Aswins are his genitors. He is the twin brother of Sahadéwa (*Adiparwa*).

Pandu Son of Ambalika by Biasa. He is weak as his mother went pale with fear on seeing Biasa when he came to sleep with her. As Dastarastra is blind he rules Nastina jointly with him (Widyatmanta, *Adiparwa* I, 1958, pp. 144–5). Pandu marries Kunti and Madrim. He is the pater, although not the genitor, of the five Pandawa brothers (*Adiparwa*).

Parikesit Son of Abimanyu and grandson of Arjuna. He briefly rules Nastina, but dies after the snake Taksaka bites him (*Adiparwa*).

Rama Son of Dasarata, king of Ayodya. He is an incarnation of the god Wisnu and the hero of the *Ramayana*. He rescues his wife Sita from the clutches of Rawana with the help of the monkey god Hanuman (*Ramayana*).

Rawana Demon king of Langka who abducts Sita. Finally Rama kills him (*Ramayana*).

Sahadéwa Son of Madrim and Pandu, but the god, the Aswins, is his genitor. His twin brother is Nakulu (*Adiparwa*).

Sakuni Brother of Gandari and chief minister of Duryodana. He is cunning and dishonest. He suffers a horrible end at the hands of Bima in the Bratayuda (*Bratayuda*).

Salya Son of the king of Mandraka and brother of Madrim. He marries Satyawati and his children are Erawati, Surtikanti, Banowati and Buriserawa. The three eldest marry Baladéwa, Karna and Duryodana respectively (Hardjowirogo, 1968, pp. 178–9). Although he is on the side of the Korawas, he secretly supports the Pandawas. In the Bratayuda he is Karna's charioteer while Kresna is Arjuna's. He prevents Karna from killing Arjuna by signalling to Kresna who presses down the front of the chariot, so Karna's arrow strikes only Arjuna's headdress. He falls at the hands of Yudistira (*Bratayuda*).

Samba Son of Jembawati by Kresna. He insults three sages who as a result curse him, saying he will be the cause of the destruction of the entire Yadus except for Kresna and Baladéwa (*Mosalaparwa*).

Sikandi (Srikandi) Son of Drupada. In the Bratayuda he enables

Arjuna to kill Bisma, thereby fulfilling the vow made in his previous incarnation. As Srikandi[6] she marries Arjuna. In the Bratayuda Aswatama kills him (Hardjowirogo, 1968, p. 150).

Sita Beautiful wife of Rama who is abducted by Rawana (*Ramayana*).

Siti Sundari Daughter of Kresna. She marries Abimanyu, Arjuna's son (*Gatotkacasraya*). In the Bratayuda she commits *satya*, following her husband to death (*Bratayuda*).

Sumbadra Daughter of Basudéwa and the sister of Baladéwa and Kresna. She becomes Arjuna's wife (*Adiparwa*).

Sutasoma Son of Mahaketu, king of Nastina. He is an incarnation of a Bodhisattwa. Through his great purity and compassion he converts the demon king Porusada (man-eater) and Kala, initiating them into the holy law, *darma*. An elephant, a tigress and a snake become his main disciples (*Sutasoma*).

Yudistira (Plate 11) More commonly called Darmawangsa in Bali: he who is descended from the god Darma. He is the eldest son of Kunti and Pandu, although his genitor is the god Darma. He is mild and gentle and does not actively participate in the Bratayuda. Only on Kresna's instigation does he kill Salya with his magical book, Kalimahosada, which becomes a flaming javelin (*Bratayuda*). Because of his compassion for a dog, who is the god Darma in disguise, he is the only Pandawa brother to ascend to heaven after the war without leaving behind his body (*Prastanikaparwa*).

Yuyutsu Son of Dastarastra and a Wèsya wife, and so the half-brother of the hundred Korawas. However, his sympathies are with the Pandawas (Widyatmanta, *Adiparwa* II, 1958, pp. 10 and 23).

Ogres (*raksasa*) or demonic beings

A large number of ogres appear in night performances. Their identity is often not fixed so they are easily substituted for one another, or they appear as a group, no single one having a defined personality. The names *dalangs* give them are often derived from the *Ramayana* as, for example, Dirgabau, Dumraksa, Marica, Prahasta, Prajangga (Plate 12) or Sukasarana (see Hooykaas, 1955). The following are some of the more important ogres or demonic beings.

Baka A fierce ogre who oppresses the people of Ekacakramandala. Every year he has to be brought a human to eat. Bima finally kills him (Widyatmanta, *Adiparwa* II, 1958, pp. 51–2).

Boma Demon king, son of the goddess Pretiwi by Wisnu. He is endowed by Brahma with great power with which he threatens the gods. Kresna smashes his head to pieces (*Bomantaka*).

Dimba An ogre who Bima kills by turning him upside down and hitting him (Widyatmanta, *Adiparwa* II, 1958, p. 47).

Dimbi Sister of Dimba, who falls in love with Bima. Kunti gives them permission to marry. Out of their union Gatotkaca is born (*ibid.*, pp. 47–8).

Dorokala Gatekeeper and servant of the god, Yama. He guards the crossroads[7] between heaven and hell (Hooykaas, J., 1955, p. 413).

Jogor Manik Black giant and servant of Yama. He is probably the first demon to meet the soul as it reaches the crossroads[7] between heaven and hell (*ibid.*, p. 243).

Kala Lord of Demons, son of the god Siwa, who threatens to devour man. The *dalang* Empu Lègèr conquers him by his shadow play and ritual exorcism (Hooykaas, 1973b, *Kala Purana*, pp. 171–87).

Ludramurti Also called Butasiyu *kèbot*, the thousandfold ogre of the left, or the lesser *pamurtian* (McPhee, 1970, p. 192). This is a malevolent form which is primarily assumed by demons (*Bomantaka*).

Niwatakawa A powerful ogre who threatens to destroy heaven and the gods. Arjuna, with the help of the celestial nymph, Supraba, kills him (*Arjunawiwaha*).

Suratma Gatekeeper and servant of Yama. He is one of the guardians of the crossroads[7] between heaven and hell. Bima fights him before obtaining his father's soul from hell (Stutterheim, 1956, p. 121).

Mythical creatures

A number of minor unnamed animals, imaginative in form (Plate 13), appear in plays. Here only two major mythical creatures are described.

Garuda Mythical bird, vehicle of Kresna or Wisnu. He frees his mother Winata from bondage to her sister by stealing the elixir of immortality from the gods (*Adiparwa*).

Hanuman Son of Anjana by Bayu, the god of wind, and so Bima's half-brother. He crosses with his army of monkeys into Langka in order to help Rama defeat the demon king, Rawana, and retrieve his wife, Sita (*Ramayana*).

The servants

The servants must be completely separated from the characters discussed above as they do not enter the epics and clearly belong to the folk tradition. However, the four Sudra servants, Tualèn, Merdah, Dèlem and Sangut, have in many ways the most important rôles in a performance (see subsequent chapters).

The earliest known Javanese literary work to include servant-like figures is the poem *Gatotkacasraya*, composed in the late twelfth century (Pigeaud, 1967, pp. 184–5). Since then they have rarely been absent from Javanese narratives. It is often assumed that they were taken over from indigenous folk tales.

There are various popular myths about the origin of the main servant Tualèn (his equivalent in Java being Semar) and his son Merdah. The first two highlight their divine status. The third myth shows why Bima has such a close relationship with these two servants, which, for instance, comes to the fore in the *Bima Suci* (p. 32–3). Here they accompany the prince on his journey to find holy water.

1. The God Sang Hyang Sepi, or Supreme Quiet, has two sons. The elder is called Ismaya and the younger Manik Maya.[8] These two gods meditate and from their concentration the other gods are created. The gods decide that mankind needs protection. So it comes about that the five Pandawa brothers, the Panca Pandawa, are born, all being descendants of gods. Sang Hyang Sepi then points out that the Pandawas have no one to guide and take care of them. He tells Manik Maya to remain in heaven, while Ismaya is to take on the form of Tualèn and descend to earth. Tualèn first meditates and creates his son Merdah. Together they go to the court of the Pandawas and become their servants.

After some time has elapsed, the Pandawas are attacked and a fierce ogre called Ari-Ari (umbilical cord) kills the brothers. Tualèn and Merdah, in fury at the gods for having let the Pandawas die, ascend to heaven. The gods are displeased to see two mortals enter their realm and fighting breaks out, in which the servants defeat the gods. Sang Hyang Sepi then intervenes and tells the gods that Tualèn and Merdah are not two ordinary mortals; Tualèn is in fact Ismaya. Sang Hyang Sepi further points out that the ogre has been sent deliberately. He represents the umbilical cord, *ari-ari*, of the Pandawa brothers. No proper rites were made for him at their birth. He is, however, one of their mystic brothers, *kanda empat* (Weck 1937, pp. 52–62, and Hooykaas 1974, pp. 3–4),[9] who has to be taken care of. Only then will he protect the Pandawas, otherwise he will bring them harm.

2. Dirt has congealed on the skin of Tunggal, the supreme god. The god meditates and the dirt takes on the form of Tualèn. Tunggal tells Tualèn that he wants him to be the servant of men who act virtuously. So Tualèn,

55

together with his son, Merdah, become the servants of the Panca Pandawa, the five brothers who have an understanding of the path of duty or morality, *darma*.

3. Bima wishes to make a cave. He digs energetically until he comes first upon a black and then a red stone which he cannot dislodge. In anger he shouts to the obstinate stones that as they are as tough and unyielding as he, he will treat them like members of the family and give them the status of brothers. Hearing Bima's words, the stones take on human shape. The black stone becomes Tualèn and the red one Merdah.

condong (Plate 14) Lady-in-waiting attached to the court. She may serve senior Satriya women, like Kunti. She is a lady of easy virtue and enjoys frolicking with the male servants.

Dèlem (Plate 15) Elder brother of Sangut. His parentage is unknown. He and his brother are said to be hereditary servants, *parekan wudun*, of the Korawas in *wayang parwa* and Rawana in *wayang Ramayana*. Although supernaturally powerful, he is stupid, clumsy and bombastic. He loves material wealth and cannot distinguish right from wrong.

Merdah (Plate 16) Son of Tualèn. No mother is mentioned in south Bali. He and his father are the main servants of the Pandawas in *wayang parwa* or elsewhere of those whose actions accord with the will of the gods. He is quick-witted and intelligent and often guides his somewhat childish, elderly father. However, he can be proud and hard-hearted.

Sangut (Plate 18) Younger brother of Dèlem. He is intelligent, shrewd and imaginative and in intelligence he is compared to Merdah. He does not approve of his elder brother, Dèlem, and is emotionally drawn to the Pandawas as they are relatively virtuous. However, he remains loyal to his masters.

Tualèn (Plate 17) Principal servant of the Pandawas or otherwise virtuous side. He is perhaps the most complex character in *wayang*. His father is often said to be the supreme god, Tunggal. His son is Merdah. Although he sometimes acts in a foolish and stupid manner, great supernatural power is associated with him and on occasions Tunggal is said to descend into his body so that he may represent the supreme god incarnate.

Scenic figures

Two scenic figures which do not occur in the Hindu-Javanese literature but are very important in *wayang* must be mentioned briefly.

Kakayonan (Plate 31) Also called Gagunungan (from *kayu*, tree, or *gunung*, mountain, respectively). Scholars (Kats, 1923; Hidding, 1931; Rassers, 1959; Bosch, 1960) have suggested that in Java the figure refers to the Mountain of the Gods, Mahaméru, the Celestial Wishing Tree or the Tree of Life. As such it represents, among other things, the sacred centre of the universe which produces and sustains all creation and into which all oppositions are resolved. The Kakayonan is the most ritually significant scenic figure and used in all performances.

Sungsang Or *kepuh* tree. McPhee (1970, p. 192) describes the figure as a large tree (*Eriodendron anfractuosum*) sacred to the goddess Durga and growing in most graveyards. *Dalangs* only need it for special performances, as, for example, *Bima Swarga* (Hinzler, 1981). It is then found in the underworld from where Bima rescues his father, Pandu.

Text in the shadow theatre

It is clear that the great Hindu epics, which ultimately stem from India, have a separate existence from both theatre and ritual in Bali. However, the epics have become deeply embedded in the Balinese sociocultural context where (*pace* Malinowski's behaviourist theory of myth) they are by no means just an adjunct of dramatic or ritual activities, an epiphenomenon of these. One can in fact safely argue that if there were no mythology there would be no *wayang* (certainly not in the way we know it today), for the two are intimately interwoven. The relationship is, however, not a passive one for the Balinese ingeniously structure and adapt the myths, taking from both the classical literature and the oral tradition to fit the idiom of *wayang*.

The night and day *wayang* must here be distinguished. As already noted, their orientation in the society differs considerably. Concomitantly with this, the relationship of the mythology to each type is very differently conceived by the people. This is discussed below.

The night performance: *wayang peteng*

In the *wayang peteng* a large number (about 60–70) of actors, i.e. puppets, may appear on the stage, the majority of whom are male aristocrats. Characters, moreover, from different literary sources may intermingle with ease in the same play, together with the four main

servants. Irrespective, however, of the source from which the characters derive their existence or which story is dramatized, all plays are
structured according to the same principle: the stage is characterized
by a strict division between two camps who oppose one another. So,
from the point of view of the *dalang*, the Pandawa brothers with their
followers in plays based on the *parwas* enter from the right of the
stage, while the less virtuous Korawas and their followers enter from
the left. In the same way in *wayang Ramayana*, Rama's group enters
from the right of the *dalang* and the group of the demon king Rawana
from the left. The Balinese seem here to be adhering to Lévi-Strauss's
(see, among others, 1969 and 1976) notion of an underlying system of
'opposition' through which the world is experienced and which
reflects the structure of the human mind. However, this system of
opposition has not got unconscious roots, for the people are clear as to
the reasons for grouping the characters into two camps. The following
analysis focuses on the *Mahabharata* because, as mentioned earlier,
stories from this are the most frequently performed.

Diagram 2.1   The protagonists in the Bratayuda: the Pandawa

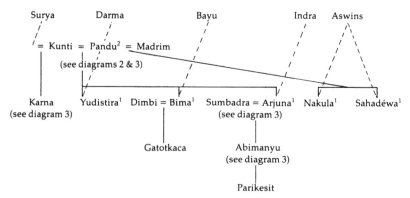

Notes

--- indicates the genitor, in each case a god according to the *Adiparwa*, where
he is not the social father.

1. The five legitimate Pandawa brothers collectively marry Drupadi
   (see diagram 3). Arjuna has a number of wives apart from Drupadi and
   Sumbadra, but his most important descendants are from his union with
   Sumbadra.

2. The earliest generation shown in this diagram is that of Pandu's genitor,
   Biasa (see diagram 2). Although earlier ones are mentioned in the *parwas*
   my informants did not know the relationships between them; nor are they
   represented by the puppets.

The kin relations mapped out in the texts, in particular the *Adiparwa*, provide the Balinese with the main grounds for uniting members of one group vis-à-vis members of another (see p. 48–53).

The conflict between the five Pandawa brothers and their cousins, the Korawas, centres around who succeeds to the throne of Nastina, the elder line of Dastarastra or the younger line of Pandu. The brothers Dastarastra and Pandu rule the kingdom jointly. By right the sons of the former, the hundred Korawas, have first claim to the throne as their father is the eldest son of the senior queen Ambika. However, the Pandawa brothers begotten by gods are more suitable rulers (diagrams 1 and 2). The problem is compounded by Widura, the younger brother of Dastarastra and Pandu, pointing out that Yudistira should be the heir as he was born before Duryodana. This is contested by Dastarastra who loves his own children and suggests dividing the kingdom and giving Yudistira sovereignty over Indraprasta (*Adiparwa*). Duryodana refuses to accept his father's advice. The conflict over who should rule forms the basis for the subsequent ever-mounting

Diagram 2.2   The protagonists in the Bratayuda: the Korawas

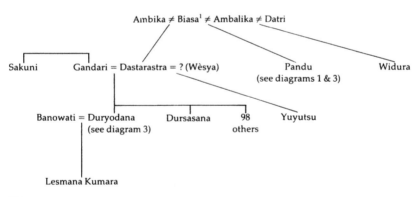

Notes

≠ impregnates

1. Anderson (1965, p. 60) shows Dastarastra, Pandu and Widura as full brothers of a single union between Biasa and Ambalika. According to the *Adiparwa* (Widyatmanta, 1958, pp. 144–6) Biasa impregnates three different women, so the source of conflict is not between full siblings, but rivalry between sons of different mothers. Widura is here of less consequence as Datri is low caste; Ambika and Ambalika are Satriyas.

antagonism between the Pandawa brothers and their Korawa cousins.

Women are instrumental in adding fuel to the initial conflict between the Pandawas and Korawas, and so polarizing the situation. Bima takes up Drupadi's vow that she will not rest before she washes her hair in Dursasana's blood in order to avenge his mistreatment of her. Banowati, the wife of Duryodana, is secretly in love with the comely Arjuna. This infuriates Aswatama who realizes that she humiliates the king of Nastina by her lack of esteem and love for him. Buriserawa's hatred of the Pandawas is related to his deep love for Sumbadra, Arjuna's wife.

Direct descendants and wives side automatically with the family into which they are born. Senior Satriyas or subsidiary males are mainly related to either the Pandawas or Korawas through marital ties (diagram 3). For example, Baladéwa and Kresna are first cousins to the Pandawa brothers as their father's younger sister is Kunti, mother of Yudistira, Bima and Arjuna. Drupada's alliance to the Pandawas is strengthened by his daughters' (Drupadi and Sikandi) marriages to the five Pandawa brothers and Arjuna respectively. Matsyapati is a firm ally of the Pandawas. This tie is strengthened by his daughter, Utari, becoming the wife of Abimanyu, the most beloved son of Arjuna. Male descendants as, for example, Drestajumena, in turn follow their fathers and are allies of the Pandawas. Altogether the Pandawas comprise a larger kin group in *wayang* than the Korawas

Diagram 2.3   Marriage alliances to powerful kings

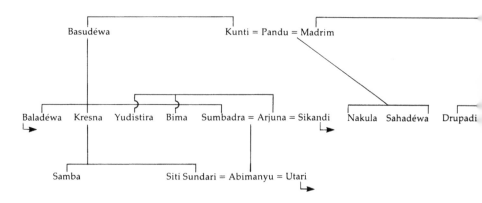

who are primarily made up of the hundred brothers. Of these, between three and seven are usually represented in a performance.

In the literature a few Satiyas have clearly ambiguous positions and this is reiterated in *wayang*. This is especially striking with Salya or Karna. Salya (diagram 3) is related to the Pandawas through his sister Madrim who is the mother of the twins, Nakula and Sahadéwa. His daughter, Banowati, however, marries Duryodana. The situation is compounded by the marriages of his other daughters: Erawati becomes the wife of Baladéwa, while Surtikanti is the wife of Karna. Karna, although he is Kunti's eldest son, allies himself with the Korawas. He is deeply hurt by his mother's abandonment of him due to shame that he was illegitimate. He also remains loyal to Duryodana who has befriended him.

Performances based on the *parwas* may incorporate a few Satriyas who are external to them. *Dalangs* link them to a given camp on the grounds of suitability. So characters like Boma or Cédi from the text *Bomantaka* may also enter the Bratayuda and fight with the Korawas. In the same way, the monkey god Hanuman may support the Pandawas in the war.

In contrast to the alliances established between the Satriyas, which are principally based on ties of kinship and descent, priests and teachers often associate themselves on religious or emotive grounds. Bisma offended the gods in his past incarnation and as a consequence

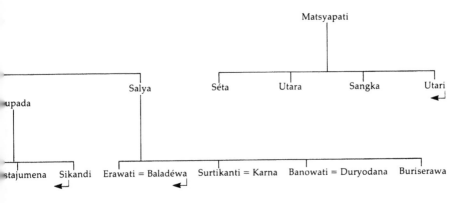

is forced to back the Korawas in the war. A bitter feud exists between Drona and Drupada⁵. The events surrounding the birth of Drona and Krépa are, moreover, inauspicious and impure. Hence these intelligent priests support the Korawas. Biasa, the grandfather of the Pandawa and Korawa brothers, has the least defined position in the literature, although in performances he enters from the right of the *dalang*, on the side of the Pandawas.

Most of the gods are associated in *wayang* with the Pandawas. From the Balinese point of view this is appropriate. Besides representing the most developed spiritual state, many of the gods are directly related to them either by virtue of being their genitors or by taking on their forms, as in the case of Kresna. Brahma and Durga, because of their association in Bali with supernatural power, in general for evil purposes, side with the Korawas.

A number of ogres generally enter the plays, the majority of whom are given names from the *Ramayana*. They actively support the Korawas in the war. The reason for this link is not immediately evident from the *Adiparwa*. As pointed out, some *dalangs* may say that the Korawas are associated with both the ogres and darkness as their father is blind and hence possesses the so-called 'body of an ogre' or a 'dark body'. There is, however, a more direct literary connection between the Korawas and the ogres which emerges in the last volume of the *Mahabharata*, the *Swargarohanaparwa*,[10] in which it is indicated that the Korawas are incarnations of demons and ogres. So the hundred brothers are regarded as having affinity of character with all ogres.

The servants stand apart from the other characters as they are not found in the epics. Yet the oral tradition explains that Tualèn is a direct descendant of the supreme god, Tunggal. The gods, moreover, have decreed that he and his son, Merdah, serve the Pandawas. Dèlem and Sangut are often said to be hereditary servants of the Korawas.

From the above it is apparent that the division on the stage is influenced by the Balinese conception of the classical literature. Although the characters in *wayang parwa* may be derived from a variety of textual sources as well as the folk tradition, they are ingeniously arranged to fit the idiom of the night *wayang*. This implies that a strict dichotomy is maintained on the stage between the two camps: most of the gods, the high castes of the Pandawa group, Tualèn and Merdah enter from the right of the *dalang* to oppose the high castes of the Korawa group, the ogres, Dèlem and Sangut who enter from the left.

The day performance: *wayang lemah*

The relationship of the classical literature to the day *wayang* is very differently conceived by the Balinese to that of the *wayang* given at night. A few figures stand motionless on the stage throughout the entire play, while two or three characters, who are usually the servants, narrate the dialogue of a short story softly. The *Adiparwa* is the text most generally used. The story is in some ways free-floating, as it is not interrelated with the quietly standing figures; moreover, the stage is not divided and no opposites confront one another (see p. 162) – a feature which is so pronounced in the night *wayang*. Only one principle seems always to be heeded: the story chosen has to be appropriate to the social occasion, a fact demonstrated in the following examples (cf. Hinzler, 1981, pp. 35–9):

Life-cycle rituals (*manusa-yadnya*)	Example of story chosen*		Text of story
One of the birthdays (*tigang odalan, oton jumu, oton*)	1	The birth of Parikesit	*Adiparwa*
	2	The birth of Bima	*Adiparwa*
Tooth-filing (*mepandas*)	1	Dastarastra performing rites after Pandu's death	*Adiparwa*
Marriage (*mekerab*)	1	Drupadi's marriage to the five Pandawa brothers	*Adiparwa*
	2	Arjuna fetches Sumbadra to become his wife	*Adiparwa*
	3	Having killed the ogre Niwatakawaca, Arjuna marries the celestial nymph, Supraba	*Arjunawiwaha*
Rites for the dead (*pitra-yadnya*)			
Cremation (*pelebon*) or other purificatory rites	1	Yudistira goes to heaven	*Swargarohanaparwa*
	2	Bisma's death in the great war	*Bratayuda*
	3	Bima fetches his father, Pandu, from the underworld	*Bima Swarga*

continued on next page

* Further details of stories are given under the summaries of the characters in this chapter.

Rites for the gods
(*déwa-yadnya*)

Temple anniversary (*odalan*)	1	Garuda fetches the elixir of immortality to free his mother from bondage	*Adiparwa*
	2	The gods recover the elixir from the demons	*Adiparwa*

Rites for the demons
(*buta-yadnya*)

Yearly rite (*nyepi*)	1	Bima kills the ogre Baka	*Adiparwa*
	2	Bima kills the ogre Dimba	*Adiparwa*

Other rites

Consecration of a building (*melaspasin*)	1	The Pandawas escape from their house before it is set on fire	*Adiparwa*

In the night *wayang* the story may also accord with the occasion. However, the *dalang* is not constrained to adhere to this principle. He mainly chooses a myth he fancies, sometimes in consultation with the sponsor, although he may consider what play is appropriate in a given circumstance. In the day *wayang*, on the other hand, a close connection is always established between the story and the rite performed.

Conclusion

In discussing the literary background to the shadow theatre one final observation is relevant. It applies in particular to the night *wayang*, which is a theatrical performance communicating to men, and less so to the day *wayang* which is a rite given for the benefit of the gods.

In the day *wayang*, as we have seen, myths are chosen which fit the social occasion. The episodes narrated are primarily drawn from any part of the *Adiparwa*. Early creation myths, which involve the fetching or rescuing of the elixir of immortality, may, for example, be recounted at the anniversary of a temple.

On the other hand, the stories dramatized in the night *wayang* all take place after the rice goddess Sri and the god Indra have been

Plate 8   Arjuna

Plate 9 Dursasana

Plate 10 Duryodana

Plate 11 Yudistira

Plate 12 Prajangga

Plate 13 Elephant

Plate 14 Condong

Plate 15 Dèlem

banished to earth to become Drupadi and the five Pandawa brothers respectively. There, like ordinary mortals, they live and die, and experience passions, pains and pleasures. The reason for this, as narrated in the *Adiparwa*, is that the gods are displeased as there is no apparent difference between heaven and earth: men, like gods, are at peace and do not become ill and die. The separation between the two cosmological spheres occurs when Sri becomes jealous when she sees the joy of Siwa and Uma in making love. Sri's weeping tears, which fall into the river to become lotuses, incite Indra to strike the couple with his thunderbolt. It is worth noting that Siwa sentences them to earth not because of their sexual desire or lust, but because of Sri's jealousy and envy, aroused at the couple's pleasure, and Indra's lack of control which results in him hurling his powerful thunderbolt.

The night *wayang* in a sense picks up at the point where the *Adiparwa* leaves off and the Pandawas are born as humans. A separation has already occurred between what the Balinese refer to as the imperceptible world, where the gods reside, *niskala*, and the perceptible world of men, *sakala*. The people clearly recognize the existence of these two spheres and stress that they must be viewed as two parts of a radically divided world. The need for such a distinction is, however, by no means confined to Bali. Leinhardt describes how, both logically and historically the Dinkas' relations with the Divinity begin with a story of the supposed conjunction and then division of the earth and the sky – the emergence of the world as it is (1978, p. 33).

In line with a *wayang* performance given to men, most stories dramatized recount events pertaining to the Pandawas and Korawas (or other aristocrats), their followers and their respective servants on earth. Yet the plays, as they unfold, hint at the possibility of mediation between the spheres – the celestial world and the world of men – and hold out the promise of untapped resources, of things to tell as yet untold, which contribute to making the hours of watching the drama significant.

Notes

1   The eight *parwas* are: *Adiparwa, Wirataparwa, Udyogaparwa, Bismaparwa, Asramawasaparwa, Mosalaparwa, Prastanikaparwa* and *Swargarohanaparwa*. The *Wanaparwa* has been added recently.
2   These myths were first chanted and translated in the field by *dalang* I Ewer (see Preface), but they tally with those in *Adiparwa* edited by

Widyatmanta. The book includes a statement by Zoetmulder saying that he approves of this edition.

3 Although the sources for Hardjowirogo's work *Sedjarah Wajang* (1968) are not known, he is mentioned when he corresponds to the Balinese view of certain characters.

4 Bisma is forced to support the Korawas because of actions in his past incarnation as Prabata. In brief, Prabata steals Siwa's sacred cow, Nandini, from the ascetic Wasista. Prabata's wife desires its milk for a friend as it bestows longevity. As a result Wasista decrees that he should be incarnated on earth and support the Korawas (Widyatmanta, *Adiparwa I*, 1958, pp. 127–8).

5 As the story is involved it is only given here in very brief outline. In their youth Drona and Drupada are close friends, they then part company. Drona's early life proves difficult as he is forced to beg for a living. After some time has elapsed he hears that Drupada has become king of Pancala. He goes to him on the strength of their former friendship and requests food. Drupada refuses, saying that it is improper for a king to help a poor, incapable Brahmana. Drona departs in fury (*ibid., Adiparwa II*, pp. 24–7).

6 Sikandi (Srikandi) is generally said to be an hermaphrodite. *Dalangs* say that an ogre gave her a phallus, after which she becomes a male.

7 The crossroads are generally described as consisting of three roads: one to the east in the direction of the mountains and the forefathers; one to the west and straight down to the sea and the underworld; and one to the parents and siblings on earth (Hooykaas, J., 1955, pp. 241–2). It is further suggested that the crossroads are on a high mountain pass in life hereafter (Hooykaas, 1956, p. 77).

8 The beginning of this myth resembles Winter's translation of *Manik Maya* which Rassers sums up as follows: out of chaos there arose one being, the highest god Wisesa; he then divides three times in succession as heaven and earth, sun and moon, and finally the brothers Manik and Maya. Manik is another name for Guru, while Maya is another name for Semar (Rassers 1959, p. 24).

9 As Hooykaas points out, the *kanda empat* personify the concomitants of a person's birth: the amniotic fluid, the vernix caseosa, the blood and the after-birth, to which the umbilical cord belongs. These represent the four mystic brothers, or sisters in the case of a female, who accompany the person through life. If properly taken care of with the correct offerings they protect him or her (Hooykaas 1974: pp. 3–4).

10 According to Uhlenbeck (1964, p. 126) the *Swargarohanaparwa* is the only *parwa* not yet translated. *Dalang* I Ewer translated this section of the volume for me and explained its meaning.

The puppets: construction, form and symbolism

The puppets are made according to a fixed scheme laid down in antiquity and sanctified by the force of the tradition. This determines their forms, costume and skin colours. The iconography is initially so important as it is through the puppets that the mythological presence of the characters is evoked during a play. During the night *wayang*, individuals may appear only fleetingly on the stage, so their contours must be precise for the spectators to recognize them.

The puppets, however, have another significance not yet touched on. Apart from representing characters derived from the myths, the iconography is considered to articulate patterns of meaning which relate to core ideals and values in the society. It is the aim of this chapter to investigate these for the villagers say explicitly that the form of the puppets and their content are one. In other words, the symbolism is seen as permeating the iconography and cannot be abstracted from it.

Puppets and puppet collections

A puppet is referred to either as *ringgit* or *wayang*. Hazeu (1897) derives *wayang* from *yang*, moving unsteadily or floating in the air, and connects the term with ghost. This relates to his view that the shadow theatre originated as a cult of the ancestors. Although my informants did not make this connection, they do consider the puppets to be sacred. This affects the place where the puppet-chest is kept, the proper order of the puppets within, and the rites that are necessary for the puppets during the course of the year, or when new puppets are made. When not in use, it is placed in a shrine in the household temple.

The order in which the puppets are stored in a chest is subject to definite rules. Those most ritually significant are always on top (*cf.* the implication of top and bottom in relation to the body, see p. 98). So the scenic item, the Kakayonan, is the uppermost figure, followed by the supreme god, Tunggal. Ogres, who usually have base characters, are placed at the bottom. The order of the puppets in the middle is not fixed, but depends on what the *dalang* thinks appropriate.

In order to ensure the spiritual purity of the puppets, small offerings are given to them throughout the year. A special rite (*ngotonin wayang*) celebrating the birthday of the puppets takes place once a year. *Dalangs* say that if they do not take care of the puppets properly the gods or the ancestors may be affronted and punish them so that they become ill. It is also thought dangerous for a *dalang* to sell a puppet which has been consecrated. Such an act is disrespectful to the gods who may curse (*tulah*) him, and his ability to interpret them during a performance may wane.

As mentioned earlier, most puppet collections are based on the *parwa* cycle. *Ramayana* sets exist, but are rarely encountered for few *dalangs* specialize in this cycle. *Parwa* collections are similar and the forms of the puppets essentially standard. The method of making new puppets, which consists of copying existing ones, ensures a unity of style throughout collections. The main difference between collections is their quality and the number of puppets they contain. A standard collection contains between eighty to one hundred and thirty puppets. Sets of simple village *dalangs* tend to have fewer high-caste characters and more ogres than do the sets of their more sophisticated counterparts. The puppets of the former are often also more crudely carved and painted.

All collections comprise the same range of the different categories of beings and things, which are as follows:

scenic figures	Kakayonan
	a few figures of trees
celestial beings	gods, *batara*
	goddesses, *batari*
	sages, *resi*
	nymphs, *widiadari*

social castes	Brahmanas
	Satriyas
	Wèsyas
	Sudras
demonic beings	ogres, *raksasa*
creatures	different animals, birds, serpents
chariots	usually drawn by one or two horses
weapons	bows, clubs, spears, knives, keris, specific weapons of individuals

In the next section the process of craftsmanship is described. This illustrates the precision with which puppets are cut, incised and painted. It also clearly indicates that the craft of making puppets is as much a religious as a secular activity.

Puppet craftsmanship

The craftsman

Craftsmen have an established place in Balinese society even though they are not recognized as a separate group. Each craftsman is designated according to his craft. Thus, a puppet-maker is referred to as *tukang wayang*, craftsman of puppets.

Puppets are usually made by specialized craftsmen; a few may also be *dalangs*. In general, the craftsmen are Sudras. Most of them make a variety of artistic objects such as masks, headdresses for operetta, or statues, and do not restrict themselves to puppets alone. As new puppets are carved from an existing model, the puppet-maker is essentially a technician. Excellence lies in the precision of the copy and the subtle beauty of the chiselwork and painting in producing a fixed form. A puppet craftsman should be seen not as an innovator, but as the guardian of a cultural tradition in which his role is subordinated to that of socially dictated ideals.

The art of making puppets in Bali is always passed on from one generation to the next. Craftsmen learn from an established puppet-maker who may or may not be their kinsman, to whom they are apprenticed for between two and five years. During this time, trainees assist their masters by running general errands and undertaking rudimentary jobs, such as preparing the hide for the puppets or grinding the colours. It is also from these teachers that the religious regulations of the craft are learnt.

The financial gain from making puppets is limited and craftsmen rarely live off their craft; they are primarily sustained by their rice fields. The motive for becoming a craftsman is neither fame nor posterity; self-aggrandisement and pride are, in any case, strongly disapproved of by the Balinese. Nonetheless, the craftsman's role – particularly if he is skilled – involves a certain respect as he is associated with the traditional arts.

Although scope for innovation is severely limited, craftsmen are sensitive to aesthetic appeal. Generally, it is agreed that the eyes and headdress are the most important parts of a puppet, the first as it reveals expression and the second as it indicates status. The bushiness of the side-burn is also a matter of some concern; it helps to show whether a face is oval and delicate or broad and heavy. A well-known craftsman defined the standards that he sought in making puppets as follows:

> Heed is the first given to the form. Then the carving is considered. It should be flat, smooth and graceful. Afterwards the colours should be correctly applied. It is pleasing if they glow. Such a puppet has *guna*.

Guna[1] is an essential attribute of puppets and in the context of the shadow theatre is best thought of as a magical device which compels and sustains the attention of the audience. *Guna* accumulates with age; thus, old puppets are preferred to new ones. The same craftsman explained that although puppets are stylized it is essential that they are modelled on the human form in order to enable the *dalang* to empathize with their characters and become their spokesman in the drama. He added, somewhat wryly, that a Balinese *dalang* would be perplexed if asked to handle Javanese puppets as they are so exaggerated and contorted.

The religous background to puppet-making

The ritual attitude towards puppet-making in Bali emerges clearly in the ceremonies and offerings which accompany the puppets' construction. There is of course some variation in the precise religious precepts followed and in the actual technique of making puppets, but there are few puppet-makers as the demand for making puppets is small.[2] Hence the following account is primarily based on the work of I Wayan Raos, the most celebrated craftsman in Gianyar, recognized for his technical skill and religious knowledge, but is supported by the work of other craftsmen in the area.

The two principal ceremonies are performed before the craftsman begins to carve a new set of puppets and on its completion. First the craftsman places offerings on a small shrine consisting of a wooden pole with a split bamboo platform (*asagan*). This is set in front of the entrance to the household temple. Balinese offerings form an extremely complex system of agreed, but unascertained, significance, based for the most part on such natural substances as banana or coconut palm leaves, sometimes woven into containers, flowers, rice and rice cakes, fruit, betelnut, and so forth (Hooykaas, 1961). I Raos explained the significance of the prescribed offerings as 'a request to Wisnu to descend and to purify the craftsman, and to beg pardon of Siwa for any mistakes made' while making the puppets.

Then each day until the collection is finished small fresh offerings of palm leaves with cooked rice are placed on the shrine. Additional purificatory offerings are given every fifteen days, and at full and new moons (on holy days, Goris, 1960, pp. 124–4). Throughout, the main concern of the craftsman is to ensure that he is in a state of ritual, and spiritual, purity; only then will the puppets be of a high standard and cast clear silhouettes on the screen. Finally, after all the puppets have been made, they are consecrated (*mepasupati*) by a Brahmana priest.[3]

The religious tradition is also evident in the actual construction of a new set of puppets. Before starting work, I Raos waits for the day of full moon which is said to be imbued with loveliness, clarity and purity. The light of the moon expresses the sweetness of the goddess Ratih, the consort of Kama, the god of love; it is a soft, subdued white (*lumbum gading*) which the Balinese often compare to the colour of the flesh of the *salak* fruit. Figuratively, it is also at this time that the celestial nymphs bathe to obtain spiritual purity. A collection begun on this day will tend to reflect the qualities associated with the full moon.

The first figure that I Raos cuts out of hide and incises is the Kakayonan. He explained that a semantic link exists between (Ka)*kayon*(an) and *kayun*, meaning to think in high Balinese. The figure is conceived to mirror his thoughts. If it is skilfully made, all the subsequent puppets will be of excellent quality.

The preparation of the hide

The craftsman only uses cows' hide. It is considered more suitable than bulls' hide, which is weak and liable to crack. Only a butcher is allowed to skin animals. He also makes the requisite offerings after the meat has been distributed. I Raos obtains the hide in this raw state, and he and the male members of his family prepare it until it is ready to be used for puppet making.

Hides come in two colours: a yellowish pink or a blackish brown. I Raos favours the former as it is suitable for all puppets, especially those with refined characters who have pale body colours.

The hide is first soaked in the river for a few days and then dried. During this time it is pulled taut on a wooden frame by straps passing through holes made all around the edge. While still on the frame the hide is scraped with a small knife until all the hair is removed and the hide is of an even thickness. Afterwards it is soaked for a day and, while wet, the craftsman cleans and scrubs it to remove grease, first using the hairy inside of a coconut and then with the stalks of freshly threshed rice plants. Once dry, it is ready for use.

Before cutting out the puppets an appropriate piece of hide is selected for each specific figure. Refined characters are made of somewhat finer, thinner hide than servants, animals or demons.

The making of the colour pigments

Balinese craftsmen distinguish basic colours from combined colours. All craftsmen use five basic colours: white, red, yellow, black and blue. Ochre may also be used, but it is not classified together with the basic colours. The five basic colours are mixed in varying proportions to produce different combined colours.

Gold leaf, *prada*, should also be mentioned in the context of colour. It stands apart from the other colours, though, and is never used on the bodies of puppets.

Some of the ingredients for making colour pigments are indigenous to Bali,[4] others are Chinese in origin. White, black and ochre are always made in Bali; this may or may not apply to yellow.[5] White is derived from certain animal bones; black from soot; ochre and Balinese yellow from stones found on Serangan, a small island in a bay on the south coast of Bali. Traditionally, special craftsmen made blue from the indigo plant; however, this skill has largely died out and Chinese blue[6] is now generally used as a substitute. Red[7] and gold leaf are imported from Singapore and Hong Kong.

The preparation of one colour (Plate 19) illustrates the making of all the basic colours. First some fish glue, also Chinese in origin, is soaked in water. The glue comes in the form of small, thin, rectangular pieces which are hygroscopic and readily soluble. The pigment is ground in a rough earthenware dish to which a small amount of water is added, ensuring that the colour will adhere to the puppet. Some chalk is then added, giving the colour its glow. Indigo, Chinese blue and yellow do not require chalk as it is said to destroy their life and clarity.

The making of black, blue and white requires particular skill. Black is derived from soot traditionally obtained from an earthenware lamp lit by coconut oil. The soot settles on the dry bark of an areca nut which encloses the wick of the lamp.

Indigo used to be favoured for its deep violet-blue lustre, but I heard of no one in Gianyar who still makes this colour. In the past, as it was time-consuming and difficult to produce, it was used sparingly. However, it was necessary for spiritually elevated characters such as Siwa or Kresna.

White is obtained from horn and two types of bone. Deer horn, which comes from Kalimantan, is considered to produce the most attractive colour as it has a soft yellowish or pinkish glow. More commonly, however, white pigment is made from chicken bones or the skull of a female pig, which are left-overs from meals. Bones from other parts of animal bodies are unsuitable as the colour is said to be dirty.

All the combined colours are derived from the five basic ones. As we shall see, the most significant aspect of the colours is the particular combinations and proportions used. However, because of the varying consistency of the paints and the different types of material which form their basis, it is difficult to calculate the exact proportions used. I Raos defines them in terms of small, moderate and large. For example, a large amount of yellow mixed with a small amount of blue produces light green. I Raos uses an unusually wide range of combined colours, numbering twenty-three (Table 1). These graduate from subdued, light tones, described as 'cool', for instance light blue, *pelung nguda*, or yellowish white, *putih susu* (literally, the milk from the mother's breast), to vivid or 'hot' ones, such as reddish brown, *soklat* (derived from the loan word chocolate).

The making of a puppet

The ten distinct stages in the making of a puppet are described in this section. The dexterity and knowledge required for puppet craftsman-

Table 3.1 Proportions for the combined colours

Balinese name of colour	English*	Proportions used		
		small	moderate	large
abu	grey		black, white	
barak nguda	light red (pink)		red, white	
barak wayah	dark red	black	yellow	red
gadang biasa	mid-green	blue	yellow	
gadang nguda	light green	blue		yellow
gadang wayah	dark green	black	yellow	blue
gadang pelosor biu wayah	blackish green	black	blue, yellow	
kedapan durian biasa	mid-olive green		blue, red, white	yellow
kedapan durian nguda	light olive green	red	yellow	white
kedapan durian wayah	dark olive green		yellow, blue, red	
kudrang biasa	mid-orange		red, yellow	
kudrang nguda	light orange	white	red, yellow	
kudrang wayah	dark orange	yellow	red	
pelung langit	mid-blue	white	blue	
pelung nguda	light blue	blue		white
pelung daki	dark blue	black	blue, white	
putih susu	yellowish white	yellow	white	
soklat biasa	mid-reddish brown	black	red, yellow	
soklat nguda	light reddish brown	black	red	yellow
soklat wayah	dark reddish brown	yellow	black	red
tangi biasa	mid-purple	white	red, blue	
tangi nguda	light purple	yellow, red	red, blue	
ulangkrik	reddish grey	black, blue		
		white		

* The simplest English equivalent of the Balinese colour is used.

ship is best shown by describing the process involved in the making of one puppet. I have chosen Kresna for the purpose because visually he is one of the most complex and elegant puppets, and the characteristic method of constructing puppets is well illustrated by examining him. Comments about the other puppets will, however, be added when relevant.

I COPYING AN OLD MODEL

An old puppet is fixed with a few nails to a suitable piece of hide, which in Kresna's case is thin and smooth. The craftsman then holds the relatively transparent hide up to the light and traces the silhouette of the copy on to the hide's surface. He concentrates at this stage only on the head, torso and legs, which are in one piece, and not on the arms which are made separately.

The parts of the puppet are drawn, and later also chiselled and painted, in a definite order proceeding from head to feet, then from headdress to dress. This process of work is said to resemble human birth where the head emerges first; so with the puppet, the head is the starting point. The craftsman would be inverting this order if he began with the legs. In line with this it is of interest that Belo (1970, pp. 90–91) points out that the inverted position of a human body in Bali is forbidden and unpropitious.

The first feature to be drawn, as well as chiselled, is always the eye. This is appropriate from a philosophical point of view (see next section). I Raos explained that the position of the eye stabilizes the composition and that all other parts must harmonize with it.

II CUTTING AND INCISING

The hide on which the character is drawn is secured with nails to a block of wood on the ground. It is then cut from the surrounding hide. I Raos first incises the internal design of Kresna's elegant headdress. After this the narrow, elongated eye is chiselled. The teeth and mouth are cut, the upper lip curling up in front to suggest an enigmatic smile. The remaining details of the puppet are then added, from the waist down to the feet. All this work is carried out with chisels of various sizes.

During the course of chiselling the puppet, the craftsman uses distinct motifs – each of which is referred to by a special name:

1 *bubuk biasa* (Fig. 3.1.): one of the most common motifs. it is used to indicate dress folds or the edges of articles of clothing where they are separated from the body.

2   *bubuk cenik* (Fig. 3.2.): used to show the contours of dress and
    decorations; sometimes also body lines, for example neck folds.
3   *bubuk pengerancap* (Fig. 3.3.): this depicts most jewellery items.
4   *util bok* (Fig. 3.4.): whorls of spirals that always imply hair.
5   *util punggel* (Fig. 3.5.): running motif depicted on the 'backwing'
    and on the scenic item, the Kakayonan, where it suggests vegetation.
6   *util bangsin* (Fig. 3.6.): found only on the Kakayonan where it is
    said to represent stones or caves.
7   *punggel* (Fig. 3.7.): is used on most jewellery.
8   *meduwin pandan* (Fig. 3.8.): patterns on the costume may be com-
    posed of this motif.
9   *patra sari* (Fig. 3.9.): floral design depicted on the headdress or the
    Kakayonan.

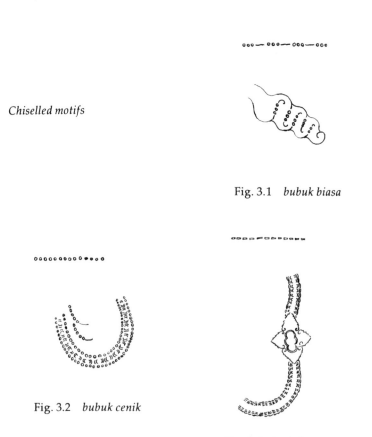

Chiselled motifs

Fig. 3.1   *bubuk biasa*

Fig. 3.2   *bubuk cenik*

Fig. 3.3   *bubuk pengerancap*

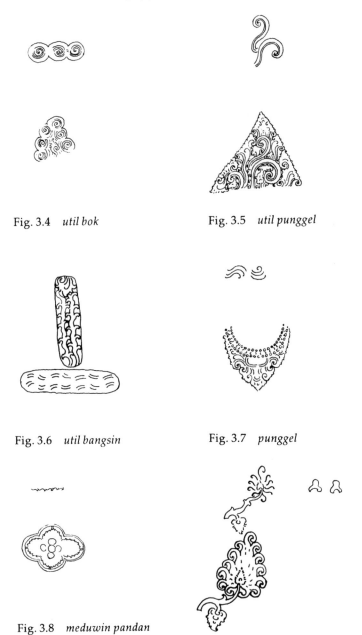

Fig. 3.4   *util bok*

Fig. 3.5   *util punggel*

Fig. 3.6   *util bangsin*

Fig. 3.7   *punggel*

Fig. 3.8   *meduwin pandan*

Fig. 3.9   *patra sari*

Fig. 3.10   *An outline of Kresna*

The chiselwork on Kresna (Fig. 3.10.) varies according to the part it depicts. Apart from *util bangsin*, all the above motifs are used on the prince. They convey a sense of movement and grace.

The arms are then cut from the hide. They are attached to the torso by inserting small wooden pegs through holes punched at the shoulders and elbows so that the arms of the otherwise static puppet can be manipulated during the performance.

The chiselwork on all other puppets, apart from the Kakayonan, is simpler than that on Kresna.

III PAINTING

Although most of the spectators see only the silhouettes during a night *wayang*, the colours are painted with great precision. This relates to the significance attributed to them, especially the skin colours (pp. 105–12).

Throughout the process, the two sides of the puppet are painted alternately. The hair of the brushes used is either of cat or goat, the former being preferred as it is soft and pliable. The entire body is first painted in successive coats of colour. On the apparel, however, progressively smaller areas are given coats of different colours. The following sequence is fixed:

1   10 coats of ochre to the entire puppet
2   2–3 coats of black only to the body
3   2–3 coats of yellow to ornaments and dress
4   5–10 coats of red to the costume
5   10 coats of cobalt blue to the ornaments and costume
6   8–10 coats of yellowish green to the costume
7   3–5 coats of Chinese yellow to the dress
8   3–5 coats of pink to all red ornaments
9   3–5 coats of light blue to the costume
10 3–5 coats of white to the body and to the costume
11 2–5 coats of light blue to the body.

In giving the body an undercoat of black I Raos is concerned above all with the shadow cast by the puppet, which must be sensitive and vital. As a result of the black base, the silhouette of the body is stronger and more distinct against the screen than the costume.[8] The undercoat of white and top-coat of light blue used for Kresna are largely of ritual significance (p. 110–11), for although the white is not visible, it signifies his purity. The final skin colour of light blue indicates his relationship with Wisnu. The craftsman has somewhat more freedom in painting the costume, although the order in which it is painted is fixed. This is especially true of the apparel of women and ogres.

Religious beliefs also determine how I Raos paints the bodies of other puppets. As he considers Siwa, Yudistira, Arjuna and Abimanyu to be spiritually elevated, they too are given a white under-coat. The servants, in contrast to other puppets, are always given a first undercoat of black. As this covers the entire figure, their shadows are more solid than those of the other characters. It is of interest to note in this context that the Kakayonan is the only puppet in a collection given no base colour of black. I Raos explained that its shadow is thus elusive, reflecting its mystical nature.

Hair or sores may be superimposed on the final body colour. A few ogres have large skin sores depicted as spots set within concentric circles of different colours.

IV   SHADING WITH COLOUR
With a fine brush I Raos shades part of the dress with the colour *ulangkrik* which is a rich, reddish-grey tone. The dress, on close observation, has thus both texture and depth.

V   DELINEATING THE BODY'S CONTOURS AND MAIN FEATURES
Using a fine brush, the craftsman paints a thin line of *ulangkrik* around the contour of the puppet. Lines also indicate neck folds, and toes, for instance, are now clearly separated from one another. Being mellower than black, *ulangkrik* is applied by I Raos to the facial features. He outlines the lips and eye, inserts the pupil, and on Kresna and other males adds the moustache and edges the sideburn in this colour.

VI   CORRECTING THE PAINTWORK
Although correcting the paintwork can be done whenever the craftsman thinks it necessary, the craftsman generally makes corrections after painting and shading the puppet, or applying gold leaf, when the figure tends to become smudged.

VII   GILDING
This is a delicate part of the work. Gold leaf is expensive, and the craftsman has to handle it with care as it is thin, soft, easily damaged or blown away. Only the yellow parts of the puppet are gilded. These are first prepared with an underlayer of fish glue. The thin sheets of

Plate 16 Merdah

Plate 17 Tualèn

Plate 18 Sangut

Plate 19
I Wayan Raos
grinding a colour pigment

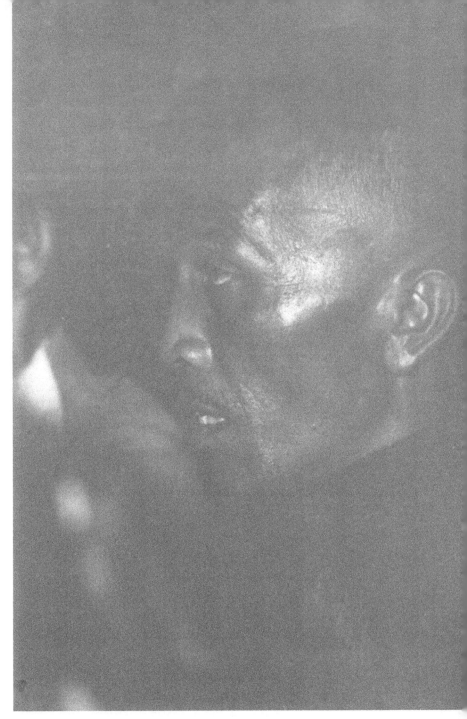

Plate 20 A spectator absorbed in a night *wayang*

Plate 21 Villagers playing gambling games
during a night *wayang*

gold leaf are placed face downwards on the glue and then smoothed out with the flattened edge of a thin bamboo stick.

The Kakayonan is usually completely gilded. Gold leaf is also applied to the costume of most senior Satriyas. Other figures tend on the whole not to be gilded.

VIII SHADING WITH FINE LINES

All the ungilded areas of Kresna's apparel are shaded with fine parallel black lines set close together. These follow the flow of the designs and garments, and function as rhythmic shading conveying movement and softness to the dress. Costumes without definite designs, like those of women, need not be shaded.

IX ATTACHING THE RODS

The handles of all characters are made either of buffalo horn[9] or wood. Wood is often used as it is less expensive. Apart from those of the servants (see below), the handles are straight, tapering rods which are split down two-thirds of their length. When a puppet such as Kresna is inserted, the rod extends to the top of the ear. The rod's thicker lower end, protruding below the puppet's feet, forms the actual handle. The handle ends in a point which can be stuck in the banana stem lying along the base of the screen.

Thin rods to manipulate the arms are attached to the puppet's hands. Their length is standard and calculated in the following fashion: the upper arm is turned out and the lower in so that it lies horizontally. In this position the rods should reach the end of the handle, although they may extend somewhat beyond this point.

The servants and one or two ogres, such as Suratma, are distinguished from the other puppets by their moveable jaws. In the case of the servants it relates to their roles as the main spokesmen in the plays. The jaw is constructed in the following manner. The back of the jaw is fastened to the head with a peg. A string is attached to the bottom of the jaw from which it extends on one side down to the handle where it is secured; on the other to the front tip of a short, thin rod (*cecantelan*), which is carved from bull's horn. As it is flexible, it acts like a buoyant spring on the puppet. The mouth opens when the *dalang* pulls the string downwards with his thumb, and it closes when he releases the string.

The handles of the servants are also distinctive. They are thick and short and extend upward only as far as the calves. Because of the lack of support to the rest of the body, the servants move in a jerky, awkward fashion on the stage.

Dèlem's head requires special comment. It is separately attached to the body, so that it jerks when he moves, and he and his brother Sangut also have tufts of cow's hair stuck on to their caps.

X VARNISHING

The entire puppet is covered in a final layer of fish glue. It is carefully painted so that the puppet's surface is smooth. This final coat is essentially a varnish which ensures that the colours remain fast and glossy.

The process of making puppets lays the foundation for the subsequent discussion on the significance of their iconography. It is evident that the craftsman is guided throughout his work by technical and aesthetic considerations; these in turn are underpinned by religious principles. As a result the forms of the puppets remain stable and constant over time, and their sacred quality is assured. This helps to validate and support the symbolic import of the iconography.

The significance of the puppets' parts

An examination of puppets shows that a unitary system underlies their iconography. Each part of the puppet is drawn from a range of possible forms. These are relatively fixed and follow rigidly prescribed conventions. The idea that puppets, like humans, are composed of separate parts, moreover, corresponds with observations by Bateson and Mead (1942) and Geertz (1973, p. 417) that the Balinese conceive of the body as divisible; references are made to battles between detachable phalluses, and to ghosts in the form of entrails. (This may also help explain the ease with which I Raos isolated and illustrated the various parts of the puppets, included here, Figs. 3.11–3.53.)

Dalangs and knowledgeable villagers can immediately recognize most of the characters which the puppets represent by their particular combination of features. A few puppets, usually minor ones, can portray up to six different characters. Major figures, on the other hand, are never interchangeable with others unless a common heritage unites them. For example, the same puppet can be used for Wisnu, Kresna and Rama as the two Satriyas are incarnations of Wisnu. Table

2 gives examples of some main substitutes which characters can assume in a performance (according to my informants).

Table 3.2

Standard character	Substitute characters
Arjuna	Laksmana
Baladéwa	Brahma
Basudéwa	Indra
Drestajumena	Yuyutsu
Drupadi	Sri or Sita
Irawan	Séta or Parikesit
Kresna	Wisnu or Rama
Niwatakawaca	Baka, Dima, Kala or Yama
Matsyapati	Dastarastra
Sikandi	Arjuna*
Supraba	Other celestial nymphs or female Satriyas, e.g. Siti Sundari
Sutasoma	Pandu
Wisnumurti	*Taken on by:* Kresna Arjuna Sahasrabahu Siwa

* Arjuna only takes on this form in the Bratayuda when his headdress almost slips off his head (see under Salya, p. 52).
For a description of the characters listed, see Chapter 2, pp. 47–54.

In every case, however, a puppet must be appropriately chosen for a given character, even if his role is small. For instance, Matsyapati can be substituted for Dastarastra as they are both elderly ruling kings.

All the puppets based on the human body have three main characteristics: costume, physical shape and colour. These characteristics can be subdivided: costume includes headdress, the different dress styles and ornaments; the facial features and hand gestures are the most important distinguishable parts of the body; colour includes skin colour and dress designs.

However, merely to classify and describe the parts of the puppet is inadequate. To the Balinese the iconography is important as it evokes explicit symbolic patterns which can be related to certain situations within their experience. It is the intention in this section to investigate this dimension and to discover the correlations that are made between the concept and the visual form. Such a survey gives some insight into the significance of the puppets and the influence they may exert on the people's thought.

There is clearly more than one source of meaning in examining the iconography. First there is what Turner called the 'exegetical meaning' (1977, p. 50), which is obtained from questioning indigenous informants. Information regarding the symbolic import of the puppet has been derived from a wide range of people – craftsmen, *dalangs*, actors from other dramatic genres, priests, as well as humble and educated villagers. Although Sperber (1979, pp. 17–34) has criticized Turner's approach, it is essential to include the exegesis, for the Balinese are verbally explicit in their interpretations of the parts of the puppets. The values they articulate are, moreover, shared to a remarkable degree across the island, or in Durkeimian terms are 'collective representations'. In line with Sperber (*ibid.*, pp. 115–49), however, the symbolic knowledge is best viewed as referring to the memory of things and words, which depends on processes of displacement and evocation. There are of course gaps in the knowledge of the natives on certain features. They know, for instance, relatively little about dress or ornaments, pointing out, as justification for their ignorance, that these items were worn so long ago that they have no more recollection of them; in contrast they wax lyrical about body colours which have a 'fan' of referents (Turner, 1977, p. 50).

Another source of information is what Ullman (1963) referred to as lexical motivation, i.e. cases when a word is found to have more than one meaning, the various meanings being associated either metaphorically or metonymically. The villagers rely on this source, for example, in their interpretation of some of the headdresses.

The meanings attributed to the parts of the puppets may, of course, change over time, and be subject to subsequent rationalizations. Yet, even when this seems to apply, as with hand gestures, the meanings are still worth including for they highlight the individual creativity of the people in the exegesis.

It is important to note, however, that the Balinese are remarkably faithful in their transmission of cultural values. A number of factors contribute to ensuring that the meaning of the symbols remains constant over time. As pointed out, the forms of the puppets are stable and they are made in a ritual setting. Moreover, many of the features of the puppets do not have meanings in isolation as they are found elsewhere in Balinese society. The exegetical meaning then often tallies with the interpretation given of the same feature in cultural settings outside *wayang*. For example, thick body hair, whether seen on a puppet, an actor on the stage or a human in daily life, generally implies a coarse character.

Comments or observations by other scholars may also be included in order to increase an understanding of the iconography or to help put the indigenous interpretations into perspective.

Illustrations of the main parts of the puppets accompany the ensuing discussion, and the most common name by which they are designated is given. They are classified according to the three characteristics mentioned earlier: costume, physical shape and colour. For the sake of clarity, tables summarizing the exegetical meanings of certain of the features are sometimes included.

Costume

I HEADDRESS

The most striking part of the puppet's costume is the headdress which is often sumptuously decorated. It sits low on the brow, covering the hair line. Most of the different headdresses are worn by male characters. It is the main item of apparel to indicate their role and status.

Headdresses can be put into one of two classes according to the meanings that the Balinese attribute to them. The first class is essentially lexically motivated, the meanings being inferred from their names; see first three examples in Table 3.

It is evident that the two imposing headdresses, the *candi utama* (Fig. 3.11.) and *candi kurung* (Fig. 3.12.) are associated by metonymy with spiritual power and the office of kingship. The Balinese do not differentiate in status between them; they simply indicate the most elevated high castes and gods in *wayang*. It is thus unsurprising that the god Siwa should be shown with the former, and Baladéwa and Kresna, also in his majestic form as Wisnumurti, should wear the latter headdress. The meanings associated with the *pepudakan* (Fig. 3.13.) are especially ingenious, with the implication that tarnished nobility will soon be dethroned. Appropriately, this headdress is worn by such characters as Duryodana or Salya who are defeated by the Pandawas in the great war.

The elegant crescent-shaped headdress, the *supit urang* (Fig. 3.14.) also belongs to this class as the name, apart from simply meaning a headdress, also denotes the pincers of a crab (van der Tuuk, 1897). Although this is the main headdress portrayed on members of the Pandawa camp, my informants were unable to explain why this is the case; no Korawas wear it. No associations are made with the name. It should be noted, however, that the small symmetrical curls of the headdress – which in operetta are made of horsehair tightly bound together – can be set in opposition to the loose hair of the ogres which sticks out in all directions (Fig. 3.15.). The form of the hair of the *supit urang* suggests order and concentration of energy, while that of the ogres suggests disorder (cf. Leach, 1958, pp. 147–64). The *supit urang anéh* (*anéh* means one; Fig. 3.16.), with its small front peak, is a simple version of the *supit urang*. It is seen on young princes.

Table 3.3 Feature: headdresses

Name and translation	Overt associations
candi utama (Fig. 3.11.) supreme royal headdress (van der Tuuk, 1897)	1 *candi* is the name given to ancient temples which during the east Javanese period were associated with ancestral royal cults (Kempers, 1959, pp. 21–2); *utama* means eminent. 2 *candi bentar*, split temple, refers to the gateway of a Balinese temple. 3 high spiritual status and kingship.
candi kurung (Fig. 3.12.) royal headdress	1 enclosed *candi*. On *candi*, see above.
pepudakan (Fig. 3.13.) unspecified headdress	1 derived from *pudak*, pandanus flower. The peak is said to resemble a large petal of this magnificent flower before it falls to the ground. 2 defeat indicated.
ketu (Fig. 3.18.) priest's hat	1 spiritual status.

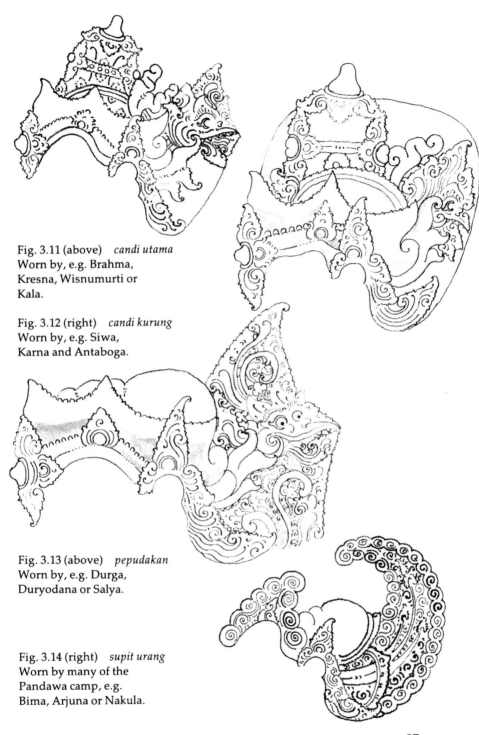

Fig. 3.11 (above) *candi utama*
Worn by, e.g. Brahma,
Kresna, Wisnumurti or
Kala.

Fig. 3.12 (right) *candi kurung*
Worn by, e.g. Siwa,
Karna and Antaboga.

Fig. 3.13 (above) *pepudakan*
Worn by, e.g. Durga,
Duryodana or Salya.

Fig. 3.14 (right) *supit urang*
Worn by many of the
Pandawa camp, e.g.
Bima, Arjuna or Nakula.

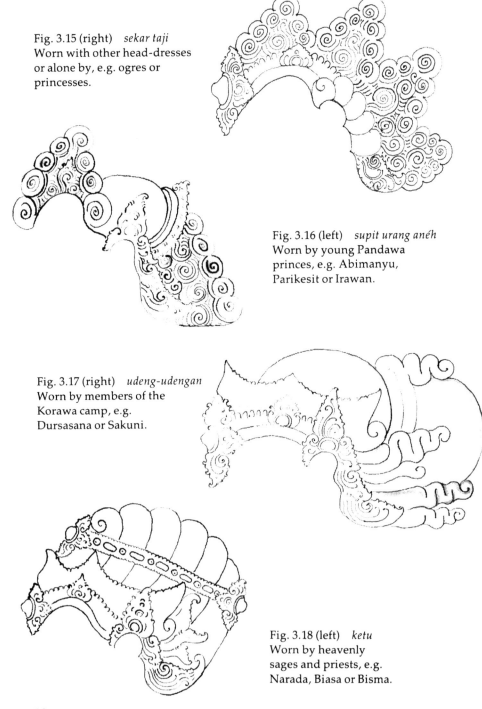

Fig. 3.15 (right)   *sekar taji*
Worn with other head-dresses
or alone by, e.g. ogres or
princesses.

Fig. 3.16 (left)   *supit urang anéh*
Worn by young Pandawa
princes, e.g. Abimanyu,
Parikesit or Irawan.

Fig. 3.17 (right)   *udeng-udengan*
Worn by members of the
Korawa camp, e.g.
Dursasana or Sakuni.

Fig. 3.18 (left)   *ketu*
Worn by heavenly
sages and priests, e.g.
Narada, Biasa or Bisma.

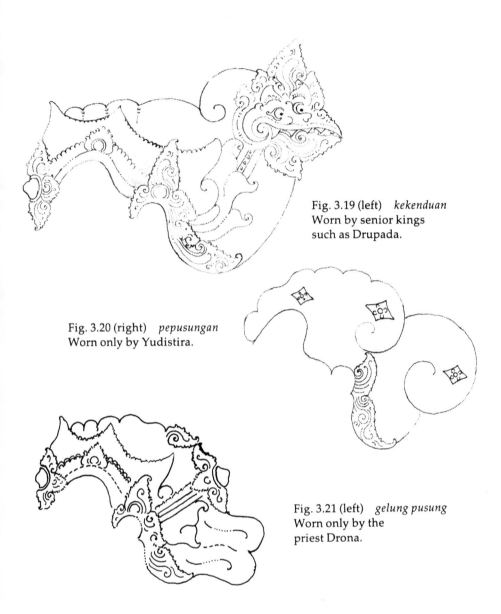

Fig. 3.19 (left) *kekenduan*
Worn by senior kings
such as Drupada.

Fig. 3.20 (right) *pepusungan*
Worn only by Yudistira.

Fig. 3.21 (left) *gelung pusung*
Worn only by the
priest Drona.

The second class of headdresses includes those which have no linguistic associations and are, or were in the past, worn in life. The most familiar present-day ones are the *udeng-udengan* (Fig. 3.17.) and the turban, *ketu* (Fig. 3.18.).[10] The first is made of cloth wound in various ways around the head. A Brahmana priest may don a tall hat called *ketu* when officiating. In the past men sometimes also wore the *kekenduan* (Fig. 3.19.) which, too, is a cloth headdress (Sukawati, 1921,

p. 528). My informants could not explain why a few kings in *wayang* should be portrayed with the *kekenduan* or courtly members of the Korawa camp should wear the *udeng-udengan*. All the male servants also wear a version of the latter headgear.

The *pepusungan* (Fig. 3.20.), also known as *gelung kaklingaan*, is only seen on Yudistira. Although most informants say it is a headdress, this is left slightly ambiguous; some describe it as a hair bun, *pusung*. Thus also Drona's headdress, where the hair is clearly arranged as a bun, is called *gelung pusung* (Fig. 3.21.). Again, as in the case of the *supit urang*, these (hair) buns suggest self-control and restraint as is appropriate for their roles. Drona is a Brahmana priest and Yudistira, who is considered the most spiritually pure Satriya, is often compared in character to a priest. It is of further interest that, according to Swellengrebel's account (1947), the king of Gianyar wore a headdress called *gelung kaklingaan* during his consecration to show his affinity to Yudistira. So we have here a recent example when a specific headdress in *wayang* may have been worn by a Satriya.

Finally, it is worth pointing out that, at least at present in Bali, the heads of both sexes are usually left bare; a man only covers his head for a ritual occasion. Most figures in *wayang* are portrayed with a headdress, or at least a crown, *sekar taji* (Fig. 3.15.). So this feature emphasizes the religious nature of the puppets.

II DRESS

Dress is standardized and found on all puppets who stand upright and have the faculty of speech in the performance. There is one exception – the supreme god, Tunggal, who is naked, and who represents an abstract idea of divinity to the Balinese.

On other male and female characters the dress depicted is a *wastra* (*kain* in Indonesian), a cloth which is wrapped in different ways around the body in life.[11] It can either hang freely or, as is often the case with males, it is swept up between the legs in a form known as *mebulat*. Tails, *lancingan*, add flourishes to many male dresses.

According to the manuscripts *Usana Jawa* and *Niti Praya* (cf. Soekawati, 1926 pp. 526–7), dress stems from the gods. Briefly, the myth is as follows:

> After creating the world, Brahma created the three sexes: males, females and hermaphrodites. They were, however, naked and lived like wild beasts.
>
> Siwa was distressed to see these people and resolved to destroy them. In due course his son, the demon-god, Kala, was born from the god's sperm which fell to earth. He grew into a giant who required his hunger to be stilled. Siwa told him that there was plenty to eat on earth. So Kala went to

earth where, as a result, the number of men diminished rapidly.

Wisnu, the god of preservation, was alarmed at this. In order to prevent Kala from eating more humans he decided, together with Indra, to ennoble men by sending them several gods and goddesses, with the necessary tools to teach them to be civilized.

Among the celestial beings who went were Ratih, the goddess of the moon, and her heavenly nymphs. They taught men how to weave from vegetable material. At first the clothes were very simple and only one colour was used for all of them.

A holy sage completed the dress. He showed men and women how to dress differently from one another, and introduced jewellery and flowers. So the Balinese learnt to dress in a similar fashion to today.

As clothes are thought to be of divine origin, they acquire special significance. Yet the Balinese are vague about the meanings of the different styles of dress seen on the puppets. By examining occasions when a particular style is, or was, traditionally worn, it emerges that dress may indicate caste, role, and sometimes age. The villagers are also sensitive about the length of dress as this tends to reflect the degree of refinement or coarseness of a character.

Three principal styles of male dress which exemplify the above points can be distinguished on puppets. There are those which cover both legs, one leg, or leave both exposed. The first style is portrayed on sages or priests who often wear a long gown and a cloak, *kewaca* (Fig. 3.22.). A few senior Satriyas, like Gatotkaca, are clad in trousers together with a loin cloth, *jalèr gantut* (Fig. 3.23.). The fact that both legs are covered is considered a mark of their distinction.

The *bulat biasa mecingcingan* (Fig. 3.24a, b), which covers one leg (*mecingcingan*), and the *bulat biasa* (Fig. 3.25.), which leaves both legs exposed from the knee downwards, are both said to belong to the second style. Here the cloth is swept up between the legs, but part droops either over or behind one leg. The *bulat biasa mecingcingan* looks especially elegant when the cloth billows out in a wide curve past the calf of the back leg, as on Kresna or Arjuna. This style often includes a dress-tail.

This second style of dress deserves singling out. According to my informants, it indicates an official role; warriors in the past probably tucked up the cloth in a similar manner for battle. Some villagers also say that a prominent dress-tail symbolizes the phallus, masculinity and sexuality. This seems to be substantiated by the fact that a man wears the dress-tail over his arm in ceremonies as it would otherwise pollute the offerings.

Fig. 3.22   *kewaca*
Worn by sages and
priests, e.g. Biasa,
Narada or Bisma.

Fig. 3.23   *jalèr gantut*
Worn by, e.g. Baladéwa
or Gatotkaca.

Fig. 3.24a   *bulat biasa mecingcingan*
Worn by such Satriyas
as Yudistira, Arjuna or
Duryodana.

Fig. 3.24b   *bulat biasa mecingcingan*
Worn by, e.g. Sakuni or
Lesmana Kumara.

Fig. 3.25   *bulat biasa*
Worn only by a few
Satriyas.

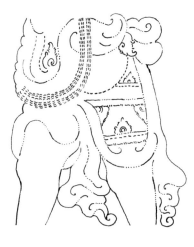

Fig. 3.26   *bulat gantut*
Worn by junior Satriyas
and a few ogres, e.g.
Abimanyu or Dimbi.

Fig. 3.27   *wastra gantut*
Worn mainly by
ogres, e.g. Baka.

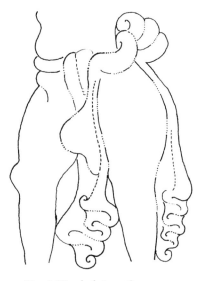

Fig. 3.28   *bulat genting*
Worn by Bayu or Bima;
without a dress-tail
by Tualèn or Merdah.

Fig. 3.29 *kimpus*
Worn by heavenly
nymphs or princesses,
e.g. Drupadi or Supraba.

Fig. 3.30 *wastra biasa*
Worn by, e.g. Kunti.

In the third style the dress is very short. This tends to suggest youth or strength and physical prowess, as in the case of Bima or Hanuman. It may, however, also indicate a coarse disposition or a lowly status – of one who works in the fields. Visually it is difficult to distinguish between the *bulat gantut* (Fig. 3.26.), when the cloth is swept up between the legs, or the *wastra gantut* (Fig. 3.27.), when the cloth is rolled up around the waist. Both may be depicted on young princes and ogres, whose ample paunches may then bulge over the dress which has slipped down to reveal an overgrown navel. The dress *bulat genting* (Fig. 3.28.), worn by Bima, Bayu or Hanuman, is striking in that it leaves not only the muscular legs exposed, but also the buttocks; the dashing dress-tail is said to represent a fold of cloth, *ngelèbèr*. The servants also wear short loin cloths.

Female dress is much less varied. There are essentially two styles: the tubular-shaped gown, *kimpus* (Fig. 3.29.), usually portrayed together wiith a tight bodice, which covers the breasts, and a dress which flows freely down from the waist, *wastra biasa* (Fig. 3.30.). The elegant *kimpus* is worn by princesses such as Drupadi or by heavenly nymphs.

Little further light can be thrown on the dress of puppets by examining the historical sources. It is, however, of interest to observe that in the Chinese chronicles of the fifteenth century (Ma Huan, 1433, p. 87 and p. 95), it is mentioned that the king of Majapahit wore a crown of gold leaves and flowers and silk kerchiefs were wrapped around the lower part of the body. Pigeaud described in greater detail the dress that members of the court of Majapahit may have worn:

> Probably in outward appearance King Hayan Wuruk and his court showed more resemblance to the Pandawas as represented in the eighteenth-century *wayang* style than to twentieth-century Central Javanese kings and nobles whose stately dress and solemn mien no doubt was influenced by Dutch gravity; . . . and [so] the traditional *wayang* clothing, however fantastically overdone, might give some idea of fourteenth-century Majapahit attire (1962, p. 507).

Although there were definite links between Bali and the Javanese kingdoms, these sources are meagre and it is on the whole more reliable to refer to Balinese culture for information on the dress of Balinese puppets. However, it does seem likely, although not conclusive, to my informants that the outfit of warriors of the court resembled that of puppets which represent Satriyas.

III ORNAMENTS

Ornaments are portrayed on all characters who are clothed, although depending on their caste, status and nature they are either richly or simply adorned. Thus senior Satriyas of both sexes are splendidly decked out, while priests and servants wear few decorative items.

Little meaning is attached to the jewellery (which may vary somewhat between collections). They mainly indicate wealth, although certain individuals are characterized by the style of their bangles or armlets, called *gelang kana* (Figs 3.31–3.37.).

Only two ornaments require special mention. The first is the *kelat bau*, which rises like a 'back wing' and which is seen on gods and high ranking Satriyas (see 'back wing' on illustration of Kresna, Fig. 3.10). Swellengrebel (1947) refers to the *kelat bau* displayed by the king of Gianyar. This suggests that, as with the headdress, *gelung kaklingaan*, such an ornament was once worn in life.

The *Garuda mungkur* (Garuda at the back; Fig. 3.38.) is the most complex and elaborate single ornament. A smaller version of it is the *guak*, or crow's head on the girdle, the *karang guak* (Fig. 3.39.). The villagers say that the mythological bird Garuda is also a crow. These birds' heads primarily connote supernatural power, an attribute traditionally ascribed to Satriyas. In folk tradition the crow is thought

Fig. 3.31 *gelang kana*
Worn by, e.g.
Kresna and
other Satriyas.

Fig. 3.32 *gelang kana*
Worn by, e.g.
Arjuna and other
Satriyas.

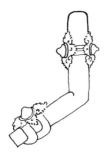

Fig. 3.33 *gelang kana*
Worn by, e.g.
Karna.

Fig. 3.34 *gelang kana*
Worn by, e.g.
Bima or Hanuman.

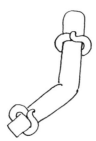

Fig. 3.35 *gelang kana*
Worn by, e.g.
some ogres; on
the wrist by the
servants.

Fig. 3.36 *gelang kana*
Worn by, e.g.
some ogres.

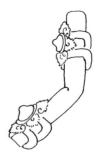

Fig. 3.37 *gelang kana*
Worn by, e.g.
Boma.

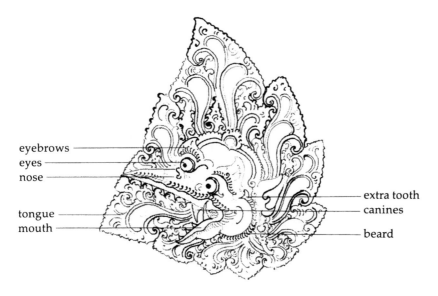

eyebrows
eyes
nose

extra tooth
canines

tongue
mouth

beard

Fig. 3.38   *Garuda mungkur*
Worn by senior characters,
e.g. Siwa, Kresna or Kala

mouth

nose

eybrows
extra tooth

eyes

tongue
canines

Fig. 3.39   *Karang guak*
Worn by many characters.

to live in the graveyard. He is powerful (*sakti*) and able to foretell the future: although his home is the graveyard he never becomes ritually impure. In view of the crow's association with mystic power, it is fitting that senior rulers like Kresna, Karna and Duryodana, or Wisnumurti, should be adorned with birds' heads.

Physical shape

Before discussing the puppets' facial features it is first necessary to understand something about the Balinese views on the body. Douglas's (1980, p. 115) approach to the body as a symbol of society is pertinent to Bali, where the people consider the head to be the most elevated part of the body. It is identified with the Brahmana caste, and the other castes with progressively lower parts. At the same time, the body is held to represent the macrocosm which consists of three spheres: the underworld, earth and sky. From the feet to the buttocks is the underworld; from the stomach to eyes is the earth; while the forehead is the sky (Weck, 1937, p. 238; Hooykaas, 1973a, p. 4).

In the light of the above it is hardly surprising that the Balinese focus on the facial features. The two most significant are the eyes and teeth. The meanings attributed to them are held for the most part by the community as a collectivity. Although little is known about hand gestures, the villagers pay attention to them as the manner in which the *dalang* moves the hands greatly heightens the impact of the figures on the stage. Other physical features are not included here as no specific meaning is associated with them.

I THE FACIAL FEATURES: EYES AND TEETH
All Balinese distinguish two basic eye shapes on puppets: slit, *sumpé* (Fig. 3.40.), and round, *dedelingan* (Fig. 3.41.). Some informants also recognize a bean-shaped eye, *pijak* (Fig. 3.42) and an eye which seems half-closed, *guling* (Fig. 3.43.), although these may be referred to as *sumpé* as they, too, are elongated and slit.

As emerged earlier, the eye is the first feature that a craftsman draws and chisels when making a new puppet. The significance of the eyes is already evidenced in the Balinese term for 'to see', *nyurianin*, which is derived from *surya*, sun. In the daily ritual, *Surya-sevana*, of a Brahmana Siwa priest, the principal god worshipped is the Sun god, Surya. Sight is also considered the most important sense in cognizing the world of men (see p. 183–84 where this is explained in much greater detail).

Fig. 3.40 *sumpé*
Seen on all refined
characters, e.g. Arjuna
or Nakula.

Fig. 3.41 *dedelingan*
Seen on all coarse
characters, e.g.
Duryodana, ogres,
or Dèlem.

Fig. 3.42 *pijak*
Seen on e.g.
Drona, Sakuni
or Sangut.

Fig. 3.43 *guling*
Seen only on
Tualèn.

In view of the significance of sight, it is understandable that the eyes in *wayang* sustain axiomatic values in the society, see Table 4. This applies especially to slit and round eyes. One or other of these two shapes is found on most puppets. Individuals with slit eyes, such as Yudistira and Arjuna, tend to be refined, controlled and uphold social ideals. On the other hand, coarse, hot-headed and often disruptive characters as, for example, Duryodana, Dursasana, the most witless of the servants, Dèlem, and all ogres, have large, round eyes.

A few characters, for instance Drona or the servant Sangut, are sometimes said to have a *pijak* eye, whereby their shrewdness is stressed.

The *guling* eye is only portrayed on Tualèn, who in many ways is the wisest individual in *wayang*.

Teeth are the most decisive feature in separating humans and gods from animals, birds and ogres. The former have flat (Fig. 3.44.) and the latter pointed teeth and sharp canines or fangs (Figs. 3.45–3.47.). The meaning of flat teeth is highlighted in the context of the tooth-filing ceremony, *mepandas*. All Balinese must have their teeth filed at some stage in their life; this often takes place at the same time as marriage.

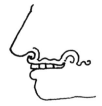

Fig. 3.44   *untu asat*
Found on all
gods and humans.

Fig. 3.45   *siung*
Found on ogres.

Fig. 3.46   *siung*
Found on birds.

Fig. 3.47   *siung*
Found on snakes.

Table 3.4 Facial features: eye shapes and teeth

Name and translation or description	Overt associations
sumpé (Fig. 3.40.) slit	refinement; an understanding of *darma*, duty and morality
dedelingan (Fig. 3.41.) wide open; round	coarseness and lack of control
pijak (Fig. 3.42) bean-shaped	intelligence and shrewdness
guling (Fig. 3.43.) half-closed	inclination to meditation; compassion for others
untu asat (Fig. 3.44.) flat teeth	ritual purity and a civilized being
siung (Fig. 3.45.) sharp canines or fangs	ritual impurity; the animal world

The indigenous explanation given of this ritual is that 'it removes the impurity which is like the thin outer skin of an onion', i.e. the last remnants of impurity are removed and then man is ritually pure and civilized. Unfiled teeth are said to be *kumel* implying a state of dirt. The term is used to refer to effluence from the nose, and mouth, and blood, sweat, pus and so forth – but not to urine or faeces.

On the other hand, it is appropriate to their low position that animals and ogres have sharp teeth and fangs. This also applies to Hanuman, although he is one of the purest characters. To the villagers, his white skin colour (see p. 111) suppresses the negative implication of the teeth.

II HAND GESTURE

Puppets are distinguished by their stylized hand gestures. Apart from the servants, these are said to be the same for both hands. This is so even if one arm is static and its gesture is indistinct because the hand is held against the dress. Informants differ more markedly in their interpretations of gestures than of any other feature. Scholarly *dalangs* say they are *mudras*, ritual hand gestures, although they do not in general know individual names or meanings. In this context it is of interest that Zoete and Spies (1973, p. 20) pointed out that the eloquent finger postures of dancers are faint relics of a sign-language, *mudras*.

As little is known about the gestures at the village level, a highly respected Siwaite priest in my area, the *padanda* from Padangtegal in Gianyar (officially known as *padanda* Gedé Manuaba) was approached. He pointed out without hesitation that puppet gestures are based on *mudras* made by a Siwaite priest. Although in life *mudras* generally require both hands to be held in identical positions and on the same level, puppets had to move their arms in accordance with the requirements of a dramatic performance. So each gesture exhibits half a *mudra*. Only the hands of the supreme god Tunggal form a distinct *mudra* (Fig. 3.48.). The servants also differ from other characters as each of their hands is in a different position, each one representing a *mudra*. Hence each servant makes, in effect, two *mudras* which are identified as *cakra-* and *padma-mudra*.

The visual evidence essentially substantiates the view that the gestures are *mudras*, although it cannot be established with certitude that they are the same *mudras* as those identified by the priest from Padangtegal. Some of them seem in fact to correspond more closely to those made by Buddha priests (see illustrations in Hooykaas, 1973c).

The priest's interpretations of the *mudras*, together with the views of a learned *dalang* on their meanings in *wayang*, are summed up in Table 5. Although these are tentative and not widely shared, they are included as they illustrate the ingenuity of individual Balinese in their exegesis. The meanings that some villagers associate with three of the gestures are also given in the table. In these instances the meanings rely on obvious visual association of the same gesture when seen in life. So, for example, an open hand is said to represent a grasping nature (see *padma-mudra*).

Table 3.5 Feature: hand gestures

Name and translation	Overt associations
redaya-mudra[1] (Fig. 3.48.) heart-*mudra*	1 *padanda* Padangtegal: it represents the creation of the universe by Sang Hyang Widi, a higher truth or transcendental world order (see p. 20). Its aim is to ensure prosperity. 2 I Ewer[2]: the above interpretation is appropriate on the god Tunggal, who is the only character to make this mudra.
saro-mudra (Fig. 3.49.) arrow-*mudra*	1 *padanda* Padangtegal: its aim is to worship the 'seat', *palinggihan*, of the goddess Gangga. 2 I Ewer: the goddess Gangga represents the holy river Gangga (Ganges), i.e. *amerta*, the elixir of immortality. The gesture indicates the desire to protect the land. 3 villagers: concentration of energy. It is not called a *mudra*.
cakra-mudra (Fig. 3.50.) wheel-*mudra*	1 *padanda* Padangtegal: its aim is to give respect to the trinity, *trisakti*, Brahma, Wisnu and Siwa (or Iswara). 2 I Ewer: on the servants the *mudra* implies the desire that the gods protect the state; on others it indicates that the aims are not always constant. 3 villagers: wavering concentration. It is not called a *mudra*.
sika-mudra (Fig. 3.51.) top-*mudra*	1 *padanda* Padangtegel: to worship the 'seat' of Brahma and his wife, Saraswati. 2 I Ewer: it is a request by ogres that they gain knowledge and develop spiritually.

padma-mudra (Fig. 3.52.) lotus-*mudra*	1 *padanda* Padangtegal: its aim is to worship the 'seat' of Widi and to ask him to descend. 2 I Ewer: to supplicate the god for protection. 3 villagers: a grasping nature. It is not called a *mudra*.
danu-mudra (Fig. 3.53.) bow-*mudra*	1 *padanda* Padangtegal: its aim is to worship the 'seat' of Widi, requesting that all diversities be unified in him. 2 I Ewer: to direct energy (*bayu*) to Widi in order to ensure that the god's concentration will not falter; then the land will prosper.

Notes
1. Hooykaas (1966) mentions all the above *mudras*, but the effects attributed to them are different.
2. The *dalang* I Ewer accompanied me to the Brahmana priest from Padangtegal. His interpretations are given in association with the meanings attributed by the priest.

Fig. 3.48 *redaya-mudra*
Seen only Tunggal.

Fig. 3.49 *saro-mudra*
Seen mainly on
Satriyas of the
Pandawa camp.

Fig. 3.50 *cakra-mudra*
Seen mainly on
Satriyas of the
Korawa camp.

Fig. 3.51 *sika-mudra*
Seen on some ogres.

Fig. 3.52 *padma-mudra*
Seen on a few ogres.

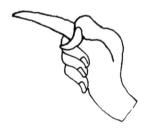

Fig. 3.53 *danu-mudra*
Seen on Bayu,
Bima or Hanuman.

103

In examining the table it should be noted how skilfully the *dalang* adapts the priest's interpretations of *mudras* to fit specific characters in *wayang*. For example, the gesture *sika-mudra* (Fig. 3.51.) is found on only one or two ogres. The *dalang* explained that it is appropriate that they should make this gesture: they are at a low stage of development and they supplicate Saraswati, the goddess of literature, so that in their next incarnation they may learn to read and write, and thereby become civilized.

In the context of *wayang*, Brahmana priests and scholarly *dalangs* point out that it is important that all puppets make *mudras*. This applies in particular to ogres. They have to supplicate Sang Hyang Widi, the transcendental unity, for his protection and to beg his pardon (*nunas ampura*) for their behaviour which is destructive and base. It is further pointed out that all *mudras* are derived from the lotus, *padma*, and represent weapons which aim to destroy witches, demons and ritual impurity in general. Through their ritual hand gestures, the characters worship Sang Hyang Widi and give him pleasure, and so ensure his continued goodwill towards the world and the creatures in it. Eventually all beings including ogres and demons, will become united with him.

Colour

I DRESS DESIGNS

The only design which has explicit meaning to the Balinese is the black and white checkered cloth, *polèng*. Its two colours are said to refer to the cosmic dualities (p. 138), and hence they reflect the state of the world and the beings in it. Some are pure and others are impure. Usually the cloth has a red edge around it. The three colours, red, black and white then represent the trinity, Brahma, Wisnu and Siwa (or Iswara) In *wayang* the cloth is only worn by characters who possess supernatural power, such as Bima, Hanuman or Tualèn.

II BODY COLOUR

The body colours of the puppets are universally agreed to be the most significant iconographic feature. Almost all the body colours, with few exceptions, are derived from mixing in various proportions the five basic colours: white, red, yellow, blue and black. An objective classification of puppets' skin colours is, however, difficult as the range of colours used varies from one collection to another. Sometimes old puppets may even be touched up with new oil paints. These are superimposed on traditional paints, which makes it difficult to determine the exact hue. However, an examination of the different collections shows that a fundamental system is being perpetuated in the application of colours. It relies on maintaining the basic relationship between hues. This means that each colour gains its identity by its relationship to the others. So while a given colour is called by a single Balinese name, its precise hue may vary from collection to collection. Within a collection, however, each colour is used consistently.

Although the body colours cannot be seen by the spectators who watch the shadows projected on to a screen at night (for reasons discussed in Chapter 5), they are semantically complex symbols, having a wide range of meanings which relate to major ideas and values in the society. In examining colour, two different aspects have to be distinguished: the meanings of the five basic colours which craftsmen use to produce the mixed ones, and the final or surface colours of the puppet's body. These are discussed separately here.

A The basic colours In order to understand the meanings associated with the five basic colours – white, red, yellow, black and blue – it is important first to realize that to the Balinese the universe is ordered according to fundamental principles of classification. The most popular system adhered to in *wayang* is known as *panca déwa* (five gods): a five-fold division of the cosmos or classifactory scheme which includes other sets such as directions, colours and numbers, see Diagram 1.

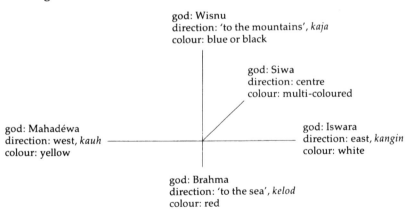

god: Wisnu
direction: 'to the mountains', *kaja*
colour: blue or black

god: Siwa
direction: centre
colour: multi-coloured

god: Mahadéwa
direction: west, *kauh*
colour: yellow

god: Iswara
direction: east, *kangin*
colour: white

god: Brahma
direction: 'to the sea', *kelod*
colour: red

Diagram 3.1 *The panca déwa (five gods)*

In this scheme the directions are defined by reference to two spatial axes which intersect at the centre. These axes differ, however, in character. In the first, the line between the east and west is fixed. In the second, the cardinal points *kaja* and *kelod* correspond roughly with upstream and downstream, from the volcanic lakes in the interior to the sea. Thus the axis linking mountain and sea describes a radius round a roughly central point to produce a circle.

'To the mountain' and east are identified in the scheme with sacredness, purity and prosperity, and 'to the sea' and west with the reverse (Swellengrebel, 1960, p. 39). As can be seen in the diagram, the gods Iswara, Brahma, Mahadéwa and Wisnu are linked with the basic colours used in painting puppets, white, red, yellow and blue or black respectively. It is relevant to mention here that a sharper distinction is made between Wisnu and Brahma than between Iswara and Mahadéwa whose names can even be used to indicate Siwa or aspects of Siwa (*ibid.*, p. 45) This has a bearing on understanding the meaning attributed to the five colours.

The five colours are said to be the purest representation of the gods of the *panca déwa*, and the symbolic values they reflect stem from the gods with whom they are linked.[12] This helps account for the axiomatic force of the colour symbols in the society. Table 6 summarizes the meanings associated with the five colours in relation to the iconography of the puppets. Informants however, agree, that their meanings are essentially the same in other artistic contexts, thus masks and facial make-up in other dance-dramas follow the same principles.

In rituals the colours only represent the colours of the gods and not their qualities. For example, the different coloured petals, rice offerings or banners then simply symbolize the gods. The clothes worn by priests, on the other hand, tend to reinforce the meanings listed above. This is especially true of white and yellow. A white dress is the standard dress of all priests. As shown in Table 6, yellow connotes attachment and compassion. Hence it is fitting that village priests, (*jèro mangku*), who are closer to the villagers than Brahmana priests, often still wear yellow sashes when officiating at rituals.

In reviewing Table 6, it is evident that white and yellow do not differ greatly in the meanings associated with them. White, and to a lesser degree yellow, mainly connote purity and refinement. Blue is associated with Wisnu and water, which is 'cooling' and refreshing. Although black is often the colour of Wisnu in literary texts, it is the most ambiguous colour in the folk tradition. It is a 'cool' colour associated with such concepts as meditation, intelligence and virtue,

Table 3.6 Feature: body colour

Name and translation	Overt associations
putih white	1 ritual purity 2 refinement, self-control, calm and an unblemished surface 3 a state of detachment parallel to that of Buddhahood (see van der Tuuk, 1897) 4 a sweet voice
kuning yellow	1 ritual purity, but less so than white 2 attachment, referred to as *semangat* (in Indonesian), active and enthusiastic 3 compassion and generosity
selem black	1 a 'cool', *etis*, colour, associated with water, which brings fertility to the land and harmony to the home (referred to as *ngetisin*) 2 intelligence, skill, bravery and steadfastness 3 meditation 4 a fluent talker 5 witchcraft and night – witches mainly emerge at night; supernatural power (black, *pengiwa*) 6 deceit
pelung blue	reflects the positive values of black (nos. 1–4) and none of the negative ones
barak red	1 a 'hot', *panes*, colour, associated with fire, which brings disturbance and strife (referred to as *manesin*) 2 courage and boldness which can be used for ignoble or noble ends 3 lack of self-control and coarseness 4 pride 5 supernatural power 6 a harsh voice

but at the same time it connotes the night, witchcraft and black magic. Because of its contradictory meanings, black is generally avoided on puppets, except on ambiguous ones, like Bima, whose genitor is a god, but who has affinity with ogres, one of whom he marries (see Dimbi, p. 54). Bima is also powerful and coarse. Red, which is the colour of Brahma, the god of fire, is clearly a 'hot' colour associated with strife, tension and lack of self-control.

In a discussion of colour it is worth mentioning that the scheme, *panca déwa*, can be related to a more elaborate nine-fold system, *nawa-sanga* (*ibid.*, pp. 50–1; see also Pott, 1966, pp. 133–6), in which 'to the mountain' and 'to the sea' become north and south respectively and the intermediate directions are ascribed with a prominence similar to that of the cardinal points. In this system black is associated with Wisnu and north, and blue with Sambu and north east. Siwa is at the centre of both the *panca déwa* and *nawa-sanga*. A few *dalangs* draw attention to this more differentiated scheme when explaining the significance of the colours in the abstract. Here mention is made of the religious incantation, *mantra Aji Kembang* which some *dalangs* chant during a *sudamala* rite (see p. 135–37). An extended version of this *mantra* is also found in the treatise *Dharma Pawayangan*, 'Laws of the *wayang*' (Hooykaas, 1973b, pp. 88–91). Although the Balinese never applied the meanings attributed to the colours in the *mantra* to the puppets, it is included for it emphasizes again the sacred nature of the colours and illustrates how they are linked to the nine gods and their consorts of this scheme, as well as to the organs of the body and the directions. The *mantra* also shows how the schemes used may differ according to context. This is primarily true of colour: the *nawa-sanga* is often said to represent a more abstract philosophical level than the *panca déwa*. The *mantra* here was recited by *dalang* I Ewer:

> In the east there is a white lotus.
> The god is Iswara.
> He dwells in the heart.
> Here he resides with his consort.
> Nature blossoms white.
> The soul who is reincarnated like this
> will be happy and fortunate
> and will enjoy rendering homage to the gods.
>
> In the south east there is a pink lotus.
> The god is Mahesora.
> He dwells in the lungs.
> Here he resides with his consort.
> Nature blossoms pink.
> The soul who is reincarnated like this
> will be able to discriminate between right and wrong
> and will be famous in the world.

In the south there is a red lotus.
The god is Brahma.
He dwells in the liver.
Here he resides with his consort.
Nature blossoms red.
The soul who is reincarnated like this
will be good-looking and live to be very old
and will be wise in the knowledge of literature.

In the south west there is an orange lotus.
The god is Rudra.
He dwells in the colon.
Here he resides with his consort.
Nature blossoms orange.
The soul who is reincarnated like this
will be patient and courteous
and popular among men.

In the west there is a yellow lotus.
The god is Mahadéwa.
He dwells in the kidneys.
Here he resides with his consort.
Nature blossoms yellow.
The soul who is reincarnated like this
will be brave in war
and knowledgeable in literature.

In the north west there is a green lotus.
The god is Sangkara.
He dwells in the spleen.
Here he resides with his consort.
Nature blossoms green.
The soul who is reincarnated like this
will be diligent in fasting and meditation
and firm and steadfast in the path of honesty.

In the north there is a black lotus.
The god is Wisnu.
He dwells in the gall.
Here he resides with his consort.
Nature blossoms black.
The soul who is reincarnated like this
will act purely
and will be good-looking and follow the path of *darma* [duty].

In the north east there is a blue lotus.
The god is Sambu.
He dwells in the peritoneum.
Nature blossoms blue.
The soul who is reincarnated like this
will be firm in *darma*
and will attain all he desires and will be loved by
the entire family.

In the centre there is a multi-coloured lotus.
The god is Siwa.
He dwells in the pancreas.
Here he resides with his consort.
Nature blossoms multi-coloured.
The soul who is reincarnated like this
will be talented and virtuous
and will be firm in fasting and meditation
in order to obtain release.

It is evident from the *mantra* that all the qualities associated with the colours on this abstract level have positive connotations. Yet it is important to stress again that the Balinese discuss the colours of the puppets' skins in relation to the *panca déwa* (the five gods).[12] Only Tualèn's body colour, *ulangkrik* (multi-colours, see p. 111), accords with the attributes ascribed to multi-coloured in both cosmological systems and befits his character.

Finally, in the context of colour, it is interesting to note that the scholar Goris has suggested that the so-called four-five part system (four and the centre) is pre-Hindu and that more differentiated systems easily linked up to it (Swellengrebel, 1960, p. 51).

B   Combined colours   Almost all the puppets' body colours are combinations (see Table 1). The five basic colours are said to retain the particular meanings associated with them (as outlined in Table 6) when they are mixed in varying proportions to produce the combined ones. So the body colour of a character subtly expresses his mystic qualities – these being reflections of the five gods of the scheme, the *panca déwa*. Although craftsmen differ somewhat in how they mix the basic colours, the proportions I Raos uses are as good an index as any of how the characters obtain significance through their body colours. For example, Kresna is usually light blue,[13] never black. His bluish skin colour is made up of white and blue, and so he is linked to Iswara and Wisnu, the god of water, of whom he is an incarnation. As already mentioned (p. 79), he is still given an undercoat of white in order to stress his purity. Many of the Satriyas in the Pandawa camp are yellowish white, while their counterparts in the Korawa camp are generally different shades of orange or brown. The former colour is made up of equal proportions of yellow and white, while the latter is of different proportions of red, black, yellow and, on rare occasions, white. As we have seen, all these colours have explicit symbolic meaning.

Tualèn (Plate 17) is the one character who stands out by his skin colour. He alone in a collection is *ulangkrik*, which is made up of all the five basic colours. The Balinese say the colour relates him to Siwa the central god of the five-fold and the nine-fold division of the cosmos. In the same way that all the gods merge into Siwa, who constitutes a higher unity and is multi-coloured, all the colours on the craftsman's palette are mixed to produce *ulangkrik*. This colour signifies the servant's role as supreme mediator in the plays, who at times show great wisdom and insight.

Red is the predominant colour used for the body colours of ogres. It links them to Brahma and reflects their coarseness and lack of control. Additional blotchers are said to be a skin (and character) disfiguration, which further emphasizes their impurity. Ogres, as well as high castes of the Korawa camp, may still have thick body hair. This is called *bulu*, feathers, and indicates coarseness and the animal world.

The only basic colour ever seen on a puppet's body is white. The god Tunggal and the monkey Hanuman are white, as are a small number of ogres. Some Balinese distinguish terminologically between the white, *putih*, on the first two characters who are very pure and the white on ogres which is called *putih melé* and described as corpse-like white. *Melé* is also associated in sound by the Balinese to the word *jelé* which means evil. Visually, however, *putih* and *putih melé* are identical colours. A possible reason for this is that the categories of gods, ogres and demons may at times seem blurred to the people (cf. Friederich, 1959, p. 54). So the gods can also take on the form of ogres. This is evident in performances where Kresna assumes the form of Wisnumurti (Plate 6) who is also called the thousand-fold ogre of the right. This figure appears terrifying with three round eyes and a massive head-dress flanked by five small heads. On top, in the centre, the head is a replica in miniature of the principal one. On one side two ogres' heads look out and on the other two tigers' heads. In addition each of the eight arms grasps an attribute,[14] referred to as a weapon. This fierce ogre-like figure is a transformation of the preserver god, Wisnu, in his transcendental state of anger.

It is evident that the iconographic elements which underlie the structure of the puppets have a more or less clearly ordered and recognized significance. The features are, however, not distributed at random, but are combined systematically to produce individuals who, as emerges in the next section, are members of groups who are part of a cosmic scheme.

The iconographic system

The iconographic system as a whole is polysemic, having multiplicity of meaning. At its widest range it implies a conception of the cosmos and the place of human society in it.

This system is essentially anthropocentric (Skorupski, 1976, p. 25) as the emphasis is on man and the moral rules which bind him with others. Most puppets in a collection are modelled on man. The largest group is the Satriyas, the majority of whom are males. The other main groups include the gods, Brahmanas, servants and ogres. Even ogres are remade in cultural or human form. Facially they resemble wild animals, yet they have human torsos and limbs, stand upright and are clothed. The same applies to such mythic creatures as Hanuman or Garuda. Apart from the Tree of Life, the Kakayonan, and the Sungsang, there are few scenic items. Unclad animals have very minor roles.

In order to understand the visual system, it is important to take into account several explanatory levels. We have seen that the parts of the puppets direct attention selectively to certain patterns of meaning. This level is explicit to the Balinese and consciously applied. The system as an integrated whole, however, gains further significance by reference to other ritual and social contexts of which the people are only marginally aware, i.e. the cultural code at this level tends to be largely latent. Yet, informants can become fully aware of this level when questioned. As in the previous section, comments by other scholars are included if relevant.

Three main issues emerge when looking at a collection in its entirety, and each will be discussed separately. The first is based on the hierarchical order into which the groups can be ranked. Here the gods are the most sublime. The second focuses on the contrasts between the Pandawas and the Korawas. Lastly, the special place of the servants is considered. They form the base or foundation of the society, as well as being mediators who have great power in the drama.

The hierarchy: the moral order of the universe

A puppet collection presents a stable view of the world which in its totality comprises celestial, human and demonic beings. In this cosmic order each group has its proper duty, *darma. Darma*, according to Zoetmulder (1965, p. 269), may also imply 'essential teaching' (*essentielled Lehre*) and 'ultimate reality' (*letzte Realität*). So, in a social context, *darma* implies righteousness, morality, i.e. the right ordering of society; at the same time the concept suggests a higher order of reality, for it can mean eternal moral law which governs all human and non-human existence (cf. Schärer on the meaning of *adat*, p. 175).

In the previous discussion we have seen how the outward appearance of the figures reflects inner states. By examining the iconographic system it is possible to gain an idea of how far individuals, and the groups of which they are members, live up to the cosmic order of which they are part.

The Balinese seem basically to agree on what the duties of the various groups are:

gods	they have a higher morality which cannot be understood by men; they may even be beyond human ideas of morality.
Brahmanas	they should follow the six moral rules: good speech, good thoughts, good actions, good use of objects and persons, good work, have only one wife and be sexually faithful. They should be learned in literary and religious matters, and maintain a state of ritual purity. They should never show fear, anger or pride, and always be generous.
Satriyas	they should be good administrators and warriors. They should protect and set a good example to their subjects. They should be virile lovers.
Wèsyas	they should engage in proper commerce.
Sudras	they should subordinate their individuality to that of the community and follow the rules and be respectful to the high castes. They should work in the rice-fields, on repairing roads and public buildings.
ogres	they should be uncontrolled, greedy, powerful, ready to devour humans or harass virtuous men.
animals	they can do no more than subsist and make themselves available to be eaten.

One point should be added here. As the focus in *wayang* is on males, the duties here mainly refer to them. In passing, it is said that women should faithfully follow their husbands. Women's relative lack of importance in *wayang* is partly due to the fact that descent in Bali is through the patriline (p. 19–20), but this will be mentioned again later.

In examining the axis which orders the hierarchical ranking of the groups, with special reference to the duties outlined above, a few pertinent comments can be made. First it is relevant to realize that the overall scheme into which the groups are integrated is essentially one of purity. The gods – in particular Tunggal who forms the apex of the hierarchy into which the *wayang* world is divided – are the most pure, while ogres and animals are impure, but it is their *darma* to be so.

In this hierarchical system gods and the different castes of men resemble each other physically: both are modelled closely on human beings and have filed teeth. Visual similarity is, however, especially marked between gods and senior ruling kings. Both groups stand out by their ornate dress and often wear the same headdresses. This affinity is reiterated in the titles by which senior Satriyas are still known, for example, Ratu Déwa Agung, supreme god, or Cokor I Déwa, the foot of the god (see p. 144, Table 1). Although my informants no longer say that the king is god incarnate, as seems to have been the case between the tenth and eleventh centuries in both Bali and Java (Stutterheim, 1935, p. 132; Schreike, 1957, pp. 9–10), the divine is thought to be immediately present in a high-ranking Satriya. Swellengrebel (1947) in his account of the consecration of the king of Gianyar, based on material collected by Schwarz in 1903, gives a good picture of the nature of the king's relationship to the gods. At one point he says that it seemed as if the king 'became a god on earth, an incarnation of the gods' (*ibid.*, p. 21). It is worth noting that the Brahmana priest, Agung Sidawa, in his report of the consecration, expresses a somewhat different view of the king's relationship with the gods. The priest did not consider him actually to embody the gods. However, what emerges clearly is that the king through his consecration takes on various attributes of the gods of the *panca déwa*, see p. 105. These are described as follows:

> god Iswara sees to it that one does not lie; god Wisnu brings happiness; god Mahadéwa ensures that alms and presents are given to unfortunate and needy people; god Brahma ensures that innocent people are not punished; and god Siwa grants an impartial judgement.
>
> (*ibid.*, p. 21; my translation from the Dutch)

Other features distinguish the Satriyas from other social groups, and unite them as a caste irrespective of their camp allegiance and individual traits. Apart from Bima, they are relatively stereotyped. They are well clad, handsome and youthful by comparison with the other castes. Together with the Sudras they are the only group whose members all stand in profile and have two mobile arms. The Balinese say that this signifies their active roles in the performance. In fact, they often fight on stage.

In looks, the Brahmana priests resemble such heavenly sages as Narada. Most priests wear the turban, *ketu*, which is a sign of their spiritual authority. There are, however, few Brahmanas in a puppet collection. The focus is on the Satriyas.

The third caste, the Wèsyas, are the least significant group in a collection. They have no individuality, and in contrast to the other castes are completely static, as they have no mobile arms. Their lack of prominence can perhaps be understood in the light of their position in Balinese society. They are effectively subsumed under the Satriyas whom they assist (pp. 18–19).

The nature of the Sudra servants is complex. Initially their portrayal suggests that they are unpolished, earthy rustics who are no threat to the Satriyas whose handsomeness and bravery are manifest in love and battle. As such they fit well into the hierarchy as *jaba* (outsiders) in contradistinction to the royal aristocracy, *dalem* (insiders). However, as will emerge clearly later and in Chapter 4, the servants are ambiguous and have multiple roles.

The ogres are ranked lower on the scale than men. Their faces, which resemble wild beasts, highlight their savagery. The villagers describe them as beings who do not know the rules of the community, and hence are lawless and disordered.

All four-legged animals are outsiders to the hierarchical system composed of completely, or at least partly, social beings. Their appearance is in line with the sharp distinction made in Bali between the human and animal worlds. For, as Covarrubias pointed out, the Balinese have a 'repugnance for actions characteristic of animals' (1965, p. 129). So children are not allowed to crawl on all fours and, up to the age of three months, are carried so that they do not touch the earth. Bestiality (*salah karma*) is considered one of the worst crimes. Traditionally, both offender and animal were thrown into the ocean; nowadays generally only the animal is drowned while the man is imprisoned or exiled. The crime is thought to make the land so impure that epidemics might break out or crops be blighted. An elaborate purificatory rite must always be performed after the event (*ibid.*, pp. 145–6).

In reviewing the iconography of the puppets, gods and high-ranking Satriyas appear to resemble one another, as do heavenly sages and Brahmanas. This suggests that a parallel is drawn between the respective groups. It also signifies the high status of senior Satriyas whose right to rule is vested in them by divine authority, by assimilating them to the gods. The four main servants are Sudras or *jaba*, who are at the bottom of the caste system, but as will emerge, their portrayal highlights their ambiguous position in the *wayang* world. It is, however, especially striking that the hierarchical order into which the groups can be classified provides a cosmic view of the world which encompasses heavenly, human and demonic beings.

The contrasts: the rival camps, the Pandawas and the Korawas

The characters in a collection form two distinct camps: the Pandawas and the Korawas (pp. 57–62), members of which confront each other in every night *wayang*.

Before turning to the actual performance it is of interest to consider how the opposition between the camps manifests itself visually. The Satriyas are the group that mainly concerns us here as it is through them that the conflict of ideals is fought in the plays. Gods, women, servants and mythic creatures are excluded from this survey as they are essentially outsiders to the war, although they may assist in the background or comment on events. On the other hand, ogres actively fight with the Korawas, as do a few Brahmanas.

It is important first to stress that the contrasts can only be drawn up on a relative basis. Although the Satriyas form a clearly demarcated group, some princes, as for instance Bima or Gatotkaca, stand out by their individual looks (for a description of individuals, see Hobart, 1985); others, as exemplified by Salya have ambiguous positions in the drama. Although Salya supports the Korawas, his sympathies lie with the Pandawas. This is reflected in his refined features. Nonetheless, it is evident that the appearance of the Satriyas, as well as their behaviour on stage, indicates the degree to which they fulfil their *darma*.

Irrespective of the variation in size and composition of the collections, the camps comprise more or less the same number of members. There are always more Pandawa than Korawa men in a collection, although this imbalance between the camps is adjusted by adding the ogres. For example, in a standard collection examined in Gianyar, one Brahmana priest and twenty-two Satriyas make up the Pandawa camp, while the Korawas' camp contains four Brahmanas, twelve Satriyas and eight ogres. So the camps contain twenty-three and twenty-four members respectively.

As emerged earlier, the five basic colours are dominant symbols in *wayang*. As a result, the iconographic opposition between the camps is most vividly expressed through their skin colours. Other features, such as the eyes or the headdresses, tend to reiterate the meanings attributed to the colours. The colour distinctions between the camps can be made at three levels of contrast. Terminologically the Balinese agree on the relationships expressed (cf. Conklin, 1955). These are:

Level 1   LIGHT *(nguda)*   as opposed   DARK *(wayah)*
                white   to   black

Level 2

                COOL *(etis)*   as opposed   HOT *(panes)*
                white, blue, yellow (black)   to   red

Level 3

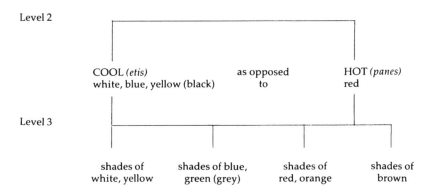

    shades of   shades of blue,   shades of   shades of
    white, yellow   green (grey)   red, orange   brown

Level 1.   *Light:dark colours::* purity:supernatural power
Level 2.   *Cool:hot colours::* refinement:coarseness
Level 3.   *(mixed colours) shades of white, yellow, blue (grey):shades of orange, red, brown::* Pandawa camp:Korawa camp

Diagram 3.2   The colour contrasts

Diagram 2 is not designed to give a complete range of meanings associated with the five colours (see Table 6, p. 107). It aims to show certain important correlates of the colour contrasts. At the first level, the opposition between light and dark colours is linked to the concepts of purity and supernatural power. At the second level, the opposition between cool and hot colours is associated with refinement and coarseness. The mixed colours absorb their meanings from the higher levels. It is evident from the above that the Pandawa camp is in relative terms purer and more refined than the Korawa camp. Hence the Pandawas are also more liable to bring harmony, prosperity and fertility to the land, i.e. *ngetesin kerajaan*, 'to cool the kingdom'. Both sides use supernatural power in the drama.

As these concepts – on the one hand, purity and supernatural power, and on the other, refinement and coarseness – are of such major importance in Balinese culture, it is worth saying a little more about them. They are also referred to in the subsequent chapters.

I PURITY AND SUPERNATURAL POWER

Purity and power are complex subjects which are only touched on in so far as they have a bearing on this genre of theatre.

The importance of purification by holy water in Balinese religion has been mentioned earlier. This purification occurs during all rites which seek to bring about both a state of spiritual purity and material cleanliness *(suci)*; these are intimately related concepts on the island (Hooykaas, 1973a, p. 6). From one point of view the Balinese ideas of purity show proximity to those of Douglas, who argues that pollution implies disorder and dirt, and that rites of purification have 'as their main function to impose system on an inherently untidy experience' (1980, p. 4). In other words, the rites, which take place continually in Bali, help reinforce the ethical values and the social rules of the community. In *wayang* this comes to the fore in the *sudamala* rite (see p. 135–37).

The visual data, however, suggests that purity has ambiguous overtones. As we have seen, gods and ogres may have completely white bodies, no humans in *wayang* possess this skin colour. White above all symbolizes purity. It appears in this context that purity, by virtue of its close association with white, is linked to the supernatural world and evokes the immensity of the universe, where ambiguity is in the nature of things. Turner's comments on white are perhaps applicable here. In his discussion of the *Chihamba* ritual he points out that 'whiteness represents an attempt to grasp the ungraspable, to embody the invisible' (1969, p. 91).

Although ritual purity seems the predominant principle when examining the iconography of the puppets, supernatural power is also important. Satriyas of both camps, ogres and the servants may possess this power which, however, only manifests itself in the performance. Initially this is indicated either by the black or red in their skin colours or by the special weapons that they own. Outstanding examples are Arjuna's magical arrow, *pasopati*, or Kresna's discus, the *cakra*.

Supernatural power in Bali is primarily obtained from the goddess Durga (see under Durga, p. 47). It may also be inherited, in which case the power is generally handed down through the matriline. An interested villager can also study manuscripts on the subject. Essentially there are two forms of supernatural power: supernatural power for good, or right-hand (white magic), *kesaktian penengan*, and supernatural power for evil, or left-hand (black magic), *pengiwa*. However, this force is inherently ambiguous and, as in other areas of the world, is easily convertible to different ends, good as well as bad.

The main feature of this mystic power is the ability to change shape, *ngeléyak*, in order to bewitch others mainly with the aim of injuring or killing them (Weck, 1937, pp. 182–203). The range and variety of forms one can assume depends on one's level of power. A man who possesses great power can even become the dreaded witch Calon Arang. Men with lesser power can transform themselves into monkeys, snails, hogs or goats, among other forms.

Gods and Brahmana priests are said to have knowledge of supernatural power, but their great purity puts them beyond the desire to use it. The Balinese say that in life it is primarily married women who use the power in left-hand magic. They attack people at night when they change shape. Such women are accused of being witches.

Traditionally, however, it is pointed out that male Satriyas used the power mainly in order to frighten their subjects and make them submissive to their rule. Their weapons are also magical. Yet this is more complicated, for mystic power is here an idiom by which the Satriyas can express their dominance. This comes out clearly in the *Ramayana* where an ideal king is described as follows:

> The power, *sakti*, of the king as hero is compared to that of the lion who endeavours to kill his enemies, for like the lion who is the protector of the forest, the king is responsible for the preservation of the splendour of his realm. (Worsley, 1972, p. 45)

In other words, mystic power is not so much an alternative to physical power as manifest in it. As such it is a demonstration of the charisma of the king and a sign of his authority in the kingdom.

In *wayang* the Satriyas use their supernatural power in battle when they change shape (p. 141). Only Yudistira's great purity puts him beyond it. Although it is never quite clear what form of power the different Satriyas have, the implication on the whole is that the Pandawas use supernatural power for good and the Korawas supernatural power for evil.

II REFINEMENT AND COARSENESS

Refinement *(alus)* and coarseness *(kasar)* are a pair of concepts which are central in Balinese culture. As in Java (Geertz, 1960, p. 232), textiles, music, dance, manner of speech, behaviour and looks, among other things, can all be described as either refined and delicate or coarse. In daily life, a person achieves and reflects refinement and sweetness in self-control and inner balance. Coarseness, in contrast, is expressed in uncontrolled feeling and energy.

Although the separation between the camps can be seen in terms of a struggle between these opposing concepts, no polarization between types of character is possible, as there are shades of difference between them. Arjuna (Plate 7) stands out as perhaps the most refined prince. It is worth noting that this manifests itself very subtly. Apart from his whitish body, his profile is straight and strong, his features delicate *(manis)*, and the lines of his apparel flow rhythmically. Indeed his appearance suggests that he is the archetypal Satriya in *wayang* who sets the standard according to which the others in his caste category should conform. On the other hand, Dursasana (Plate 9), the crudest Korawa prince, has round eyes, thick, heavy lips and a hairy orange body. He looks so angry and sullen that my informants compared him to an enraged cow whose tongue lolls out and whose eyes glow.

Ogres and servants in *wayang* are also coarse, but it is their *darma* to be so. However, as mentioned earlier, the conflict of ideals is essentially expressed through the appearance and concomitant behaviour of the Satriyas on stage.

The base figures: the servants or mediators

The male servants, *parekan*, are also called the *pandasar*, the base or basic ones. The second designation is especially fitting as the Balinese say they are the basis of society: without them the kingdom could not exist.

The extraordinary portrayal of the four main servants highlights their special place in *wayang*. Initially, as we have seen, their forms indicate that they are Sudras or common peasants who are the lowest rung of the caste system, as such they are royal retainers of the court. Tualèn and Merdah serve the Pandawas and Dèlem and Sangut are the servants of the Korawas. This role is one that the villagers know well and can empathize with. Although the power of the aristocrats has waned they still keep retainers at the court.

The servants are, however, clearly more than, in Turner's words, 'social personae' (1982, p. 47) whose innovative expression is held in check by the rigid jural-political rules which dominate the hierarchical caste structure. They stand out as distinct individuals. While they are all fat and uncouth, their bold idiosyncratic lines – reminiscent of those a caricaturist may use – conjure up their essential traits to the Balinese. Tualèn's inward-looking eye, usually described as *guling*, reveals a wise and contemplative character. This eye is fitting because Tualèn requests the gods to favour him *(nunas ica ring ida batara)* so that he can protect the descendants of kings and ensure harmony in the country. At the same time he has a thick jaw which is said to give him a foolish expression. As the villagers point out, Tualèn is after all old, and so he sometimes behaves childishly. Merdah has a large bulbous nose which, together with the upward tilt of his head, gives him an audacious, intelligent expression. Dèlem's round eye, set within a large circular head which jerks when he moves, admirably expresses his pompous, coarse and doltish character to the villagers. His neck is also uncommon. It is short and the swelling in front is described as goitre *(gondong)*, which is a sign of *mala* (spiritual impurity; Hooykaas, 1973a, p. 6). Sangut has a narrow, protruding mouth and a thin neck with a large Adam's apple. His looks are said to reveal a shrewd, resourceful character, who thinks ahead. Although Merdah and Sangut are considered the most lucid talkers, all the servants can move their jaws, an ability that makes them eminently suitable to act as chief spokesmen in the plays.

The individuality of the servants comes especially to the fore when they are compared to the relatively stereotyped Satriyas. In fact, among the Satriyas, caste and status seem effectively to eliminate individuality, while among the Sudra servants, personality seems to predominate over caste roles. As individuals with forceful personalities, the servants represent the ideas of equality which are distinct from those of hierarchy which permeate the wider society (p. 19). This emerges vividly in the plays, as we shall see.

It is interesting to speculate for a moment on the nature of the servants. Several theories have been advanced about them in Java, most of which are based on literary evidence (see Hobart, 1983, p. 167). The opinion put forward by Pigeaud (1938, pp. 361–2) is perhaps in this context especially pertinent. He emphasizes more than other scholars the peculiar iconography of the Javanese servants. He argues that their appearance resembles animals, in particular the dog; it also indicates that they are hermaphrodites. A bisexual being is a mediator figure par excellence in Javanese culture (*ibid.*, p. 362).

The strange forms of the Balinese servants, like those of their counterparts in Java, require special comment. Their stumpy legs are dwarf-like beneath their towering torsos and huge heads. Their features are exaggerated and awry. Tualèn and Merdah have the large breasts of hermaphrodites.[15] Although Dèlem and Sangut are flat-chested, a touch of femininity is exhibited in their inflated nipples and soft, fleshy bodies. It is evident that they do not fall into a neat, standard category. Their appearance suggests that they are both anomalies and misshapen wards of the court; historically dwarfs and grossly distorted men were taken under the protection of a prominent prince. (In Java they were known as *polowijo*; Holt, 1967, p. 83.) It was thought that they had supernatural power which had to be contained and would augment that of the prince. As bisexual beings and anomalies, they are excellently suited to being the main mediators in the performance. Douglas (1980, pp. 5–6) has argued of anomalies that on the one hand they are dangerous, but can be controlled by men; yet on the other, that they enrich meaning or call attention to other levels of existence.

The supernatural power of the servants seems in some way connected to their roles as mediators. Tualèn, as indicated by his unique skin colour (p. 111), is the most important of them. Yet all the servants, as will emerge in the next chapter, give shape to the mythology when on stage and thus exercise influence by interpreting the tradition. In so doing they mediate between the mythological world of cosmic events where the heroes are gods and the realistic time-bound world of the village which they represent.

Conclusion

A puppet collection thus consists of a series of figures, most of which are derived from the great epics, but which are more than this. Their iconography articulates select patterns of meanings which relate to the core values, norms and rules found in the society and such abstract concepts as rank and refinement, or purity and supernatural power. At the same time, the puppets can be regarded as temporary loci of the sacred. This comes to the fore during a performance. Before beginning to narrate, the *dalang* requests Brahma to give the puppets life so they may 'glow' and 'dance' (p. 134). Thus the values expressed by the puppets acquire special significance on stage as they evoke the presence of the gods.

The servants deserve final comment. It is evident that their extra-ordinary appearance emphasizes their complexity and ambiguity vis-à-vis the other characters. It amply justifies their designation as the basic ones, who have multiple roles in the drama, and who are the basis of society.

Notes

1 Van der Tuuk (1897) translates *guna* as a means used by a woman to make someone enamoured of her, or to bring ruin. In my area *guna* is primarily used as a formula or substance to attain a desired effect on another person by postulated supernatural means. There are two principal categories of *guna*: love *guna* and hate *guna*. The former is used most frequently to make a member of the opposite sex fall in love with one and can be used by either sex.

2 This has been confirmed by Hinzler (1975, p. 54). Therefore any account must rely on a small number of craftsmen. Variation is mainly apparent in the religious regulations followed (cf. Pink-Wilpert, 1975, pp. 59–61).

3 McPhee (1970, p. 187) calls the ceremony for the consecration of new puppets *melaspasin wayang*. This name was not used by my informants who referred to it as *mepasupati*, derived from Pasupati, the name for Siwa as Lord of the Beasts.

4 Nowadays some younger craftsmen use oil paints, but these are not considered as attractive as the traditional ones and have less *guna*, super-natural power.

5 Chinese yellow or orpiment *(atal)* is yellow sulphide or arsenic. This was confirmed by Bambang Gumarjo, director of the Wayang Museum in Jakarta, in a personal communication. Chinese yellow is preferred to indigenous yellow because of its luminosity.

6 Chinese blue may be azurite (Gettens and Stout, 1966, pp. 95–6).

7 Red is probably vermilion, a red mercuric sulphide known in China since prehistoric times and held in high esteem there (Gettens and Stout, 1966, pp. 170–2).

8　Other craftsmen often paint the entire puppet completely first in black and, while building up the subsequent colours in the same order as I Raos, ignore the distinction between body and costume that he makes.

9　Horns are usually obtained from Kalimantan or Sulawesi.

10　Kunti also wears a turban called *kupa* which is not illustrated here.

11　Dress includes additional items such as waist cloths, chest bands, sashes or shawls which are not mentioned in the text. No meaning is attached to them. Articles of dress also often have designs. Most of them are vegetal. Some suggest stylized blossoms. While the main designs are fixed, they are not designated. My informants either disagree on their names or do not know them. The designs are moreover difficult to distinguish as they are often very intricate or look alike. No specific meaning seems to be associated with them.

12　Scholars such as Kats (1923), Pigeaud (1929, pp. 285–9), Mellema (1954, pp. 58–77) and Holt (1967, pp. 142–3) already drew attention to the relationship which exists between the facial colours of the Javanese puppets and their character. None of these scholars, however, associated the colours and their referents with the gods and their work throws little light on the colours found on Balinese puppets. However, Pigeaud (1929) pointed out the existence in religious texts of four- or five-part systems of classification which relate the colours of the gods, the directions and the emotional states.

13　Kresna is sometimes painted a light or mid green. Green indicates fertility which is the result of sufficient water and thus this colour too is appropriate.

14　These are from top to bottom the discus *(cakra)*, club *(gada)*, incense bowl *(dupa)* and forked spear *(canggah)* on one side, and on the other the lotus *(padma)*, serpent-arrow *(naga-pasa)*, lance *(tumpak)* and trident *(trisula)*. One of the main central arms holds in its hand a long sabre *(berang)*.

15　Although my informants never said that the servants are hermaphrodites, they agree that Tualèn and Merdah in particular show bisexual tendencies. Hermaphrodites have an accepted and sometimes honoured position in Balinese culture. So, they are included in the myth of the origin of clothes (p. 90) and in the *mantra panggègèr* (p. 134).

4

The audience and the performance

The last chapter focused on the symbolic import of the puppets. We are dealing, however, with theatre and not with a static art form and it is on the stage that the characters come alive or, as the villagers put it, 'wake up' (*metangi*). This is vividly illustrated by the Balinese proverb 'like war in the shadow play', which is said of a man and a woman who quarrel during the day but sleep together at night. The analogy is taken from the puppets who are thought of as sleeping in their chest when off stage out of sight of the public, but who confront and fight each other during a night *wayang*. It is then that the nexus which binds individuals and groups is dramatized.

During the performance the iconography of the puppets is presented as part of a complex set of dramatic stimuli. These include patterns of light, rhythm, movement and sound. The latter is especially important in this genre of theatre. As in the case of most western drama from Aristotle onwards, a *wayang* performance can be considered as a branch of poetry. During each show a mythic story is narrated and an illusory experience created which is meant to be heard as well as seen. As we will see, a *dalang* has a certain amount of freedom to improvise and elaborate on the basic story; at the same time he is bound to a definite framework by the specific constraints of this type of theatre.

In the ensuing discussion both the audience and the performance are considered, for one could not exist without the other. Yet the purposes of the two types of performance, the night and day *wayang*, are quite distinct, and concomitantly they are directed to entirely different spectators. Hence they are clearly distinguished throughout the chapter.

Audience and stage

The night performance: *wayang peteng*

As the shadow theatre is a type of entertainment, going to a performance is a relaxed, informal occasion. Most of the spectators know one another as they come from the same area or vicinity. There is no admission fee as a performance is not a commercial enterprise. It is the temple congregation, village council or head of a household who hires a *dalang* and pays for a performance. A *dalang* of repute is of course more expensive to hire than one who is not yet established or is unknown (on the cost, see p. 29).

There are usually three to five hundred spectators at a performance. Although all castes are represented, the majority are Sudras. This is hardly suprising in view of the fact that the Sudras comprise about 90 per cent of the population. The audience is primarily made up of adult men and boys for reasons which are discussed in Chapter 5. Only a small number of women watch a show. In my area these tended to be older or Chinese women. When asked, women point out that it is inappropriate for them to be interested in such scholarly subjects as the shadow theatre, or for that matter the masked dance, *topèng*, or the chanting of classical literature. Nor do they enjoy the plays which focus on war and conflict.

During the play the spectators stand, squat on the ground, or sit at stalls, most of which have been set up for the occasion. Sometimes they seem deeply absorbed in the story (Plate 20), but often they chat quietly or eat and drink coffee, tea or lime juice at the stalls. Here all sorts of food is sold, such as nuts, fruit, rice cakes or betel-nut. In the background a few groups of villagers may sit huddled round dimly lit tables, staking money on gambling games; *ceki*, which is played with small cards, is especially popular (Plate 21). The barking of dogs prowling around looking for refuse may be heard. It is relatively easy to slip in and out of the crowd, and spectators arrive at any hour during the performance. They can also easily walk away if the show fails to stimulate them.

The attention of the audience, like those Peacock described watching proletarian drama, *ludruk*, in Java, 'flickers on and off' (1968, p. 242). The villagers are acquainted in general with the main outline of the plot and the somewhat disjointed quality of the play, interspersed with humorous self-contained episodes, allows the spectators' concentration to wander in this way. The relaxed atmosphere of a per-

126

formance also enables the villagers to comment, criticize and speculate freely and imaginatively on the merits, or demerits, of the show.

The essential illusion of the *wayang* world is, however, set off clearly from the actuality of the audience's surroudings. This is especially so as the *dalang* sits in a raised booth and the shadows (Plate 22) projected on to the screen are remote from the spectators, thereby establishing a great distance between the medium/message and the beholder. In contrast to the current practice in Java, where the play is watched from either side of the screen (Mellema, 1954, pp. 66–7), only a few Balinese observe the play from the same side as the *dalang*. This is made the more difficult as he is enclosed with the musicians in the booth.

The stage with screen

The booth for a night *wayang* is set up in a secular area in the village compound, the courtyard of a home, the outer court of a temple, or on the grounds outside the temple. A pavilion may also be used as a stage if the play is given within a temple or home. As the shadow theatre is concerned with the welfare of the community, it is properly oriented to the propitious direction of 'to the mountain', *kaya*, or east (on directions, see pp. 105–6).

The booth is temporarily erected for the play, usually by members of the household or community who have commissioned the performance. It is taken down in the next day or so. The walls and roof of a standard booth are made of coconut or bamboo woven mats which overlap at the edges (Diagram 1). The floor consists of wooden planks covered by mats. A vertical screen (*kelir*) of cotton cloth about six feet in length makes the background against which the puppets are moved. There are generally nine holes along the top of the screen through which string is passed and wound round a bamboo cross-bar. The screen is bordered with black cloth at the top and bottom, and small squares of red cloth are fastened to either end at the top. A cocount-oil lamp (*damar*) is suspended from the ceiling. A thick banana palm stem (*gedebong*) is placed along the base of the screen (Diagram 1).

The *dalang*'s puppet-chest is to his left. He taps against it with gavel in accompaniment with the play (p. 31). He inserts the handles of the puppets in the soft pulp of the banana stem when they are stationary. The four musicians sit behind the *dalang*. One or two assistants (*tututan*) sit to either side of him, passing him the puppets (Diagram 2).

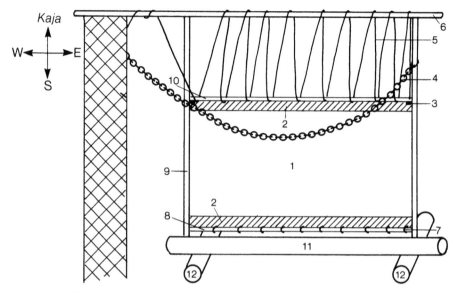

1. screen: white part
2. screen: black part
3. screen: red part
4. chain from which the lamp is hung
5. string with which the screen is tied to the top cross-bar of the booth
6. top cross-bar of booth (bamboo)
7. iron clamps with which to stabilize the screen
8. bottom cross-bar (bamboo)
9. side bar (wood)
10. top cross-bar (bamboo)
11. base (banana stem)
12. sides (banana stem)

Diagram 4.1   View of the inside of the booth

It is important, however, to realize that the stage, together with the equipment, is not just a technical device enabling a drama to be enacted, but is symbolic. Its symbolism is known to all my informants. According to them it replicates the macrocosm:

> The screen is the sky or face of the world. The puppets are all the animate and inanimate things which exist. The lamp is the sun which enables there to be day and night. The banana stem into which the puppets are placed is the earth. The *dalang* is god who is invisible to the audience.

Some informants add that the music of the *gendèr* orchestra represents

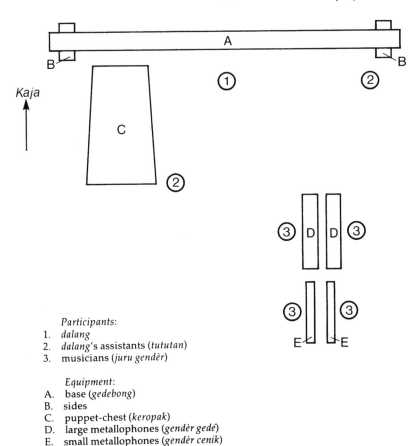

Participants:
1. *dalang*
2. *dalang's* assistants (*tututan*)
3. musicians (*juru gendèr*)

Equipment:
A. base (*gedebong*)
B. sides
C. puppet-chest (*keropak*)
D. large metallophones (*gendèr gedé*)
E. small metallophones (*gendèr cenik*)

Diagram 4.2 Spatial layout for the night performance

the harmony and interrelationship of all things in the universe. A less elaborate version of this underlying model of the stage is found in the treatise *Dharma Pawayangan* (Hooykaas, 1973b, p. 25).

Stage details also reflect religious principles. The nine holes along the top of the screen refer to the nine-fold division of the cosmos, *nawa-sanga*. The lamp is usually lit with three bundles of wicks. This number and the three colours of the screen, white, red and black, represent the trinity, *trisakti* – the gods Siwa (or Iswara), Brahma and Wisnu.

So the stage offers an ideal setting for enacting a play which has cosmic dimensions.

The day performance: *wayang lemah*

The day *wayang* is said to be given primarily to an invisible audience, i.e. the gods, the human spectators being essentially irrelevant. Indeed during the one- to two-hour performance only a few adults and some children stand around curiously listening to the story which in any case is almost inaudible.

As the day *wayang* is simpler and shorter than the night *wayang*, its cost is relatively low.

THE STAGE WITHOUT A SCREEN

The day *wayang* takes place on the ground in the special area set aside for the ritual (Plate 23). This is always either within the household or in the innermost courtyard of a temple. The *dalang* faces either *kaja* ('to the mountain') or east – the two most propitious directions. A Brahmana priest (Plate 24) sitting in an elevated pavilion prepares holy water while the *dalang* enacts the play.

Diagram 3 shows the layout of the various shrines in the temple of the dead, *pura dalem*, in Sukawati, and the different activities which were performed during one of its anniversaries (*odalan*). It is rare for a standard masked dance to be performed, as on this occasion, in the inner court of a temple. Generally only *topèng pengajegan* (p. 190) would be danced here. In the diagram the *dalang* faces *kaja* and the Brahmana priest east.

Neither a lamp nor a screen is used during the day *wayang*. A string consisting of threads in the three colours of the trinity: white, red and black entwined together is stretched between two branches of a luminous plant, *dapdap* (*Erithrina lithosperma*), about a foot above the banana trunk. The *dalang* manipulates the puppets between the branches and only two musicians accompany the performance.

Although the stage is so simple, its few constituents have deeper significance. The three colours of the string represent the trinity already mentioned. *Dapdap* is also known as *kayu sakti*, a tree with supernatural power, and priests burn its wood in an earthenware bowl in all rites. In folk belief the leaves can be used as charms against witches; the juice from the leaves can be given to someone who is ill to help cure him, and the branches are used to form a pillow under a dead person.

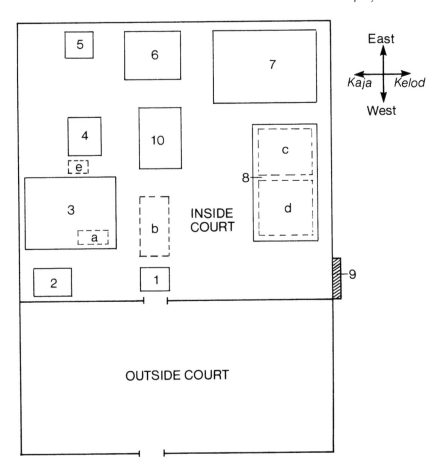

Shrines and pavilions:

1. *balé patok*
2. *balé* (unspecified pavilion)
3. *pengaruman*
4. *pengaruman alit*
5. *padmasana*
6. *gedong pesimpangan*
7. *balé peseleng*
8. *balé gong*
9. (kitchen)
10. *asagan**
    *temporary shrine for offerings.

Activities taking place:

a. *pedanda mebakti* (Brahmana priest worshipping)
b. *topèng* (masked dance)
c. *wayang lemah* (day wayang)
d. *gong* (orchestra)
e. *gambang* (orchestra)

Diagram 4.3 Spatial layout of the shrines and activities during an anniversary at the death temple in Sukawati

The ritual activities of the *dalang*

The ritual activities of the *dalang* are complex and elaborate. These mark him off from ordinary villagers and indicate something of the powers attributed to him. This perhaps becomes most apparent in the religious incantations, *mantras*, which he recites (Plate 25), most of which are found in the *Dharma Pawayangan* (ibid., 1973b). He also makes offerings before and after each performance (Plate 26). Although the details of the rites may differ, variation in my area was slight.

The *dalang*'s role as priest comes to the fore in the *wayang sudamala*. This rite is only touched on in this chapter as it is a subject in itself. Yet it is of special interest as it highlights the power of certain puppets.

The night performance: *wayang peteng*

Before any performance the *dalang* dresses himself as is appropriate for the occasion. His three standard items of wear are the headgear, waist cloth and dress (Plate 3). These are said to represent the three spheres of heaven, earth and underworld.

It is, however, mainly through the rites that the *dalang* attains the temporary status of a ritually marginal person who stands outside ordinary life while performing and is in contact with powers that are ambiguous and asocial. During the performance he also conjoins the three spheres of heaven, earth and underworld. Before entering a booth, a *dalang* tests his breath in order to see which god will descend and communicate through him while he speaks. If the breath exhaled from the right nostril is stronger, it means that Brahma will perform; stronger breath from the left nostril means that Wisnu will perform; equally strong breath from both nostrils indicates that Iswara will perform.

Numerous *mantras* are recited before a standard night *wayang*. *Dalangs* agree that these, together with the accompanying rites, have essentially a three-fold purpose: to protect the *dalang* from dangerous spirits such as witches and demons; to invoke the gods to descend and enter both him and the puppets; and to ensure that the spectators enjoy the performance and believe the higher truth in the sacred mythology.

A *dalang* mainly tries to protect himself from evil spirits who may attack him when he is still at home, just before setting out to perform. The *mantras* recited by the *dalang* I Ewer give good examples of how and from whom the *dalang* seeks to protect himself. The first is the *mantra pasikepan* (cf. *ibid.*, 1973b, p. 51):

> Yes, supreme god, Tunggal,
> Grant me magical power,
> (So that) demons and witches are happy,
> (So that) the people are happy,
> (So that) the gods are happy,
> All that exists in the world be happy and worship,
> and so depart in happiness.
> AM AH (Sky Earth)

While reciting this mantra, the *dalang* chews a special form of betel-nut, called *lekesan*. This betel-nut, together with its contents, symbolizes the *kanda empat*, the four mystic siblings of the *dalang* (See Chapter 2, note 9, p. 66), who protect him while performing.

Before departing from his home, I Ewer also calls on the five semi-divine Pandawa brothers, the Panca Pandawa, to protect him, by reciting the *mantra* of the *Dharma Pawayangan* (cf. *ibid.*, 1973b, p. 61). In the *mantra* the Pandawa brothers are said to reside in the palm-leaf manuscript, as well as in heaven. Thereby the *mantra* also stresses the sacred nature of classical literature in general, and the *Dharma Pawayangan* in particular:

> Yes, Sang Panca Pandawa who live in heaven,
> Nakula (and) Sahadéwa who are in the front and back cover
> (of the palm-leaf manuscript),
> Arjuna who is in (the pages of) the palm-leaf manuscript,
> Darmawangsa who is the literature (i.e. the written word),
> Bima who is the string (of the manuscript), imparting strength,
> Remove all that is dangerous.
> AM UM MAM UM OM.

Further protection from evil is still required on the stage before a *dalang* begins to narrate. As one *dalang* put it, witches in particular are active at night and can cause havoc: for instance, they may make a *dalang* stumble on entering the booth; they may shake the screen or put out the lamp. In these unpleasant ways they try to prevent him performing. It is on the stage that the *dalang* carries out the most complex rites. By sprinkling it with fresh water and presenting offerings to the gods, he creates a pure area in which to perform. He also recites incantations invoking the gods to descend into him and into the puppets. For it is their presence which ensures that the audience will enjoy the play and believe what is said. The *mantra panggègèr* (cf. *ibid.*, p. 39) and *mantra pangurip wayang* (cf. *ibid.*, p. 45), again recited by I Ewer, are included as they demonstrate this:

Yes, I am god Trinity,
Who possess *guna*, or magical power (see Chapter 3, note 1, p. 123).
Attract men,
Attract women,
Attract hermaphrodites,
(So that) they gather in front of me,
To listen attentively to me,
My body is the god of love, Semara,
If the spectators are bored on looking at the god of love, Semara,
They will be bored watching me.
May their happiness not flag (repeated three times).
AH UM MAM.

Wake up, god of the puppets, Sang Hyang Ringgit, and dance,
Brahma, give them life,
So that the puppets will glow.

Each puppet is thought to have a soul and it is the god Brahma who enables them 'to glow', *mecaya*, on the stage. Only then can they move or dance with fluidity and grace.

Fewer rites are carried out after the performance. Most *dalangs* seem first to request the gods to bring back to life those characters who have been killed during the drama. Afterwards, the god of the puppets, Sang Hyang Ringgit, is requested to go back to sleep and the puppets are placed in their chest. Finally, the demons are appeased with offerings, which include local spirits – arrak, palm wine (*tuak*), and white rice wine (*berem*); these are poured over the banana trunk. The demons are then sent home.

The day performance: *wayang lemah*

The preparations a *dalang* makes before a day *wayang* are much less elaborate than before a performance given at night. There seem to be two main reasons for this. First it takes place in a ritually pure area in a temple or household compound during the day (or when conceptually still light). Secondly, it is not intended for a human audience, but for the gods. In order to attain a pure state of mind *dalangs* agree that it is sufficient to say the *mantra Kakayonan* (cf. *ibid.*, p. 45):

On waving the Kakayonan believe that:
Samba returns to Wisnu,
Wisnu returns to Sangkara,

Sangkara returns to Mahadéwa,
Mahadéwa returns to Rudra,
Rudra returns to Brahma,
Brahma returns to Mahesora,
Mahesora returns to Iswara,
Iswara returns to the Kakayonan,
The Kakayonan takes the place of the pure all-powerful mind,
The pure mind takes the place of the god-poet,
The poet's [or *dalang*'s] skill consists of the faculty of speaking
all that can be expressed in words.

This *mantra*, which is also recited before the night *wayang*, can best be understood in the light of the Balinese beliefs in the nine-fold division of the cosmos, *nawa-sanga* (p. 108). The god Sambu who starts the movement is located in the north east. When the *dalang* waves the Kakayonan, it is thought that he causes the gods of the nine-fold division of the cosmos to enter one another in an anti-clockwise motion until they become one with Siwa in the centre or, in this case, the Kakayonan. The above suggests that the figure may be used as a 'tool', *yantra* (Pott, 1966, p. 26), in meditation. It is with the Kakayonan, the symbol of a higher order of reality, that the *dalang* identifies before narrating. This *mantra* is said to be one of the most important that a *dalang* recites.

A few simple ritual activities are carried out after the performance.

Wayang sudamala

The *dalang*'s role as priest comes to the fore in the *wayang sudamala*, a somewhat unusual type of performance which is mainly exorcistic in intent. It seems to deal with people who are in some way out of place either through death, illness or danger (i.e. being born in the week of Tumpek Wayang). The actual *sudamala* rite, which is highly elaborate, is carried out by a *dalang* after either the night or day *wayang* (Plate 27).

During the rite certain high-ranking puppets are stuck into the banana stem. Diagram 4 gives an example of the puppets used during such a rite. This one was performed by I Ewer after his night *wayang* and its overt purpose was to ensure the continued health of a child who had previously been very ill. The grandmother held the child during the ritual activities. His illness was conceptualized in terms of the demonic, and the child had to be purified to avert further attacks from demons. For this particular occasion, I Ewer chose nine important puppets, five of which represented the gods of the five-fold division of the cosmos, *panca déwa*.[1]

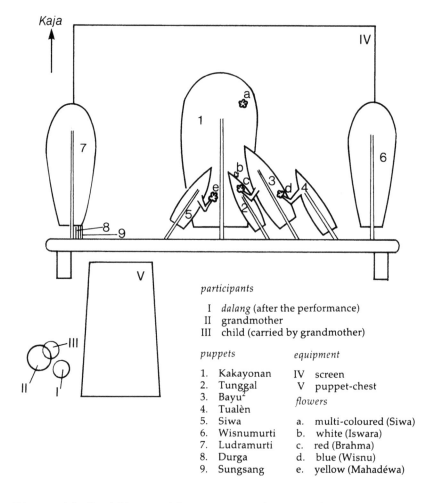

Kaja

IV

participants

  I   *dalang* (after the performance)
  II grandmother
  III child (carried by grandmother)

puppets		*equipment*	
1.	Kakayonan	IV	screen
2.	Tunggal	V	puppet-chest
3.	Bayu²	*flowers*	
4.	Tualèn		
5.	Siwa	a.	multi-coloured (Siwa)
6.	Wisnumurti	b.	white (Iswara)
7.	Ludramurti	c.	red (Brahma)
8.	Durga	d.	blue (Wisnu)
9.	Sungsang	e.	yellow (Mahadéwa)

Diagram 4.4   Spatial layout of the puppets, equipment and main participants during the *sudamala* rite

As the diagram shows, the flowers which were stuck behind the five puppets also symbolized the gods.

The ritual acts of I Ewer were primarily concerned with preparing special purificatory water, *toya penglukatan*. The puppets and *mantras*, one of the main ones recited being the *mantra Aji Kembang* (p. 108–10) always play a relevant part in the preparation of this water. Each of the five puppets representing the gods was taken in turn out of the banana stem; the handle of each was waved through the flame of the lamp; and the tip was then placed momentarily in the container of fresh water. The *dalang* also threw the petals of the flowers into the container. Finally, he sprinkled some of the purificatory water, which had just been prepared, over the child, who was held by his grand-mother, and gave him some to drink.

I Ewer explained that the purificatory water spiritually 'cleansed' the child and so restored order and a sense of well-being in the family (on purity, see p. 118). The *dalang*'s action of waving the handles of the puppets through fire reiterated this purpose, for it caused the god of fire, Agni, to burn away all ritual impurity. It seems worth recalling Eliade's ideas on water here, for they are reminiscent of those expressed by the Balinese. The scholar (as quoted by Douglas, 1980, p. 161) points out that water nullifies the past, for in it everything is dissolved; hence it has the power of purification, regeneration and restoration.

So the *sudamala* rite illustrates the power of certain important puppets in preparing purificatory water used in special circumstances of danger and disorder. It is of interest to note that the grouping of the puppets emphasizes Tualèn's mediatory role. He is generally the only human figure used in the rite. On this occasion he represented the preserver god, Wisnu.

The performance

Each play is a creative work. The dramatic skill of a *dalang*, however, comes to the fore in the night *wayang* as it is directed to villagers. Varied stimuli are then orchestrated to set up a complex and some-times critical response in the audience. The day *wayang*, as we will see, is more rigid and much simpler.

The night performance: *wayang peteng*

In describing the night *wayang*, three issues are distinguished: the dramatic quality of the play, the structure and development of the plot, and the themes and poetic imagery of the *wayang* stories. The setting, movement, voice, language and background music all con-tribute to establishing the tone of the play, the peculiar intensity known as 'dramatic quality'. This aspect of the play, as well as the structure and development of the plot, remains essentially constant in all performances. On the other hand, the themes of the stories are wide-ranging.

I   THE DRAMATIC QUALITY OF THE PLAY

A   The setting   The Kakayonan, the cosmic Tree of Life, creates the setting for the performance. It marks the beginning and end of a play or scene, its elusive shadow flickering to and fro on the screen as the *dalang* waves or 'dances' it. The *dalang* can also use it to represent a wide range of phenomena: the sea, bathing places of the celestial nymphs, forest, wind, rain, fire or a palace.

Educated *dalangs* explain that the Kakayonan's preliminary dancing on entering the stage signifies the *panca-maha-buta*, the five great elements, air, wind, fire, water and earth, which are responsible for creation and form the essence of both the macrocosm and microcosm.[3] Before beginning to narrate, the *dalang* first sets the Kakayonan into the centre of the main banana stem. It can be suggested that this implies the suspension of profane time and the entering of a consecrated area, which Eliade (1974, p. 17) has referred to as the 'centre' of the universe from which the whole habitable world extends.

It is against this background that the story unfolds. As mentioned earlier, in every play there is conflict between two camps, the Pandawas, or relatively virtuous side (who enter the stage from the right of the *dalang*) and the Korawas, or less virtuous side (who enter from his left). An invisible vertical line down the centre of the screen separates the two camps. In line with the cosmological setting of the performance, the division of the Pandawas and Korawas is linked to the binary opposites, *ruwa-binèda* (cf. Weck, 1937, pp. 39–52), found in Bali and Java: right/left, day/night, young/old, male/female, sun/moon and so forth.

In this cosmological scheme, the evil of the Korawas is necessary to offset and complement the goodness of the Pandawas. This view is laid out in the Old Javanese treatise, *Korawaçrama* (Swellengrebel, 1936, p. 25), known also in Bali, and summed up by Bosch (1960, p. 87) as follows:

> While both groups, the Pandawas and Korawas, are bitterly opposed, they 'are each other's counterparts and indispensable completion . . . The equilibrium between the groups should ever be maintained. If the Korawas have been humiliated they shall have their revenge on the Pandawas; but not by killing them, as the Pandawas, too, are indispensable. How would things be right with the universe without the existence of the Korawas and Pandawas who fill the whole world . . . ?'

Indeed, as already mentioned, most *dalangs* recite a short *mantra* after a performance in order, symbolically, to bring back to life any hero killed in battle, regardless of his camp allegiance.

So the Kakayonan sparks into life the struggle between the complementary opposites which is only resolved at the end of a play when the purer and worthier Pandawas defeat the Korawas. Yet this is a temporary victory, for the struggle between the divine and demonic forces is constantly renewed in every night *wayang*.

B   The dancing on the stage   The Balinese say that the puppets dance, *mesola*, on stage, so manifesting the cosmic rhythm of the drama. Zoete and Spies reiterated this idea when they wrote that 'drama [in Bali] is not the telling of a story, but action, dancing; the same word applies to both, for drama is only conveyed through the heightened rhythm of dance, never at the flat pitch of actuality' (1973, p. 18).

The dance movements of the puppets are highly stylized. Most of them can move either one or both arms. Only the servants and one or two ogres have, in addition, moveable jaws. All speeches are punctuated with tense, nervous gestures (Plate 28). In passing, it is of interest to note that such gestures in the village context would indicate arrogance and lack of control. Yet in *wayang*, the disproportionately long arms are one of the principal means of communication.

Although *dalangs* vary somewhat in the way they dance the puppets, a consistency is generally maintained between the appearance of a character and his actions on stage. Movements can, however, be considered an extension of appearance and establishes relationships whereby the figures are incorporated into a dynamic sequence of events. A *dalang* mainly uses his ingenuity to illustrate details of the plot. So a character may strike his chest in sorrow, shock or surprise, or fold his arms gracefully or extend them to convey his seductive or amorous intentions. The *dalang* also has some freedom in depicting battle scenes.

Apart from the above incidents, however, the *dalang* adheres to definite conventions when dancing the puppets which determine their style of dancing, actions and position on stage. The style seems primarily to reflect the continuum between refinement and coarseness (see p. 120). Individuality is for the most part subordinated to these two criteria. This also means that movement is a decisive factor in uniting groups. Refined high castes and gods (with slit eyes) dance gracefully, swinging their arms gently, while their coarse counterparts (with round eyes) dance in a proud, overbearing manner and move their arms flamboyantly. Gods are primarily distinguished from men as they enter from on high, suggesting heaven. The dancing of ogres, on the other hand, is often violent and terrifying. Some of the more comic ogres also walk with a rolling, unsteady gait. The towering figures of Wisnumurti (Plate 6) and Ludramurti sway backwards and forwards, *ngelayak*, in front of the screen. Van der Tuuk (1897) points out that girls in the Javanese court dance, *serimpi*, sway in this manner: the body is curved backwards until the head almost touches the ground.

The *dalang* moves animals according to their genre. Birds, for example, swoop down, while monkeys leap and run with agility.

Only a few of the prominent Satriyas and servants stand out by their dancing. Arjuna is known for his fluidity and grace. Bima bounds audaciously across the screen. The dancing of Duryodana is stiff and gauche. Although all the servants walk with their arms swaying jauntily in accompaniment with the movements of their bodies, each still has a particular style of dancing. Tualèn shuffles along, while his son, Merdah, who is able and quick, moves rapidly. Dèlem struts around in an aggressive, uncontrolled manner. His bombastic nature is underlined by the ornate umbrella Sangut often holds over his head as he enters. Sangut walks very slowly, almost sluggishly.

The behaviour of the characters also provides a framework within which the castes can be identified and differentiated: the Brahmanas often teach; Satriyas are mainly involved in battle, love and courtly exploits. Of these, the first predominates. In fact the vast array of battle techniques displayed on the stage is a reflection of the *wayang* world where there is always conflict between two opposing camps. The techniques are specified. One *dalang*, known for his skill with battle scenes, described the main ways Satriyas can fight. They beat with clubs, shoot with bow and arrow, stab with keris, slice with knives, hurl stones, punch with fists, strangle, wrestle, fling the opponent on the ground, submerge him in water, or tear him apart. A few heroes possess their own special weapons. For example, Kresna flings his discus, *cakra*; Bima uses an unusually big club; and Arjuna has his special arrow, *pasopati*. Whichever method is chosen, however, combat is always a personal contest. Two characters attack each other; then one flees and the other pursues.

Senior Satriyas may also use supernatural power, *kesaktian* (pp. 119–20) in battles in order to transform themselves into ogres. Bima, Gatotkaca and Arjuna who are thought especially powerful (*sakti*), can transform themselves into up to seven fierce ogres in succession, in order to frighten and kill their opponents. Kresna can take on the form of Wisnumurti, the terrifying thousand-fold ogre of the right (p. 48, p. 111–12).

Wèsyas, in line with their insignificant role in life (pp. 18–19) hardly enter the plays, except as followers of the Satriyas. They never talk, and flash fleetingly across the screen.

The servants, who are not directly involved in battles between the Satriyas, may kick and hit each other or the ogres. Tualèn is distinguished by his large and, as McPhee (1970, p. 154) aptly describes it, phallic-shaped arrow which he mainly uses to beat up ogres. More commonly the servants simply abuse each other verbally (*saling bat-bat*), and this often with irony and wit (see subsequent sections). The servants' caste position is primarily indicated by their uncouth behaviour on stage, which is less formalized than that of the high castes. Attention should in this context be drawn to their distinctive attitude when they are in the presence of high castes or gods. They always lower themselves bodily on such occasions. They also often clasp their hands together in a gesture which in both *wayang* and life shows subservience and respect to the king (*ngastawa Ida Sang Prabu*), see Fig. 4.1.

Fig. 4.1   *Ngastawa Ida Sang Prabu*

The positions the puppets can assume on stage are also important (Plate 29). When the *dalang* installs the puppets in the main banana stem for a given scene, he considers their camp allegiance, their status and the aesthetic principle of creating a balanced composition. Members of the Pandawa camp, for instance, are placed to his right and members of the Korawas to his left. A position near the centre usually indicates seniority.[4] When, however, a scene involves characters of only one camp, some transgress the invisible central line in order to ensure a charming visual symmetry.

Finally it should be recalled that most of the audience watch the shadows during the play. As the *dalang* dances the figures at a slight distance from the screen, their shadows are vibrant and sensitive. When they stand still in the banana stem, their heads are small, dark and crisp; in relation to them the torsos and limbs appear large, light and fuzzy. To the spectators the shadows are the mirror images of the puppets. Essentially they see the reverse of the scene the *dalang* sees: depending on whether one watches the puppets or the shadows, right becomes left and left, right.[5] The shadows, in their disembodiedness, also suggest metaphysical or even transcendental overtones. This point is taken up in Chapter 5.

C **Voice and language** Voice and language follow set patterns which lend further formality to the relations depicted on stage and reiterate the mythic nature of the play. They crystallize the emotive attitude of the characters. Speech and language are more closely linked to the plot than the voices, which generally accord with the puppets' appearance.

While a *dalang* changes his tonal quality to suit the story, the pitch of the voice is standardized. Similarly to dance, it relates to social category and type, refined high castes speak in high voices which are thin in quality, their laughter is delicate and sweet. Coarse-looking high castes speak in low voices indicative of their roughness, and their speeches are interspersed with throaty laughter. Gods, irrespective of physical type, usually announce themselves in deep, booming voices in order to make their supernatural status felt. The speech of ogres is low-pitched, and they may also snort or wheeze while talking, thereby showing affinity to the animal world. Most *dalangs* have great virtuosity in portraying the different animal species, making apt and humorous sounds: monkeys chatter, pigs grunt and snuffle, horses neigh, crows caw, snakes hiss, and so forth.

The servants can be clearly distinguished by their voices. They vary their pitch considerably more than the other characters. It can be high and thin or drop a few octaves to be low and sonorous. The changes in vocal quality convey different emotions. One *dalang* listed the following which occur in most performances. They weep, primarily after a prince has died. When aroused, they shout. Their voices often express amusement and drollery. Tualèn, who is old, and Dèlem, who is especially crude, fart. In plays Dèlem and Sangut still stand out by their voices. Dèlem, in accordance with his character, slurs his words and speaks in an arrogant manner, while Sangut talks in a slow, syrupy fashion.

Language in *wayang* is of special interest. It does not neatly overlap with that used in life. A clear division is maintained between the servants and the other characters. The servants mainly speak colloquial Balinese, while the others use *kawi*, a form of Old Javanese (Robson, 1972, pp. 308–26). The high castes only use Balinese when they address the servants, to emphasize the difference in status between them. A note should here be added on the prince Bima. Defying the ordinary forms of courtesy maintained by the Satriyas, he may speak Balinese even to the gods.

The majority of *dalangs* are not fluent in Old Javanese, and incorporate Balinese words into it. In my area this was called *kawi nguda* ('young' *kawi*). Yet in the performance they disguise their inadequacy in Old Javanese by running together words deliberately in order to render them indistinct. The Old Javanese of the ogres tends to be much less pure than that of the high castes and gods, as *dalangs* feel at greater liberty to add Balinese words which do not have the same reputation as the sacred idiom of the classics (cf. Tambiah, 1968, pp. 17–18, on the hierarchy of language). At any rate, most of the spectators do not understand the Old Javanese spoken in *wayang*, which is translated or paraphrased for them by the servants. This is referred to as *melut*, literally 'peeling' the words, i.e. unveiling the sacred language and so making it accessible to the audience (This is illustrated later.) Geertz (1960, pp. 248–60) has argued that language in Java involves a defined system of etiquette. This also applies to Bali, where different language levels are spoken (see Preface). In *wayang*, however, it is mainly through the Balinese spoken by the servants that the audience is made aware of the relative status of those conversing. Table 1 gives an indication of how the servants uphold the status of the others through correct use of language level, as well as title.

It is evident that the language used by the characters on stage and the sweetness and harshness of their voices help create that special dramatic tension which is intrinsic to the world of *wayang*.

D   The music   Rhythmic music played on four metallophones known as *gendèr wayang* accompany all *parwa* performances.[6] Each *gendèr* has ten keys which are suspended over bamboo resonators. The musicians strike the keys with light, wooden hammers, the shock of which produces a clear ringing sound. The ethnomusicologist McPhee has described this music as 'perhaps the highest, and certainly the most sensitive form of musical expression existing in Bali' (1970, p. 146).

The music provided by the *gendèr* ensemble is a complex, specialized subject (for a detailed analysis of the music see McPhee, 1960, pp. 201–33 and 1970, pp. 146–97). Comments will mainly be made here on how it is interwoven with the other dramatic elements. The *gendèr* are

Table 4.1   Examples of Balinese language used in *wayang*

servants to:	gods	high castes: Brahmanas	Satriyas	Wêsyas	one-another	ogres & 'low' creatures	
	titiyang	*titiyang*	*titiyang*	*tiang*	*cang*	*kai*	self
	ratu batara (lord god)	*i ratu*	*i ratu*	*jêro*	*cai(m) nyai(f)*	*iba*	you
		ratu padanda (lord priest)	*cokor i ratu* (at the foot of the lord) *cokor i dêwa* (at the foot of the god) *cokorda aji* (father cokorda) *dêwa agung gedé* (great supreme god) *ratu dêwa agung* (great supreme god) *ratna diyah* (royal princess)	*i gusti aji* (prime minister)	*bli* (older brother) *mbok* (elder sister) *adi* (younger brother or sister) *bapa* (father) *nanang*[1] (father) *nani*[1] (father)		titles or kin names
	nunas	*nunas*	*nunas*	*nunas*	*medaar,* *ngalih nasi*	*medaar* *ngamah*	I eat[2]
	ngaksi	*miunan,* *merayunan*	*miunan,* *merayunan*	*ngajengang,* *merayunan*	*medaar,* *ngalih nasi*	*medaar,* *ngamah*	you eat

Notes

These three words, I, you and eat, have been selected as they, among of course others, are particularly sensitive to differences in social relationships.

1. Merdah often calls his father *nanang*, and Tualin calls his son *nani*. These terms are only used in the shadow theatre and not in life.
2. 'Eat' has a referential, *singgih*, and deferential, *sor*, form. These are included in the chart.

Plate 22 Shadows cast on the screen during a performance.
From right to left are Arjuna, Kresna, Tualèn, Yudistira and Bima

Plate 23 The day *wayang*

Plate 24 Brahmana priest officiating during a day *wayang*

Plate 25
Dalang I Wija reciting *mantras*
before beginning to perform

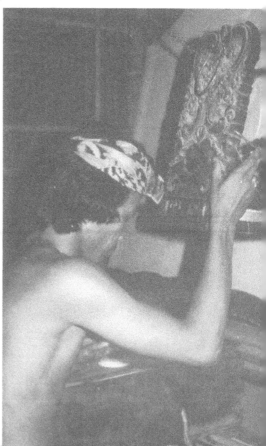

Plate 26 *Dalang* I Wija
placing incense sticks
into a basket of offerings
(containing, among other things,
Chinese coins, *kèpèng*,
a coconut and an egg)
before beginning to perform

Plate 27
Dalang I Badra preparing purificatory
water during a *sudamala* rite.
He holds the supreme god, Tunggal,
in his left hand.

Plate 28 Silhouette of Kresna while punctuating his speech with his hand

divided into two pairs: a larger *pengumbang* and a smaller *pengisep*, which is higher pitched. The larger *gendèr* form the leading unit; their music ranges from simple, unison passages to intricate four-part polyphony. The smaller pair of *gendèr* enrich the tonal quality by doubling their parts an octave higher (McPhee, 1970, p. 160). The scale peculiar to the *gendèr wayang* is pentatonic and known as *slèndro*.

Each district and ensemble has its own style of playing. This is unsurprising in view of the fact that it is preserved by memory; there is no notation. Despite this, McPhee (1966, p. 225) points out that the repertory played during a performance is standard.

The role of the music is integrative. It announces entrances, supports the dialogues, creates a gracious atmosphere for romantic scenes, and adds excitement to scenes of conflict. There are basically two types of composition. Soft (*alus*) compositions form the background to certain stanzas and quiet scenes. These are two-voiced, non-rhythmic, archaic and static. The second type is vigorous and dynamic and accompanies departures to wars, battles, pursuits and flights (*ibid.*, p. 225).

The most elaborate composition is the opening one, *Pemungkah*, played while the puppets are taken out of their chest and installed in the main banana stem in front of the *dalang*. This can last up to one hour. The mood changes constantly from calm to agitated. It is followed by a quiet melody, *Alas Harum* (perfumed forest), while the *dalang* chants the opening stanzas to the play. From then on the music is largely incidental, accompanying different situations.

Soft music of the first type is primarily played during love scenes and moments of grief. Love episodes in particular demand close coordination between the *dalang* and musicians. As the prince makes overtures to the princess, the *dalang* sings in a high, langorous voice to the melody called *Rebong*, which is soft and slow in tempo. It changes to become loud and animated when the scene closes with burlesque advances made by one of the servants to the lady-in-waiting, the *condong*. *Masem* is played during sad events involving refined characters.

The second type of music includes principally the *Angkat-angkatan* for departures and *Batèl* for battles. A loud, vigorous composition, *Runduh*, also accompanies ogres and Duryodana's entrance on stage. My informants explained that a special composition is played as each of the four main servants enters. McPhee (1970, pp. 177–8 only draws attention to the *lagu* Dèlem, which belongs to the category of forceful music.

Mention should also be made of the rapping sound which punctuates the dialogues. The *dalang* produces this by hitting the side of the puppet-chest with his gavel which is held between the toes of his right foot. During battle scenes it is tapped energetically and loudly, accenting the gestures of the warriors.

The delicate yet poignant *gendèr* music is intrinsic to every performance. It is to this sonorous image of progress, abstracted from the mundane world of the spectators, that the *dalang* dances the puppets and recounts the story.

II   THE STRUCTURE AND DEVELOPMENT OF THE PLOT

Each play, *lelampahan*, is a work of art brought to life by the *dalang*. Yet definite rules underpin his performance, which is best viewed as an example or, as Wollheim (1970, p. 90) put it, a 'token' of a specific genre of theatre. The plays flowing from this genre are all based on myths known to the *dalang*, traditional melodies and songs, standard patterns of dialogues[7] and a specific style of performance.

Lévi-Strauss (1976, pp. 16–22) has described creation by fragments or odds and ends as *bricolage*. This, he argues, is characteristic of mythical thought and governed by a logic very different from, but certainly as rigorous as that of science. The *dalang* is eminently suited to being called a *bricoleur*, or handyman, in the sense implied by Lévi-Strauss. During a performance he shifts and rearranges existing dramatic elements into new arrangements. These, like the patterns of a kaleidoscope, are regroupings of the same basic elements, and produced by the conjunction of contingency and constraint.

The *dalang*'s role as a *bricoleur* is vividly illustrated in the way he constructs the plot. The classical literature forms the basis of the plots, which are never written down. It is essential though to distinguish between the literary source and the plot. The *dalang* only uses the bare skeleton of the myth from the text. He develops the entire plot himself and improvises extensively. He may also insert short stanzas, *peretitala* (see McPhee, 1970, p. 134) in Old Javanese. These derive from the classics, but not necessarily from the same text as the plot. They are sung or chanted. The *dalang* may also include light-hearted Balinese songs.

A plot has been defined as motivated action, involving some conflict or issue which is finally resolved, even if this implies no neat ending, but only the attainment of an implicit conclusion (Danzeger and Johnson, 1967, pp. 19–22). A set of constraints further determines the selection and sequences of the dramatic episodes, i.e. the cultural fragments. A *wayang* plot corresponds on the whole to the standard definition of a plot. A number of constraints are also imposed on the *dalang* in his narration. *Dalangs* stress that it is essential that a thread, known as *giing satua*, runs through the story which is always concluded on the night of the performance – unlike Java, where stories often continue for several nights. In passing, it is worth noting that this contrasts with Becker's (1979, pp. 224–6) account of the plot in Javanese *wayang* which, he points out, does not observe Aristotle's unity of action, i.e. a continuous action, with a beginning, a middle and an end. While a *dalang* in Bali may begin the story at any point, a well-planned plot has a linear unity. The conflict or problem is first introduced, it is then developed and at the end some sort of solution is worked out. While coincidences (causeless interactions, *ibid.*, p. 224) do occur, they are generally related to the plot. Either they illuminate an issue in it, or at the very least involve some of the main characters.

All plots also have complicated sub-plots within which the *dalang* often skilfully ad libs. Most of them take place outside the court in the middle of the story. The servants are the main actors in these. It is then that they may dance, sing, weep, tell jokes, frolic around, make advances to the opposite sex or become involved in skirmishes, especially with the ogres. Such motifs are considered to be embellishments to the main plot, and hence are called *penyelah*, or 'beautifiers' (van der Tuuk, 1897). The *dalang* tries to relate them to the main action as a parallel, contrast or complement in order to prevent the plot from 'zig-zagging' (*sarag-sirig*).

A plot has spatial unity. Usually it begins and ends at the court. A substantial part of the middle section often takes place in the forest or some other place in nature. Additional structuring of the plot is apparent on several levels. Essentially three basic scenes can be distinguished: audience scenes, scenes outside the audience hall, and battle. These scenes can crop up on several occasions, but again the *dalang* links them consistently to establish a continuous sequence of events.

Each scene includes three components: description, dialogue and action. The *dalang* always starts a performance with a long poetic description which is obligatory (*pamabah*, followed by *panyarita*) where he introduces the story; he also refers to the text on which it is based. After this, the description, the actions and the dialogue appear to be equally developed. This means that the characters are revealed not so much by what they say, but by their behaviour and what is said about them. As mentioned earlier, the servants' role here is crucial for they translate and paraphrase into Balinese what the others say. In fact little motivation for action is evident in the plot. As will emerge when we examine the thematic content of the stories, it is the servants who bring a performance to life by mediating between the past and present, between the world of mythology and that of the spectators.

III   THEMES AND IMAGES IN *WAYANG* STORIES

The plays deal with numerous subjects, ranging from lofty moral themes to love and spiritual striving, or political intrigue. They all seem also to contain comic interludes, social commentaries and ethical dilemmas. Although here we are dealing with the surface level, it is on stage that the *dalang* explores and amplifies the skeleton of the plot derived from the text. The dramatic impact of the narrative is best illustrated by stories and extracts from dialogues taken from actual performances. The outlines of four such stories, together with dialogues, are presented in this section. Each of them was dramatized by a different *dalang* from south Bali all of whom are married (see p. 29). Thereby the reader can obtain an idea of the variation which exists between *dalangs* in their thematic content and their narrative style. The standing of the *dalang* in the community is also mentioned and the response of the audience to the particular performance reviewed.

In these four *wayang* stories the gods and high castes say little and speak the form of Old Javanese, *kawi*. The servants translate into colloquial Balinese and often comment at length on their words. They speak high Balinese to high castes and gods, generally low Balinese to ogres and, unless otherwise indicated, ordinary Balinese when they address one another. This pattern is standard for all night performances. As the language used in the plays is highly repetitive and idiomatic, the passages are paraphrased. The speech level is included in brackets when thought helpful for the reader.

A   *Lelampahan wayang*: Gatotkaca's meditation   *Dalang* I Wija gave this performance during the anniversary of the temple of the dead, Duurbingin, in the village Tegallalang in Gianyar. He is a Sudra from Sukawati and still relatively young. He is married to an American and has travelled to the United States. He is widely recognized as the best *dalang* on the island today. As a result he is often asked to perform, especially in the regencies of Gianyar and Badung.

The villagers say that his greatest ability lies in narrating a *wayang* story which is exciting and thought-provoking. It is also skilfully composed, with the plot having a definite unity. He also dances the puppets elegantly. He may be mildly criticized for his voice: it is melodious, yet somewhat soft and hence not always heard.

Because of I Wija's skill in telling a story, a number of extracts from dialogues are included here which involve gods, high castes and the servants. The dialogues are taken from the *wayang* story *Gatotkaca's meditation* which is said to be based on the text *Cantakaparwa*.[8] The myth tells of the prince, Gatotkaca, who is seeking through his meditation (*yoga*) to transform earth into heaven. His brothers question the merits of this pursuit, while the gods strongly disapprove of it. The main problem posed is whether the categories of heaven and earth should be kept distinct, or whether they can merge. This is an unusual myth, because the gods in it fight the Pandawas, so it does not follow the standard pattern of *wayang* stories where the virtuous princes confront the princes of lesser virtue. In the play Dèlem and Sangut serve the gods and Tualèn and Merdah the Pandawas.

As the story unravels, we are taken to three places: the court, heaven and Mount Kailasa in the forest. I Wija introduces the play with the following speech:

Dalang   (*kawi*) Yes, it is early in the morning and the gamelan and the trumpets can be heard. The populace is cheering to the music. They are walking in a procession. The kings, who are splendidly clad, are riding in chariots. Darmawangsa, Bima, Arjuna and Nakula, who are the leaders in the war, are heading the procession.

The *parwas*, composed long ago by the sage Biasa, are still in use.

(The puppets are taken out of the chest and placed in the banana stem).

Sang Hyang Ringgit [the god of the puppets) is now ready to dance. The god Iswara will narrate.

A meeting is called to discuss whether Gatotkaca ought to be stopped in his meditation as he is trying to convert earth into heaven. It is questionable whether this is virtuous. Yudistira, Kresna, Bima, Tualèn and Merdah are present.

Kresna   (*kawi* to Yudistira) Why are you troubled?

Yudistira   (*kawi*) It is true that Sang Gatotkaca is meditating on Mount Kailasa. He wants to transform earth into heaven. Kresna would then become Wisnu. Surely, this is wrong.

149

Tualèn	(high Balinese) Excuse me for translating what you, Sang Darmawangsa, have said to Sang Kresna. Darmawangsa is troubled as Gatotkaca is trying to transform earth into heaven [*makariya swarga ring jagaté*]. Darmawangsa, Bima, Arjuna, Nakula and Sahadéwa would then become the gods Darma, Bayu and Indra and the Aswins respectively. Kresna and Baladéwa would become Wisnu and Brahma.
Yudistira	(*kawi*) Yes, Gatotkaca is too bold in assuming that he can equal the gods. As a result, the gods will make war on us.
Tualèn	(high Balinese) Hence Darmawangsa feels troubled. The sage Narada has already told him that if Gatotkaca does not stop meditating within the next three days, the gods will make war on us.
Yudistira	(*kawi*) It is difficult to know how to act. I would be showing disrespect to the gods if I did not heed their request. At the same time, I would be considered ignorant of religious matters if I tried to prevent someone from meditating.
Tualèn	(high Balinese) If Darmawangsa stops Gatotkaca from meditating, the populace will certainly think he is at fault. Yet, if he does not stop Gatotkaca, mankind will be in danger as the gods will make war on us. He does not know how to deal with the problem.
Yudistira	(*kawi*, to Kresna) What is your opinion about this?
Kresna	(*kawi*) Gatotkaca should be left to meditate. Yet he is not showing the gods their due respect as he is not heeding their request to stop in his endeavour to transform earth into heaven.
Merdah	(high Balinese) Forgive me for explaining what you, Sang Kresna, have said to Darmawangsa. It is true that Gatotkaca is too bold in assuming that he can equal the gods. It is difficult, though, to know whether he is acting virtuously or not. He can only be considered virtuous if the entire family is in unison about his conduct. However, Sang Arjuna is displeased that Gatotkaca is meditating.
	In the same way there are many religions: some search for virtue from the north, some from the east, some from the south and some from the west. Harmony can only be achieved when they all agree that their final goal is to worship the supreme god, Sang Hyang Widi [who represents a transcendental unity, see p. 20].

Bima	(*kawi*, to Arjuna who has joined the group) Why did you previously say [before the meeting took place] that Gatotkaca is in the wrong?
Tualèn	(high Balinese) Forgive me for translating what you, Bima, have just said. Why is Gatotkaca in the wrong? You (to Arjuna) are jealous that he is able to transform earth into heaven.
Arjuna	(*kawi*, to Bima) Your child is stupid!
Merdah	(high Balinese) In the same way as a newly hatched bird is like his father, Gatotkaca resembles his father. He is coarse and ugly. His body is huge and ungainly. His voice is as loud as a buffalo, and he is dumb for he never learnt literature at school.
Bima	(*kawi*) It is true, younger brother, what you say. I am ugly and stupid. None can be compared to you in looks.
Tualèn	(high Balinese) It is true what Bima says. Yet if Bima were not ugly, who would call Arjuna handsome? Ugliness and beauty must both exist.

This conversation continues for some time. It ends with the servants fruitlessly disputing on the merits or demerits of Gatotkaca's meditation.

The story now turns to heaven where the god Indra and his servants, Dèlem and Sangut, are present. Indra has sent his heavenly nymphs to Mount Kailasa to try and disrupt Gatotkaca's meditation. In consternation, and mounting anger, the god discusses the situation with the servants.

Indra	(*kawi*) The celestial nymphs have fled from Mount Kailasa without being able to disrupt Gatotkaca's meditation. They became frightened when Bima hit them with his club. I am very angry with Gatotkaca and will now go with the god Yama to Mount Kailasa.
Dèlem	(ordinary Balinese) The celestial nymphs were unable to disrupt Gatotkaca's meditation as Bima, who is protecting his son, hit them with his club until they fled. Indra is very angry. Gatotkaca is too bold. He is a mere human who is trying to equal the gods.
Sangut	(ordinary Balinese) Why are you saying, brother, that there is no proper purpose to Gatotkaca's meditation? You are blustering! You must consider why he is meditating. Perhaps his motivation is good [*mawinan becik*] and he wishes to bring peace to the world.

Dèlem	(ordinary Balinese) You speak as if you were on the side of our enemies. The gods in their anger will kill us all. Now Indra and Yama are going to Mount Kailasa to ask Gatotkaca why he is meditating.

Indra, Yama, Dèlem and Sangut descend with their attendants to Mount Kailasa. There they meet Bima and the monkey god Hanuman who are guarding Gatotkaca.

Indra	(*kawi*), My child, Sang Bima, I have come here as the gods are distressed that Gatotkaca wishes to transform earth into heaven. If he does not cease to practise ascetism in the woods [*tapa berata*] the gods will kill him.
Bima	(*kawi*) Forgive my stupidity, Indra, but why is Gatotkaca in the wrong? Why are you trying to prevent him from meditating? It is worthy to practise ascetism and to meditate. This way a person purifies himself and banishes the three states of impurity, *tri mala* [unvirtuous thoughts, speech and action] and the six enemies, *sad ripu* [lust, greed, anger, disrespect, pride and envy].[9]
Tualèn	(high Balinese) Yes, Indra, forgive Bima's stupidity. He wishes to know why Gatotkaca is acting virtuously. He is, after all, purifying himself so that the three states of impurity, *tri mala*, and the six enemies, *sad ripu*, of a person are banished. As a result there will be peace and prosperity in the land.
Merdah	(ordinary Balinese, to his father) Do *tri mala* and *sad ripu* imply impurity [*leteh*]?
Tualèn	(ordinary Balinese) *Tri mala* and *sad ripu* prevent a person from following the path of *darma* (duty and virtue).

Indra then explains that humans should not try to transform earth into heaven, as this would imply the destruction of both spheres. After this, Yama confronts Gatotkaca and war breaks out between the gods and the Satriyas. At this stage the gods of the nine-fold division of the cosmos, *nawa-sanga*, enter, as do the ogres in support of them. Kresna and Baladéwa fight with Wisnu and Brahma while Yudistira, Bima, Arjuna, Nakula and Sahadéwa fight with their respective genitors, the gods Darma, Bayu, Indra and the Aswins. Hanuman first confronts the elephant god, Gana, and then fights fiercely with Yama.

Finally Siwa arrives and tells them all to cease fighting. He explains that Gatotkaca is meditating in order to obtain his reward promised to him as a child. When still young, the prince killed a powerful ogre who was threatening to destroy heaven. As a reward for his brave deed, Siwa had assured him that he would become a god. So far this promise has not been fulfilled. Siwa then requests the gods to return to heaven. The story concludes with Siwa telling Gatotkaca that he would become a god and should go home in peace.

The play was heatedly discussed the next day by numerous villagers. Two main issues were raised. Should heaven and earth be kept distinct? Was Gatotkaca in fact given his due reward as promised to him by Siwa? The villagers unanimously agreed that the two spheres must remain separate, as only then can there be order in the cosmos (see p. 64–5). The second issue was more difficult to settle, for the story did not reach an obvious solution. Finally one of the village priests pointed out that Gatotkaca had in fact received his reward as Siwa enabled him to become aware of his true god-like nature, and so he could remain content as a human on earth. The priest's opinion was generally accepted by the others.

This was an unusually complicated story and not all the spectators entirely understood it. Even such terms as *tri mala* or *sad ripu*, which were not elucidated in the play, were only understood by some of the adults. Yet the villagers all conceded that it was a stimulating play which was excellently dramatized.

B *Lelampahan wayang*: rivalry between the Korawas and Pandawas

Dalang I Berata is the second most popular *dalang* in Sukawati after I Wija. His stories are, though, less well planned and the dramatic elements less smoothly interrelated. His voice, however, is fuller than that of I Wija. He stands out for the moral content of his stories and thus many villagers enjoy watching his plays. He is of low caste, middle-aged and married. He often performs in Gianyar. This performance was given during the anniversary of one of the village temples in Tegallalang in Gianyar. The story is based on the *Adiparwa*. The play begins after the incident in the epic when the Pandawa brothers escape from their home which the Korawas had set on fire in the hope of killing them (cf. Zoetmulder, 1974, p. 71). Only the dialogues of the servants are presented in this example; in fact, the high castes say very little in the play. The speeches are of interest as they illuminate the qualities of the main protagonists of each side. They also illustrate how pithy sayings and buoyant songs may be incorporated in the narration.

The following scene is set at the court of Nastina. The old King, Dastarastra, is grieving as the five Pandawa brothers and Drupadi are no longer with him,

153

but somewhere in the woods. Sangut translates and comments on the king's words:

Sangut   (high Balinese) Oh dear! I beg your pardon, elderly king, I will explain what you said. He feels heartbroken and frail, like a man with no bones, as the five Pandawa brothers are no longer with him. No one can equal them. If you look in the world, Darmawangsa truly represents the god Darma, who strengthens *darma*. Bima is firm and determined. Where would you meet someone as handsome as Arjuna; it is as if the god of love, Semara, had descended to earth. Nakula and Sahadéwa have great loyalty for Kunti (who is not their real mother). Also the princess Drupadi's beauty is unparalleled. It is on remembering them that the king grieves.

Duryodana, Karna and Sakuni, who are also present, pretend to grieve with Dastarastra. Sangut, who is shrewd and intuitive, sees through their deception and comments on it to Dèlem.

Sangut   (ordinary Balinese) Yes, he [Duryodana] is really clever. You are often taken in by others who are clever, Dèlem. This is like an expression at the coffee stall: everyone knows now and has known in the past that there are three things, *bayu-sabda-idep*: action, speech and thoughts. These cannot be separated. That which appears as one has diverse elements. That which appears diverse has an underlying unity.

Dèlem   (ordinary Balinese) What do you mean?

Sangut   If the thoughts are evil, it is clear that the actions are evil. If the actions are evil, it is clear that the thoughts are evil. It must be so. If only the speech is clever, the actions and thoughts are still evil.

Dèlem   Oh!

Sangut   Why do you say Oh? As he [Duryodana] is clever with words, he can hide his thoughts and actions from others.

Dèlem   Oh, Sangut knows how to philosophize (*ngupas pilsapat*).

The lady in waiting, the *condong*, enters on stage, dancing coquettishly. Both Sangut and Dèlem flirt with her. Dèlem bombastically announces that he wishes to marry her:

Dèlem   Who is this woman who looks like a lotus?

Sangut	(singing sweetly) Her scent is fragrant and poignant.
	Her lips are like a red flower.
	Her teeth are level and cast a glow like that of the insect *tibangbang* that shines at night.
	Her hair is worn in two coils at the back of the head.
	Her breasts are firm and smooth like the inner side of two coconuts.
	Her arms sway gracefully to and fro.
Dèlem	Sister (as he boldly approaches her).
condong	Good heavens (*déwa ratu*)! Elder brother, speak from further away for your breath stinks!
Dèlem	But every day I brush my teeth with toothpaste and now you say my breath is foul!

The servants continue to banter for some time, after which they depart. The story then turns to the Pandawas in the forest. First only their servants are present. Tualèn is grumbling at all the ceremonies he has to perform for his son:

Tualèn	I have spent so much money on my child [*nani*]. Since his birth I have had to prepare life-cycle rites [*manusa-yadnya*] [on the *yadnya*, see p. 26] for him. Now again he asks for money!
Merdah	Oh, why does father [*nanang*) reproach himself? I am not brave enough to admonish him as he is old, but I can point out his mistakes. He is like one who did not wish to learn when he was young. Such a person can be compared to grass. While young he is agile, but when old he is feeble. Later on after your death, father, I shall have to perform the rites of the dead [*pitra-yadnya*].

Later on in the same scene Tualèn complains to Merdah about the hardships that they have to endure in the woods, and the following dialogue ensues in which Tualèn says he will return home in the disguise of an indigenous medical practitioner, *balian*, in order to make some money:

Tualèn	I will disguise myself as a medical practitioner. The last time I was at home I gave my friends advice as to what medicine to use.
Merdah	Father was once a medical practitioner?
Tualèn	Indeed, and I was a supernaturally powerful medical practitioner, renowned for my ability to cure conjunctivitis.

Merdah	How did father cure illnesses?
Tualèn	When a patient came with conjunctivitis I closed his eyes. When a sterile person came I stroked his stomach and told him not to eat rice for fifteen days.
Merdah	Oh, father is skilled! How did you train to become a medical practitioner?
Tualèn	One should not ask such a question.
Merdah	If you are not trained, you are pretending to have a skill you do not possess [*nyolog karma*]. Retribution will be great. If father does not know the palm-leaf manuscripts on medical matters, *usada* [see Weck, 1937, p. 6], the religious incantations, the causes of illness or how to cure them, and never practises meditation, but asks money from patients, he is in effect stealing from them. It is also not proper that you should want to make a profit from curing others.
Tualèn	(looking after Merdah who runs off) He is ashamed of me.

In the meantime Duryodana, Karna and Sakuni have discovered the whereabouts of the Pandawas, who are residing near a lake in the forest. There fighting breaks out between the two camps. Indra and the celestial beings, *gandarwa*, descend from heaven to support the Pandawas while fierce ogres assist the Korawas. The latter are finally defeated and the Korawas and Pandawas return to their respective homes.

This play was well received by the audience. They drew special attention to I Berata's skill in characterizing, through the eyes of the servants, the main Satriyas of each camp: the virtuosity of the Pandawas was vividly set against the dishonesty of the Korawas.

C *Lelampahan wayang*: Baladéwa sent to the Valley of one Thousand Waterfalls I Déwa Rai Mesi, who narrated this story at the anniversary of a village temple, is a Wèsya from Bangli. He is middle-aged, married and used to travel around selling his merchandise of medicines and indigenous charms to villagers. He only became a *dalang* fairly late in life. He often performs in isolated hamlets in the remoter mountainous regions of Gianyar or Bangli. This performance, too, was given in such a hamlet. Although the episodes of his stories are somewhat aimlessly strung together, humble or young villagers enjoy them as they are sprinkled with jokes and spicy puns. In contrast, older or more educated Balinese may disapprove of the stories which do not adhere closely to the texts. The *dalang* also departs from tradition by speaking Indonesian at times on stage. Like I Berata, he is praised for his strong, clear voice. Many spectators enjoy his war scenes, which are lively and exciting.

This particular story is said to be derived from the *Cantakaparwa*.[8] It is set before the great war, the Bratayuda, breaks out. The Pandawas and Kresna are trying to think up ways to prevent Baladéwa from joining the Bratayuda on the side of the Korawas, because Baladéwa is very powerful, being an incarnation of the god Brahma, and could affect the outcome of the war, enabling Duryodana to win. Finally, by a ruse, the Pandawas succeed in sending Baladéwa to meditate in the Valley of One Thousand Waterfalls and hence he is away from the battlefield.

As the *dalang*'s knowledge of Old Javanese is limited and his sub-plots humorous and long-drawn-out, only extracts of dialogues from the servants are included here.

The story takes place at three places: the court of the Pandawas, the forest and Baladéwa's court. The first dialogue, between Tualèn and Merdah, takes place at the court of the Pandawas near the beginning of the play. Merdah is pointing out to his father that he is looking for a wife who should, however, be an older woman. Tualèn mildly reprimands him:

Tualèn	You like older women, son?
Merdah	That is so, Father. They are more experienced with men and can give a young fellow like me more pleasure!
Tualèn	A young girl would be a much better choice.
Merdah	But I am ugly and unprepossessing to girls.
Tualèn	I will find you a loyal wife. Then the two of you can settle down happily together. The Bratayuda will break out soon and were you to die, you would then have descendants.
Merdah	Where do I find such a wife and how do I propose to her?
Tualèn	You have been to school. What were the first letters that the teacher taught you?
Merdah	A I U E O.
Tualèn	A I U E O. Now try to interpret their meaning, for the letters stand for words which, if correctly understood, indicate how best to obtain a wife.

157

[In brief, the letters stand for the following words: A =*angkuwang*, endeavour; I = *itungang*, discuss; U = *usahang*, borrow; E = *erangang*, proceed earnestly; O = *orahang*, inform.]

> You must first endeavour [*angkuwang*] to work hard so that you have enough money to marry. You must then discuss [*itungang*] your intentions with your parents so that they consent to the union, as you will all be living in the same household together. If you have no money, borrow [*usahang*] some, so that the two of you can start a life together. Proceed earnestly [*erangang*] with your plans; tell your friends what you have in mind so that they are willing to back you. Finally, inform [*orahang*] the girl's parents of your intentions. Having done all this, you must obtain a marriage certificate, as this is necessary nowadays.

Merdah   And if her parents don't agree, what then?

Tualèn   Try again. But if they refuse again, you will have to give up your marriage plans.

A number of such sub-plots are loosely interwoven with the main plot. In due course the story turns to Dèlem and Sangut who are at the court of their master, Baladéwa. They are animatedly disputing the pros and cons of supporting the Korawas or Pandawas in the coming war:

Dèlem   I will tell the populace to follow Baladéwa and the Korawas in the Bratayuda. Although Kresna is on the side of the Pandawas, it would be foolish to back them as they are very poor. This is especially so as they have just come from the forest, where they lived for twelve years. During that time Bima worked as a cook at the court of Wirata. Arjuna became a dance teacher there so that he could fondle the girls, and Darmawangsa taught literature whereby he hid his poverty from others. The Korawas, on the other hand, who are rich, can ensure their subjects an easier life. If the Pandawas become the rulers, we shall have to work hard for our living. Moreover, they have caught illnesses in the woods. Darmawangsa has lice. Bima has ringworm. Arjuna caught syphilis from sleeping around. Insufficient vitamins have resulted in Nakula and Sahadéwa developing beriberi.

Sangut   I beg to apologize for my brother, as he is unable to distinguish right from wrong. It is better to support the Pandawas in the war as they are virtuous. They have suffered poverty and sickness, as they are not overcome by greed like the Korawas.

Darmawangsa is in fact a priest. Bima is as strong as a mountain and, although stupid, he is honest. Arjuna is never defeated in battle. Nakula and Sahadéwa are pure.

Now, if we look at the leaders of Nastina, Dastarastra is blind, Widura lame, Sakuni squints, and Drona's arm is crippled. How can their thoughts be pure if their bodies have defects?

Dèlem   This is mere propaganda for the Pandawas!

The conversation continues in this vein for some time, but then it becomes more personal as Dèlem and Sangut begin to tease and upbraid oneanother as follows:

Dèlem   Ngut [Sangut], Ngut, Ngut!

Sangut   Ngut, Ngut, Ngut! Why are you calling me Ngut? You are not showing me my due respect. Older and younger brother should be respectful to one another.

Dèlem   (boasting about his master) Baladéwa is like the sun god, Surya. If enraged he will scorch the earth [as he is an incarnation of Brahma, who is associated with fire, heat and the colour red]. No-one can withstand him in battle.

Sangut   True, it will become hot, but perhaps the heat will derive from the swelling in front of your neck. It hangs there like a light bulb!

Dèlem   You too should show me more respect. I would not describe you in such words. In any case many villagers when they see me do not even think I am a servant as I possess a golden kris.

Sangut   Is that true?

Dèlem   Villagers think I am a public official.

Sangut   Oh, perhaps an official electrician! You may even attract an elderly woman with money and then you can gamble. There is a song about such an incident in a palm-leaf manuscript.

Dèlem   I know of no such song in a manuscript.

Sangut   You do not know how to chant the classical texts [*mekakawin*]. Very few people nowadays – perhaps no more than ten – know the texts or the different metrical forms.

The story then turns to Kresna and Arjuna who are discussing how to prevent Baladéwa from joining the war. After due consultation, they decide to change shape and unify to become the heavenly sage Narada. In this form they descend to Baladéwa and tell him that the gods wish him to hold a ceremony (*déwa-yadnya*) before the war begins. Baladéwa, beguiled into thinking that Narada has indeed arrived, agrees to do as the gods desire. He then tells his subjects that any request made during the period of preparing the ceremony would be granted to them.

Arjuna and Kresna again change shape to become an ugly, decrepit couple. Arjuna is the wife and Kresna the husband. The man begs Baladéwa to give him his wife, as his own is barren. Baladéwa, in fury at hearing this request, kills the couple. Yet they possess a sacred flower which enables them to come back to life.

In the form of Narada, Arjuna and Kresna again come to Baladéwa. The sage tells him that he has become impure as he has killed innocent villagers. In order to purify himself, he should go to meditate in the Valley of One Thousand Waterfalls. Baladéwa has no alternative but to do as the sage demands.

While he is in the valley the war breaks out, but the gushing waters deaden the sound of the fighting. Hence Baladéwa remains in the valley as he does not realize that the great war has begun. As a result the Pandawas eventually emerge as the victors.

Most of the audience found the play highly entertaining, though some of the older villagers said that the *dalang* spoke too frivolously about the Pandawas. The first dialogue was considered especially humorous. It also illustrates modern trends, for it is common nowadays for villagers to choose their own marital partners (*pada pada demen*).[10] It is still proper, however, to obtain the parents' consent to the union.

D *Lelampahan wayang:* **King Pretu requests** *amerta*   *Dalang* I Ewer, a Sudra, lives near Ubud and is one of the most learned *dalangs* left on the island. He has excellent knowledge of Old Javanese and often led *mekakawin* sessions (see p. 37) in the past at the Ubud court, *puri* Sarèn Agung. The Satriyas of the court are also his patrons and he was always called upon when a performance was required in their family. Now elderly, I Ewer only teaches Old Javanese in his home and performs the day *wayang*, as he does not have sufficient stamina for the night *wayang*. His voice is also rather jarring as he only has a few teeth left. The villagers respect him perhaps more as a scholar and a ritual practitioner than as a dramatic performer. This applied also in former times as his sub-plots were sometimes said to lack sprightliness, although the stories themselves were considered erudite and reflective.

I Ewer narrated this story some years ago in conjunction with the *sudamala* rite, described earlier, in a small hamlet outside Ubud. The story is derived from the text *Catur Asrama* and tells of a severe drought in the kingdom of King Pretu. In order to bring fertility back to the country, the king and his ministers decide first to perform rites to the gods (*déwa-yadnya*) and then to go with their servants, Tualèn and Merdah, to Indra in heaven (Indraloka) to ask the god to send rain so that the land will prosper again.

The following dialogue shows how a scholarly *dalang* may weave Old Javanese stanzas into his narrative to enhance the poetic experience of the play. The hymn that Tualèn chants here is based on the *Arjunawiwaha* (Zoetmulder, 1974, pp. 234–7).[11] The dialogue takes place at the court of King Pretu before he goes off to heaven. In his speech, Tualèn explains to Merdah in what frame of mind rites should be carried out.

King Pretu	(*kawi*) In a country all the five ritual cycles, the *panca-yadnya*, form a unit and the correct rites must be carried out. Now there is no *amerta*, elixir of immortality. Hence nothing is growing on the land. Let us perform the rites to the gods, *déwa-yadnya*, and visit Indra.
Merdah	(ordinary Balinese, to his father) I agree with the king's plan.
Tualèn	(ordinary Balinese, to his son) In order to perform *déwa-yadnya*, the people must have pure thoughts. The feelings of those women who make the offerings must not be impure, insincere or gloomy. For as it is said in the *Arjunawiwaha*:

(*kawi*) Like the shadow of the moon in a vessel filled with water,
If it is clean and pure, the moon will be visible.
In the same way god is present in every creature.
If you perform *yoga* god will be manifest.
To meet god whose form cannot be met.
To understand god whose form cannot be understood.
To grasp god whose form cannot be grasped.
To confront Siwa who is eternal.

(ordinary Balinese) If a jar is filled with clean water, the reflection of the moon will be clear. This also applies to mankind. If their thoughts are pure, a higher truth, Sang Hyang Widi, will be reflected within.

Merdah	(ordinary Balinese) Come, let us prepare for *déwa-yadnya*. It is unnecessary to talk further.

The story soon turns to heaven, Indraloka, the abode of Indra. The god is furious at seeing humans enter heaven and he refuses to grant the king *amerta*, the elixir of immortality. War breaks out between Indra, who is supported by Yama, the black giant Jogor Manik and his army of ogres, and mortals. King Pretu is seized, but he manages to escape. He then departs with his servants, Tualèn and Merdah, to Siwa in Siwaloka and requests the elixir. This is granted. Siwa orders Wisnu, his wife, Sri, their servants and the ascetic Wiswakarma to accompany the king back to earth. Wisnu's servant is told to become maize and Sri's servant sweet potatoes. Wisnu, Sri and Wiswakarma should show the people how to grow rice.

Tualèn's role as mediator between the spheres of the gods and the humans is stressed in the story. The servant in his speech also focuses not only on the proper actions, but also on the intentions underlying them. The older men in the audience considered this story very appropriate for the *sudamala* occasion as it stressed the need for ritual purity – a condition which ensures prosperity and harmony in the land. In the rite that followed, I Ewer prepared purificatory water for the previously ill child; his actions reiterated the meaning of the story.

The Day Performance: *Wayang Lemah*

I THE DRAMATIC QUALITY OF THE PLAY
The day *wayang* is much simpler than the one at night. About five to fifteen puppets are stuck close together into the banana stem, where they remain during the entire narrative, forming a quiet, static backdrop to the play. The Tree of Life, the Kakayonan, and the supreme god, Tunggal, are generally installed in the centre of the banana stem.[12] There is little or no conflict during the day *wayang* and the division between the camps is not prominent.

The servants and a few other characters through whom the *dalang* recounts the story, are not stuck into the banana stem. They are held by the *dalang*, but their movement is slight. Often they are leant against the immobile puppets, and only their elegant arms punctuate the speeches. In as far as the other dramatic features are developed, they mirror the principles already discussed.

Only two large metallophones, *gendèr pengumbang*, accompany the play. As a result the music is less rich in tone and colour than during the night *wayang*.

II STRUCTURE AND DEVELOPMENT OF THE PLOT
While the outline of the plot is derived from the classical literature, the *Adiparwa* is the text most often used as *dalangs* hold it in such high esteem (see pp. 41). It is considered essential in the day *wayang* that

the plot adheres closely to the text, hence there are no sub-plots. The plot itself involves a unified sequence of events. The two dramatic components, description and dialogue, predominate in the scenes as there is hardly any action.

The *dalang*, however, develops the plot primarily through the servants. As there is no struggle between the two camps, two servants may even suffice in a play. Although the use of Old Javanese is deemed especially important in the day *wayang*, it is thus again the servants who interpret and elaborate in Balinese on the events and characters in the story.

III THE THEMES AND IMAGERY OF THE STORIES

The stories deal mainly with moral or spiritual themes, and stress the importance of the quality of a man, and only to a lesser degree his achievements. There are no comic interludes. It is also essential that the story chosen should be appropriate to the social occasion (p. 63–4).

Lelampahan wayang: **Yudistira goes to Heaven**   One such story is presented here. It was narrated by I Ewer (see night *wayang*) during a cremation *(pelebon)* in Ubud. As he is a highly esteemed scholar, the pattern of episodes worked out in the play tally with those in the epic literature. The story also fits the occasion. It is based on the last part of the *Prastanikaparwa* and the subsequent *parwa*, the *Swargarohanaparwa* (Zoetmulder 1974, pp. 81–3). The myth tells of Prince Yudistira's release by ascending to heaven without leaving behind his body *(moksa)*.[13]

The story begins with the *dalang* narrating the fate of the Pandawa brothers and their wife, Drupadi, who had failed to accompany Yudistira on his way to heaven. One after the other they had fallen into a sea of mud and died. The reason for this was their unvirtuous behaviour in life, i.e. the 'seven darknesses' *(peteng pitu)* had overcome them. Drupadi was too easily enraptured by men and so had five husbands. Sahadéwa boasted too much about his intelligence. Nakula was too proud of his looks. Arjuna had lusted after too many women. Bima thought he was the most powerful man on earth; he also drank too much. Only Yudistira's faithful dog continued to accompany his master. Indra then appears in order to take Yudistira to heaven in his chariot. The following dialogue ensues between the god, Yudistira and his servants:

Merdah	(ordinary Balinese, to Tualèn) Father, father, Ida Sang Indra is descending from heaven [*swargaloka*].

Tualèn	(*kawi*, to Yudistira) He is accompanied by gods, celestial musicians and sages. His mount is the white elephant Erawana who is bedecked in gold and jewels. He carries a thunderbolt and a splendid umbrella made out of birds' feathers.
Merdah	(ordinary Balinese) Father, the sages are reciting from the sacred texts, the *wédas*. Flowers are raining down from heaven and the air is filled with sweet scent.
Indra	(*kawi*, to Yudistira whom he embraces) Oh, my child, you have never swayed from the path of *darma*. Enter my chariot and ascend with me to heaven.
Tualèn	(high Balinese, to Yudistira) Permit me to explain your words, Lord [*ratu batara*]. You have acted virtuously and the god now desires you to return with him to heaven.
Yudistira	(*kawi*, to Indra) Thank you, Lord, for inviting me to enter your chariot and ascend with you to heaven.
Merdah	(high Balinese, to Yudistira) My father and I, too, wish to enter the chariot and remain with you.
Yudistira	(*kawi*, to Indra) This dog is tired and wishes to come with me. My brothers and my wife failed to accompany me on my path. However, my faithful dog followed me and I feel compassion and pity for him.
Tualèn	(ordinary Balinese, to Merdah) Sang Darmawangsa wishes to go to heaven with his faithful dog for whom he feels great pity [*kangen*]. He also promised the dog that they would always be together. He would not be pursuing the path of *darma* if he broke his promise.
Indra	(*kawi*, to Yudistira) The dog is impure and so cannot enter heaven.
Tualèn	(ordinary Balinese, to Merdah) Oh, son, Darmawangsa is distressed by the god's request.

In fact Yudistira steadfastly refuses to go to heaven without his loyal dog. Suddenly the dog becomes the god Darma who embraces Yudistira. The god tells the prince that he has indeed proved that he is a man of *darma*. Yudistira, without leaving behind his body (*moksa*), then ascends to heaven in the company of the god Darma and the other celestial beings.

Yudistira is horrified on reaching heaven to find there the hundred Korawas and not his own brothers and wife. The sage Narada tells him to calm himself, and the following discussion takes place with Indra explaining to the prince why the Korawas are in heaven:

Indra	(*kawi*, to Yudistira) Stay, child, with your cousins, the hundred Sang Korawas, in heaven.
Merdah	(high Balinese, to Yudistira) The Lord wishes you to remain in heaven with the Korawas.
Yudistira	(*kawi*, to Indra) Oh Lord, perhaps you did not know that when I was young, and still being taught by Bisma, Drona and Krepa, I promised my brothers that we would always remain together in good and bad times. How could I, moreover, remain in heaven with the Korawas as they had evil intentions towards us at that time?
Tualèn	(ordinary Balinese, to Merdah) Yes, Darmawangsa promised his brothers that they would always be together in good and bad times. I, too, realized that the Korawas were jealous of the Pandawas. The Korawas tried to poison Bima when he was young and then threw him in the river. They also tried to kill the Pandawas by burning down their house.
Yudistira	(*kawi*, to Indra) In life the Korawas never followed the path of *tapa* [ascetism], *yoga* [meditation] and *semadi* [concentration]. They never acted virtuously.
Tualèn	(*kawi*, to Indra) You are silent, Lord. Perhaps it is difficult for you to know how to answer Darmawangsa. Why are the Korawas in heaven?
	(ordinary Balinese, to Merdah) It is true, the Korawas never performed ascetism, meditation or concentration.
Indra	(*kawi*, to Yudistira) Your father will explain why the hundred Korawas are in heaven. They fought bravely and were killed in battle. The celestial nymphs bring directly to heaven anyone who is killed in battle.
Tualèn	(high Balinese, to Yudistira) Your father is explaining to you, his child, why the Korawas are in heaven. They fought bravely and were killed in battle. Anyone so killed, need not be cremated; his soul is taken directly to heaven by the celestial nymphs.
Yudistira	(*kawi*, to Indra) Oh Lord, in that case why are Karna, Gatotkaca, Irawan, Séta, Utara and Sangka not in heaven?
Tualèn	(*kawi*, to Indra) The gods are not righteous.
	(ordinary Balinese, to Merdah) Yes, Karna, Gatotkaca, Irawan, Séta, Utara and Sangka, who all fought bravely and were killed in battle, are not in heaven.

> (high Balinese, to Yudistira) In the beyond it is only Sang
> Hyang Widi [a higher truth], who knows what is just (*uning
> sané iwang patut*).

Irrespective of the god's words, Yudistira refuses to remain in heaven, distressed that his brothers, their children and his wife are not there. He then proceeds with his servants to the underworld in quest of his family.

At the crossroads (Chapter 2, note 7, p. 66) between heaven and hell he sees the land of the dead (Yamaloka) stretching out in front of him. In this realm there is a large lake called the Lake of Suffering (*tegal penangsaran*). Tualèn and Merdah describe what they see in hell (*kawah*). Merdah first compares heaven to earth.

Merdah	(ordinary Balinese, to Tualèn) Only daytime is known in heaven. Hence the petals of the lotuses never close as on earth when it is night.
Yudistira	(*kawi*) We have now reached the crossroads between heaven and hell.
Tualèn	Dah [Merdah], Dah!
Merdah	(ordinary Balinese) Look father, heaven lies in the direction of *kaja* [to the mountains] and hell *kelod* [to the sea; on the directions, see p. 105–6). There are three gatekeepers protecting the crossroads.
Tualèn	(ordinary Balinese) The three gatekeepers are Sang Dorokala, Sang Suratma and Sang Jogor Manik. They are the judges in life and in the hereafter. Suratma carries a manuscript [where the deeds of each person while on earth are recorded]. Dorokala talks to the souls as they arrive at the crossroads and Jogor Manik tells them where to go. In front of us must be the Lake of Suffering. From its centre rises a large tree with leaves shaped like keris. Many souls are drifting in the lake. As the water is very hot, they are trying to climb up the tree. The followers of Yama, however, are shaking the tree so fiercely that the souls are falling back into the water and the leaves are dropping on to them. Depending on where the leaves strike, the souls will be reincarnated either with hare-lips or with crippled arms or legs. In this way the souls are punished for their misdeeds on earth.
Merdah	(ordinary Balinese) Father, look. Jogor Manik is there with a crowd of souls.
Atma (soul)	(*kawi*, addressing Jogor Manik) I know that in life I practised witchcraft.

Tualèn	(ordinary Balinese) Those are souls who were witches. Durga enabled them in life to practise witchcraft. Jogor Manik is telling them that as punishment they would remain in hell for one thousand years. Never, son, become a witch!
Merdah	(ordinary Balinese) I would never learn witchcraft, father.
Tualèn	(ordinary Balinese) Jogor Manik is now with souls who were once beautiful and delighted in many men. Yet they never had husbands and no children. Jogor Manik is placing large ants on their breasts. These ants feed off them.
Merdah	(ordinary Balinese) More souls are arriving. They are clad in rough goatskins as they never learnt to weave. Dogs are biting them.
Tualèn	(ordinary Balinese) What is that big fire?
Merdah	(ordinary Balinese) Look, father, at those large stones which are closing and opening, crushing souls caught between them. Now another soul is coming up to Jogor Manik.
Jogor Manik	(*kawi*) Oh, soul, you are pure (as he shows him another path).
Tualèn	(ordinary Balinese) Yes, this soul was virtuous in life and so he will go to the east [to heaven].
Merdah	(ordinary Balinese) So, it is like that, father. A soul who performed ascetism and meditation in life is not punished by Jogor Manik.
Tualèn	(ordinary Balinese) Darmawangsa is tired from walking on so many slippery stones. We are now in hell. Listen to all those souls calling out to us.
Yudistira	(*kawi*) All these souls are suffering terribly. My brothers and my wife are calling out to me that I should purify them.

Yudistira then recalls his promise that his family should always remain united in sorrow and happiness, and he descends to them. Suddenly hell changes into heaven and heaven becomes hell. The Pandawas go to the former and the Korawas to the latter. Tualèn points out that Yudistira had briefly to experience hell to atone for sin in lying to Drona (p. 50). The story ends with Merdah telling his father that the time had come for them to return to earth (*manusaloka*).

As a day *wayang* does not communicate to humans, no particular reaction was forthcoming from the few who watched the show. The adults only mentioned that the story was appropriate for the cremation.

Creativity and the servants

In dramatizing a play the *dalang* is bound by a set of criteria which are culturally standardized. These determine to a large degree the structure of the plot, the movement, voices and language of the characters in *wayang* and the background music. The *dalang* must have an intimate knowledge of these criteria in order to recombine or go beyond them to create a play which is acceptable to the audience as well as being stimulating. This is especially true in the night *wayang*, on which this section focuses, for the villagers tend simply to walk away if they are bored.

The spectators at a night *wayang*, as we have seen, are primarily interested in the content of the stories, the qualities of sound and form, the overall composition of the play, as well as the sheer technical skill with which the *dalang* enacts the drama. The *dalang* should also consider the area in which he performs. Spectators from isolated hamlets seem mainly to enjoy the comic interludes, whereas sophisticated villagers from traditional areas, like Ubud or Peliatan, are more aware of the basic themes in the story, which should have moral overtones, and the precision with which the language levels are used. In any case, it is essential that there is some feedback between the *dalang* and the audience for the play to be successful. In fact, creator (*dalang*), performers (the puppets) and beholders should be viewed as an entity forming a tripartite notion of communication. All three are involved in a performance given at night.

Structural analysis has emphasized the binary structure in myth and its hidden significance. Although the myth enacted on the stage abounds in oppositions – human and animal, god and demon, day and night, heaven and earth – what stimulates the audience is the telling of a story in dramatic form. Each play is ephemeral and each story in its narration is a unique event. Steiner has drawn attention to the openness of language which he compares to 'an intensively energizing beam of light, shaping, placing, and organizing experience' (1975, p. 142). In view of this, it is hardly surprising that a *dalang*'s creativity seems primarily to occur in his narration.

A *dalang* can be creative in several ways in telling a story. As this is a complex subject, only a few of the more obvious ones are mentioned. It is perhaps important to point out first that each story is created by aesthetic discourse, i.e. the *dalang* is involved in systematic and sustained reflexive dialogue on stage when he explores and questions the meaning in the story. At the same time, an accomplished *dalang* interweaves the other dramatic elements such as the dance and voices of the characters so ingeniously with the narrative that they contribute to the meaning of the story, while adding vitality and colour to the play as a whole.

It is interesting to note how the *dalang*'s freedom in exploring themes in the text and iconography may express itself. The latter is an important referent in the play, constraining even the humblest of *dalangs* with limited textual knowledge. Yet I have heard one such *dalang* wax lyrical on Drupadi's coquettish and fickle character although she is generally portrayed as beautiful, refined and dignified in both the literary and depicted tradition.

However, it is mainly in the speeches and antics of the servants, who are outsiders to the events revolving around the Satriyas, that the *dalang* gives reign to his imagination. They are the principal actors in any performance as they translate and paraphrase the archaic language spoken by the epic characters which most Sudra audiences do not understand (cf. Forge, 1978 p. 81, on the role of the Sudras in interpreting the arts). Yet, apart from being the translators, they have a multiplicity of other roles in a play. As the extracts from dialogues from actual performances highlighted, they also act as social commentators, instructors, clowns or jokers, and intermediaries (see Hobart, 1983, pp. 159–69). Tualèn often has a special role as he may mediate between the divine and the human world. This comes to the fore in the *sudamala* rite. Some *dalangs* even say that the 'supreme god, Tunggal enters his body during a performance' *(Sang Hyang Tunggal dadi nyusup di awak I Malèn).*

It is of interest that in the folk and literary tradition the *dalang* is linked to Siwa (p. 105), the centre, and the servants Tualèn, Merdah, Dèlem and Sangut to the gods of the cardinal points, Iswara, Mahadéwa, Brahma and Wisnu respectively (Hooykaas, 1973b, pp. 126–7). It is evident that a special relationship is envisaged between the *dalang* and the servants, which is particularly marked in the case of Tualèn.

It is largely through these ambiguous figures who stand on the borderline between reality and illusion that the *dalang* creates an open space in which he can explain and elaborate on such core concepts as *darma*, duty or morality, *karma* or *karmapala* (as it is often called), and *kesucian*, purity, often adding a personal touch to the interpretations given. Moreover, like King Lear's Fool, the servants are granted 'sanctioned disrespect' on stage which allows them to see and speak the truth about the other characters. In fact in their speeches they frequently allude with wit and discernment to the virtues, as well as the foibles and vices, of their masters. At the same time the servants express either explicitly or at least implicitly their beliefs and feelings about the epic characters and their pursuits. In other words, the servants are the village philosophers who in a serious playful tone ponder and speculate on their culture.

It is evident that the process of the *dalang*'s creativity is reflected in the play itself, with particular reference to the spoken word. While the deeper symbolic level underlies the articulate or surface level of the story, it is only given plastic life in the performance when all the dramatic stimuli are orchestrated together. It is then that the *dalang*, largely unconsciously, scans and integrates these levels to produce a play which, if skilfully enacted, stimulates and entertains the audience.

Conclusion

So the *dalang* in the night *wayang* is the creator of a performance during which shadows are projected on to a screen. There they dance in accompaniment to a story set in a consecrated space. Although the play is removed from the spectators, they are still an integral part of the drama, the essence of which seems to be elusive, contradictory, enigmatic and illusionary, *maya* (cf. O'Flaherty, 1984, pp. 117–19 on the various meanings of *maya*; see also p. 177). In the day *wayang*, on the other hand, the *dalang* conjures up an immobile, still world which does not set out to communicate to humans.

Yet in both performances, it is mainly the servants who enable the *dalang* to express his inner vision and intuitive perception. At the same time he is constrained by his particular artistic medium which reflects symbolic patterns of the community to which he too belongs.

Notes

1 There is some variation in the puppets a *dalang* may use for the *sudamala* rite, although those of Tunggal, Siwa, Durga, Tualèn and the Kakayonan seem always to be required.

2 I Ewer pointed out that he chose Bayu to represent Brahma because of the relationship between them: Brahma was the creator god. He first created *bayu* (wind or energy) which enabled there to be life.

3 Hinzler (1981, pp. 248–58) further suggests that the movements of the Kakayonan during each play enact the Hindu cycle of creation.

4 Heine-Geldern (1943, pp. 15–27) drew attention to the significance of the centre of the kingdoms in South East Asia, where the king was identified with the axis of the universe. While this applied to Java, this is somewhat more complex in Bali. Here sacredness is attributed to both *kaja*, 'to the mountains', and east (see p. 105–6).

5 Anderson argues that this reversal expresses 'the ambiguous interconnections of human existence . . . by the irony that left and right are not absolute' (1965, p. 6).

6 A percussion group, *batèl*, is added to the *gendèr* quartet for *wayang Ramayana* which is not dealt with here (McPhee, 1966, pp. 201–2).

7 These may also include exhortations, *tandak*, which cannot be literally translated (see Hinzler, 1981, pp. 280–2).

8 Ensink (1967, p. 51) mentions that Balinese *dalangs* often base their stories on the *Cantakaparwa*. This text consists essentially of folk myths which, however, involve heroes from the great epics. According to Ensink it has not yet been translated.

9 I Ewer gave this interpretation of *sad ripu*. Some variation may exist here. Cooper-Duff (1985, p. 82, note 5), for example, says that the six enemies are lust, greed, anger, drunkenness (of which there are seven kinds), confusion and envy.

10 Important traditional forms of marriage in the village sphere were 'agreed', 'mock capture', 'forced', 'capture' and 'elopement'. The parents agreed to the first three forms of marriage; the last two forms indicate that the girls are married in the face of parental protest (Hobart, M., 1979, p. 357). Girls are neither captured nor forced into marriage these days.

11 In the original hymn Arjuna is on the verge of being defeated by a hunter who, however, takes on the form of Siwa as *ardhanariswara* (half man, half woman). Arjuna worships the god with this hymn of praise (Zoetmulder, 1974, p. 234).

12 Hinzler (1981, p. 253) also points out that the most authentic way of performing the day *lemah* is with the Kakayonan set in the centre of the banana stem.

13 My informants pointed out that three types of *moksa* are recognized in Bali: to die without leaving behind the body (like Yudistira); to cremate oneself with the strength of one's thoughts; and to leave behind the body without having been ill, knowing that the time has come to die.

5

The place of the shadow theatre in Balinese culture and society

The Balinese tend to agree in saying that the shadow theatre, *wayang kulit*, has a three-fold significance in the society. It is instructive, entertaining and religious in intent. Thereby they establish the dominant frame from which I wish to proceed and examine this genre of theatre. However, throughout the book I have taken the position that the indigenous interpretations are part of the data to be explained. By adopting such an approach *wayang kulit*, together with its mythological system, is set within its wider cultural and social context, and not just viewed in isolation. In this chapter we further see how *wayang kulit* acquires its meaning as an active force and organizing principle in the daily life of the people. It has also profoundly affected the other arts, particularly the other popular genres of dance-drama given in the village to the community at large.

In any case, it will emerge that *wayang kulit* performs several linked functions and contains different levels of meaning which intuitively correspond to one another. At a deep level of reality it may even come closer to the truth, where things are revealed in their essence, than the other art forms in Bali, which is perhaps why it is so highly esteemed by the people.

The significance of the performance

The night performance: *wayang peteng*

The night *wayang* is a contrivance of great complexity. Insight can only be gained into its significance when its form and content or thematic material are examined together, for they are interrelated on stage into a rhythmic single structure. This implies looking at the myth in its dramatic setting and not as an isolated entity. Much has been written about myth, but rarely in association with theatre. In the play the spoken word is interwoven with the other dramatic stimuli to affect the audience in various ways. Here it is relevant to note that in all performances the stimuli tend to harmonize with one another and so accord with the message in the *wayang* story. (This is expanded upon later). A distinction should, though, be made between the story and the iconography. In telling a story, as we have seen, the *dalang* explains and questions issues. On the other hand, the iconography, and by extension the dance, the voices and the language level used by the characters, are essentially fixed, and seem rather to evoke shared values and experiences of the community.

It seems evident that such an elaborate genre of theatre would fulfil a number of functions simultaneously. It is of interest that spectators and *dalangs* alike stress its instructive role. They point out that the *dalang* in telling a mythic story dramatizes values which often have moral overtones. These are then picked up and given depth and texture by the other dramatic elements. The Balinese seem here almost to be echoing Durkheim who saw the traditional mythology as embodying the representations, the system of belief and the moral order of the society.

The symbolic complexes expressed by the iconography have already been noted. However, the villagers are also aware of the deeper meaning of the mythic stories. These, too, often articulate values, norms, rules and ideals which relate to the social life of the people as well as to certain features of the social structure. A few examples suffice to illustrate this. For the sake of clarity I am using the *wayang* stories discussed in Chapter 4. Although such statements as those included below belong to the surface level and are as fleeting as the plays are ephemeral, they give a good indication of the tone of the stories flowing from this genre of theatre.

In the performance given by I Berata, Merdah admonishes his father, Tualèn, by saying: 'He is like one who did not wish to learn when he was young. Such a person can be compared to grass. While young he is agile, but when old, feeble' (p. 155). Such a statement touches on delicate inheritance matters in the society. Descent and inheritance in Bali are through the male. Towards the end of his life the elderly father will have to let his more capable son take over, and the son may make pointed references to this fact. The tension on stage between Dèlem and Sangut (p. 159) are also reminiscent of actual life in a Sudra family. Dèlem is stupid, greedy and pompous; Sangut clever and philosophical. Although brothers are expected to live and work together, they often have little in common.[1] The inheritance system singles out one heir, who is usually the younger brother.

In a similar although less overt manner, plays also allude to the complex rules of inheritance and succession in a traditional Satriya family. Primogeniture is the ideal rule, but it is mitigated by a preference for selecting the most suitable heir. In the plays, as in life, it is not immediately apparent who are the rightful heirs. The Pandawas, however, in the contents of their speech (once translated), their behaviour and their looks, demonstrate during the course of a performance their fitness to rule the kingdom.

In I Wija's performance Tualèn eloquently expounds on Bima's words 'Yet if Bima were not ugly who would call Arjuna handsome? Ugliness and beauty must both exist' (p. 151). This statement has to be seen in relation to *ruwa-binèda* (p. 138), the principle of binary opposites in Bali, which includes among its opposites that of man and woman. As will be shown again later, this principle is also mirrored in the social organization, for ideally the sexes are seen as forming a complementary relationship over the public and domestic spheres.

In I Dèwa Rai Mesi's performance, Sangut describes to Dèlem the leaders of Nastina in the following poignant terms:

> Now if we look at the leaders of Nastina, Dastarastra is blind, Widura is lame, Sakuni squints, and Drona's arm is crippled. How can their thoughts be pure if their bodies have defects? (p. 159).

In other words, the leaders are in a state of ritual impurity, *mala* (cf. Hooykaas, 1973a, p. 6). The statement reflects an important philosophical concept in Bali. Similarly to the ancient Greeks, the Balinese do not draw a sharp distinction between the physical and the spiritual, i.e. the inner life of a person is reflected in his outer appearance and behaviour. In this context, it is unsurprising that men who are severely handicapped by being, for example, blind, lame or hare-lipped, or women who are menstruating and so considered ritually unclean, are not allowed to enter a temple.

Such statements are sprinkled throughout all performances, irrespective of who the *dalang* is or where he performs. They refer to axiomatic values embedded in the social life of the people. Their impact is of course increased as the *dalang* is thought to be divinely inspired while narrating on stage – the microsm of the macrocosm (p. 128) – and hence a mouthpiece of the gods.

Plays seen in their entirety also provide the spectators with a blue-print for living, a design for selfhood. As one *dalang* poetically explained when asked the meaning of the night *wayang*:

> Like the bumble-bee who ceaselessly smells the fragrance of the flowers,
> Like the stag beetle who day and night never forgets to smell the putrid and
>   wallows in excretion,
> So too there are good and evil actions.

Selfhood, however, is only achieved through social interaction with other men. This is vividly expressed in *wayang* where there is always war between two sides : in *parwa* stories the relatively virtuous Pandawas oppose the ignoble Korawas. Besides the victory of the former over the latter, there is also the triumph of the gods over the ogres. The tension which builds up on stage adds force to the conflict of ideals. So a night *wayang* presents a powerful scheme which 'exemplifies', *ngelawatin*, the different paths open to a person in pursuit of selfhood: he can dissipate his energies in selfish, unworthy causes, or become an upright member of society – and, as the servants indicate, these paths are open to all people irrespective of their social category.

As implied by the above, a person's pursuits and actions have also to be seen within a cosmic order. In this order not only the individual but also the group has its proper duty or morality, *darma* (p. 113). In life *darma* can be identified with *adat*, the rules which govern all relations between men and the cosmos. *Adat* has been translated as customary law (Boon, 1977, p. 51) or traditional rules of behaviour (Geertz, C. and H., 1975, p. 197), but these do not take into account its full nature, which has been well summed up by Schärer on *adat* among the Ngaju Dayak in Kalimantan:

> It certainly means more than simply 'usage, custom, habit'. We can only grasp and interpret its significance through the conception of God. Seen in this context the notion has a double meaning. Firstly that of divine cosmic order and harmony, and secondly that of life and actions in agreement with this order. It is not only humanity that possesses *adat*, but also every creature or thing (animal, plant, river etc.), every phenomena (e.g. celestial phenomena), every period and every action. (1973, pp. 74–5)

In this cosmic order Schärer (*ibid.*, pp. 40–3) further points out that there are two groups of people: a superior group who are ideally well-balanced, good-looking, elegant and virtuous and an inferior group who are bad people: ugly and deceitful. Although the separation between the camps in *wayang* is not as extreme as that described by Schärer, as there are shades of differences between characters, a performance presents a similar world view.

However, another characteristic is evident in *wayang* which does not occur in Schärer's model of the universe. As we have seen, the servants have multiple roles in all plays. They seem at times comparable to men awake who stride in and out of the dream-like mythic story as they comment on and explain the speeches and behaviour of the other characters who are remote from the spectators. The servants clearly represent the egalitarian system in Balinese society which cross-cuts the hierarchical structure of demarcated ranked divisions.

Apart from the socio-cultural implications of the night *wayang* some *dalangs* may also interpret it in psychological terms. According to them, the five Pandawas are said to represent the five senses as follows: Yudistira represents hearing, Bima feeling, Arjuna sight, Nakula taste and Sahadéwa smell.[2] Only when the five brothers are in harmony with one another and united, i.e. the five senses are correctly ordered, can the wishes and desires be controlled. The latter are represented by the Korawas and the ogres in a play. This symbolism gives another conception of 'self' in Bali, but this time in relation to the subjective experiences of man.

Certainly the above remarks indicate how core values reverberate below the surface of the plays which pertain to the Balinese system of belief and moral order. As already noted, the night *wayang* also entertains, thereby compelling the attention of young and old alike during a performance. The sub-plots in particular are often set in a ludicrous context. It is then that the servants clown around or become involved in horseplay, when they may upbraid one another bawdily or tell witty jokes. They may also frolic around and make advances to the *condong*, or lady-in-waiting. As she is attractive and her caste unspecified (or at the most Wèsya), the servants are free to woo her with songs and romantic allusions.

A performance is also an aesthetic experience. In fact the spectators may comment at great length on the technical merits of a given show. While the story should be stimulating and have humorous interludes, the villagers are acutely aware of the voice of the *dalang* during the narrative. At best it is described as 'sweet' (*manis*), and at worst as rough or hoarse. The *dalang* should also show a sense of symmetry, form and elegance when he dances the puppets and composes scenes on stage, irrespective of whether they involve battles or not.

Although the Balinese emphasize the instructive and to a lesser degree the entertainment or aesthetic value of the performance, it still

Plate 29 The *dalang* entering
Yudistira from his right.
A gendèr musician is visible
behind the *dalang*.

Plate 30 An offering

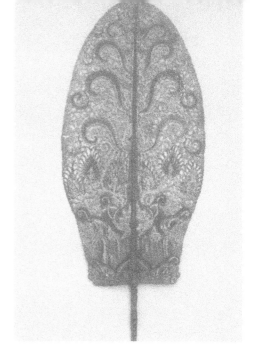

Plate 31 The kakayonan

Plate 32 The night *wayang*. The kakayonan appears fleetingly on the left.

Plate 33 Painting by a student of Nyoman Mandara. Scene from the *Bagawadgita* with Kresna and Arjuna in the chariot and Tualèn and Merdah behind. Hanuman is shown on the flag.

Plate 34 Statue of winged lion in front and a scene from *Sutasoma* in back at Kreta Gosa. Sutasoma is teaching the tigress; the servants squat below.

Plate 35 Carving of Hanuman
on temple gateway

Plate 36
The servants, the *penasar*
and *wijil*, in *topèng*

has profound religious significance for the people. This is illustrated by the indigenous interpretations of the shadows (*lawat*). Scholarly *dalangs* may refer to the shadows by the Sanskrit term, *maya*, illusion. The name alludes to the illusory nature of all categories of manifestation and enables the shadows to act 'as a bridge', *sekadi nitinin*, between this world and the next. Texts may also attribute special value to the shadows. The Old Javanese poem *Arjunawiwaha* is outstanding in this respect. In the poem Indra explains to Arjuna that all appearances merely ensnare the senses and are an illusion by making the following analogy:

> For it is as with spectators of a puppet performance (*ringgit*). They (are carried away), cry, and are sad (because of what befalls their beloved hero or heroine) though they know that it is merely carved leather that moves and speaks. That is the image of one whose desires are bound to the objects of the senses, and who refuses to understand that all appearances are only an illusion and a display of sorcery without any reality (Zoetmulder, 1974, pp. 209–10).

So the shadow play emerges as a vehicle which, in an almost Platonic sense, encourages the ascent of the mind to a higher intelligible region or transcendental metaphysical reality. Yet the Balinese do not make the same radical distinction between 'appearance' and 'reality' as did Plato, but suggest instead that there are different levels of comprehension. As man gains in wisdom, so too does he enhance his awareness of the transcendance.

Attention should here be drawn to the terminological link which exists in the Balinese language between *ngelawatin*, to exemplify, and *lawat*, the shadow. To the villagers this illustrates the inter-relationship between man's experience, as exemplified on stage, and the ideal which hovers on the edge of actualization.

Finally, from a broader perspective, it is of interest to note the indigenous correlation which is often made between the performance, the microcosm, and the macrocosm. *Dalangs* mainly explain this in terms of supernatural power for good and purity. These forces are thought to run down over time as evil increases, bringing decay and degeneration in its wake. While these conflicting forces are intrinsic to the cosmological order, their ever-precarious balance must be maintained; one must not engulf the other.[3] Through the performance the *dalang* strives to counterbalance the opposing forces of supernatural power of purity and pollution. So the night *wayang* emerges as a paradigm of the cosmic process which directly relates to events in the world of men. Order in the microcosm implies that order is reasserted in the macrocosm.

The day performance: *wayang lemah*

The day *wayang* is the most revered form of theatre in Bali (cf. Hinzler, 1981, p. 18), yet it is hardly theatre in the standard sense of the word for it does not set out to communicate to humans. It is essentially a rite which is directed to the invisible beings or powers. As such it plays an essential part in the five ritual cycles, *panca-yadnya*, on the island (pp. 26–7). In this light it is fitting that the villagers consider it an offering, *banten*. In what is probably folk etymology, *banten* is derived from *enten*, to wake up, implying to be conscious. Van Eck (1897) translates the term as to wake up momentarily, then to fall back to sleep again. So the day *wayang* shows that one is conscious, even if only temporarily, of the gods (*matur pekelingan ring batara*).

As an offering the day *wayang* mediates between men and gods. In fact *dalangs* explain that figuratively the play takes place in heaven where there is always light, *lemah*. Here, in this pure setting, it is given to the gods. Certainly the few villagers who watch the show are irrelevant. The story, moreover, is hardly audible. The pleasure that the gods receive from the day *wayang* is said to be essentially the same as the essence, *sari*, that they obtain from other offerings. Thus the performance sets up a reciprocal relationship between men and gods.

In view of the sanctity of the day *wayang*, it is also fitting that the colours are visible during the performance. As mentioned earlier, during the night *wayang* the colours are hidden from the audience, who watch the shadows projected on to a screen. The colours are the most sublime of all the puppets' features (pp. 104–12). They are said to be derived from the gods, whose presence they evoke during the rite. It is interesting that western scholars, too, have drawn special attention to the significance of colour. Ehrenzweig, for example, says that form and colour belong to different levels of experience, and drawing on Gombrich, he points out that 'the experience of colour stimulates deeper levels of the mind' (1971, p. 155). Experiments with mescalin, the scholar argues, show how colour in certain conditions can detach itself from concrete objects and attain an independence of its own. So the colours of the puppets during the day *wayang* enhance in an unobtrusive way the participants' experience of the ritual.

Another characteristic of the day *wayang* is the relative absence of conflict or movement on stage. The stillness, it can be suggested, creates a cultural realm which is outside or beyond the time which measures secular processes. This marks a transitional phase of the rite, or a period of 'liminality' as Turner (1982, p. 25) referred to it. So the story that the *dalang* narrates unfolds outside society in a period of timelessness. Van Gennep (1960) distinguished three phases in a rite: separation, transition and incorporation. It is interesting that in telling a story, *dalangs* focus on the intervening phase of transition: the hero, having left one place, passes through an intervening, often ambiguous zone, a sort of social limbo, before reaching another place. The story tends also to stress his purity and nobility, achieved by overcoming some obstacle, which justifies the transition to what is usually a more elevated state. This emerged in the story-telling of Yudistira's ascent to heaven which I Ewer narrated during cremation. (p. 163–7). Yudistira, with his family, only enters the celestial sphere once he has experienced the underworld and he and his brothers have been purified. Two other stories are summarized as they show that this pattern of events is general.

The first is based on the *Arjunawiwaha* (Zoetmulder, 1974, pp. 234–7). The play was enacted by I Ewer in conjunction with a marriage ceremony and subsequent tooth-filing ceremony in a high-caste family in Ubud. The story is popular and often chosen by *dalangs* on such an occasion (see pp. 63–4 on how stories fit the occasion).

> Arjuna has been steadfast in his meditation on Mount Indrakila. Thereby the prince demonstrates his spiritual power. With the help of the beautiful heavenly nymph, Supraba, he then kills the fierce demon king, Niwatakawaca, who has been threatening heaven. As a reward Indra invites him to marry the seven celestial nymphs, Supraba being the most senior of them, and to remain in heaven for seven days (which equal seven human months). The prince then returns to earth. The play concentrates on his sojourn in heaven. The servants, Tualèn and Merdah describe how attractive heaven is, where the colours of the flowers reflect the colours of the nine-fold division of the cosmos, the *nawa-sanga*, by reciting a very abridged version of the *mantra Aji Kembang* (p. 108–10).

The second story was narrated by the late *dalang* I Badra on the occasion of an *odalan* (anniversary) of a temple of the dead in Tegallalang.

> Garuda's mother, Winata, has become a slave of her sister, Kadru, as the result of a wager which she lost. She would only attain freedom once she had obtained the water of immortality, *amerta*, for her sister's children. These consisted of numerous serpents. The story focuses on Garuda's ascent

to heaven in his quest for the vessel containing the elixir. Indra tries to stop the bird, but without avail. Having succeeded in his mission, Garuda returns to earth and brings the elixir to the serpents.

(The story is mainly told by Tualèn and Merdah.)

This second story marks the transition from one year to another and is dramatized on behalf of the community. *Dalangs* may say that the elixir of immortality symbolizes the prosperity and welfare which the congregation is seeking from the gods.

So the stories enacted during the day *wayang* parallel and accompany a person's passage from one status to another in rites of passage or, in the case of the community, the collective movement from a previous socio-cultural condition to a new one.

The day *wayang* is of course only one of a number of rites which take place during the occasion in question, but it is among the most important. The emphasis in the play seems to be on the mythical incident when profane time is suspended. At the same time, the motionless puppets in the background evoke through their colours the presence of the gods. Although it is evident that the day *wayang* does not actively communicate to the humans gathered at the ritual, it can be suggested that it helps them to reflect upon self and other, and hence may effect a transformation in individual understanding which is consistent with the overt aim of the ritual.

In view of what has been said, it is unsurprising that the day *wayang* is considered the quintessential form of dramatic art on the island and called an offering (Plate 30), which is the purest man-made creation thought to exist.

Interpretation: the dynamic equilibrium of the cosmos

The night and day *wayangs* can be contrasted to one another within a total system. Already the names by which they are designated – *wayang peteng*, night performance, and *wayang lemah*, day performance – indicate that the Balinese conceive of them as complementary opposites. As such they also accord with the important philosophical principle of *ruwa-binèda*, the theory of binary opposites, mentioned earlier. Both forms of performance of course exist in their own right and have been discussed as such so far. (In other countries in South East Asia, for example, only the performance given at night with a screen is known.) However, *wayang kulit* is deeply embedded in the social and cultural life of the people; the day *wayang* is, moreover, a rite essential to religious occasions. When the night and day *wayangs* are seen as inter-related within a system they present powerful metaphors of the world and man's place in it. Thus *wayang kulit* acquires definite ontological status on the island.

A few remarks about the Kakayonan (Plate 31) are pertinent. In Java much has been written about this figure, or the Tree of Life which it is said to represent. As its symbolism is far-reaching and complex, I will restrict myself here to Bali. It is, though, worth recalling Eliade's words on this tree as they pertain also to the Balinese Kakayonan: 'The Tree reveals the World as a living totality, periodically regenerating itself' (see Werbner, 1984, p. 268). Yet the figure has additional significance when examined within the indigenous context.

Its iconography provides in a distinctive way insight into reality. Its two main components link the three zones of underworld, earth and heaven. Figuratively the mountain rises from the abyss into the sky. So, too, the roots of the tree descend into the earth while its branches penetrate the heavens. The mountain represents the material world, permanence and stability; the tree, on the other hand, represents the vegetal world, transience and mutability. The integration of the puppet's simple outline and tree formation with the swirling background design further highlights the contrast between the serene and the turbulent. Both extremes are interwoven to express their mutual dependence on one another and a sense of unity. So the Kakayonan's form suggests mediation; at the same time it combines harmoniously contrasting poles.

However, while its iconographic elements remain constant, the figure's actual appearance and movement on stage during the night and day *wayang* differs considerably. During the night *wayang* the story only unfolds once the *dalang* has set the Kakayonan in the banana stem. Henceforth, until the end of the play, its silhouette is only fleetingly glimpsed on stage which is a replica in miniature of the macrocosm. (Plate 32). Its initial appearance sparks into life the danced-out fight between the two camps, i.e. the cosmic dualities. The fluctuating tension between them suggests a world of flux where opposites are subject to constant strife. It is tempting here to think for a moment of the early Greek philosopher Heraclitus for whom conflict between opposites constituted the universe and who propounded the idea that war was the prime creative force (Guthrie, 1980, p. 446). This view is echoed in the Balinese shadow theatre. The struggle between the camps, in which the more refined and purer side emerges as the temporary victor, gains further impetus as it is set within a transcendental order which is an intelligible moral universe. This cosmic drama is renewed in every performance whereby consecrated life is perpetually regenerated.

Yet the dancing shadows on the screen point to the illusory and transitory nature of all appearances within human experience. This is reiterated by the Kakayonan. Its elusive shadow, which is seen now and again on the screen as the story is told, hints at a cosmos of harmony, when opposition is mediated and, at last, balance transcending all polarities is achieved.

The day *wayang*, however, provides a strikingly different view of reality. There is no screen, and the Kakayonan is generally placed in the centre of the banana stem. There, together with other puppets, it remains motionless during the entire play. It can be suggested that the performance represents a more complete vision in which the temporal world of illusion with its inherent conflict between opposites is felt to be transcended and sacred time is played out.

From the preceding discussion it seems evident that the night and day *wayang* can be placed on a single thematic or semantic axis, but contrasted to one another. Their opposition then suggests different ways of thinking about reality and time. The night *wayang* refers to the time-bound world of men which is in constant flux and shrouded in darkness (*peteng*).The day *wayang*, on the other hand, refers to the timeless heavenly abode of silence where there is light (*lemah*). When seen as complementary opposites within a system, each makes the other more valued. Taking a large panoramic view, the perspective provided by *wayang kulit* into ways of 'seeing' may have more general significance. For, following on from Langer (1976, p. 66), one can say that nothing is as fundamental in the fabric of our feeling as the sense of flux and stillness and their intimate unity.

It is of interest here to examine briefly the relationship of the mythology to the night and day *wayang* as it reflects the above-mentioned opposition. As discussed in Chapter 2 (see pp. 41–2, 64–5), most stories dramatized in the former take place after Sri, the rice goddess, and Indra have been banished to earth (or *sakala*) where they are incarnate as humans. Thereby the night *wayang*, as it were, 'anchors the present in the past' (cf. Cohen, 1969, p. 349, on the functions of myth), set in heaven before the spheres have become separate. In contrast the myths enacted in the day *wayang* are primarily drawn from the *Adiparwa* and for the most part they unfold in the imperceptible world (*niskala*).

So the skilled *dalang*, who is remote in both performances, emerges as a highly creative artist and poet-priest. While bound by the constraints of his art, each play is a unique event when the *dalang* revitalizes and reactivates the deeper symbolic linkages that give life to the villagers' experiences.

The shadow theatre in village life

Wayang kulit thus emerges as a vehicle which articulates a distinctive conception of the universe and the rules governing the moral order. This view is objectified and presented for contemplation during each play given at night which unfolds on a stage aloof from the humdrum existence of everyday life. As the dramatic content of the day *wayang* is negligible, it being basically a rite which does not communicate to men, it is not discussed henceforth.

Yet a night *wayang* is more than a work of art to be enjoyed and contemplated in an attitude of disinterested attention. It imbues the villagers with an intense sense of the continuity of tradition. It is also an important organizing force in the community. In this section I want to consider why the night *wayang* is so highly regarded as an idiom concerned with ethics. This leads to a further examination of how the villagers internalize and perpetuate the pattern of values and ideals expressed by this genre of theatre.

Philosophical background: the sense of sight

All the traditional arts, but in particular the night *wayang* and to a lesser degree the masked dance, are considered important, albeit informal, means of education. In order to understand the reasons for their didactic impact, it is relevant to stress the value accorded to the eye at the expense of the other senses. Here the Balinese seem almost to be reiterating the ancient Greeks. Aristotle said that of all the senses trust only sight, and Plato pointed out that sight was related to a divine source. It is in conjunction with this that the philosopher could write that ' "blind" is just how you would describe men who have no true knowledge of reality' (Plato, 1981, p. 277). While the Balinese recognize that there are various levels of comprehension, sight is deemed the principal sense of knowing in the world of men. This sense is also associated with daylight, *lemah*, and virtue, as the ability to distinguish things visually is thought crucial in enabling man to discriminate between right and wrong. In contrast, blindness is linked to the night, *peteng*, which is ambiguous and may even have evil connotations (on black, see p. 107). It is therefore not surprising that one of the greatest misfortunes is to be born blind, *buta*, a term that also means ogre or demon. In this hierarchy of the senses sight is the highest, hearing is the lowest. The villagers point out that in life words are tenuous and unreliable – in fact nothing is deemed more deceptive than words. This is lucidly expressed in I Berata's performance when Sangut describes the ignoble king Duryodana to his brother Dèlem:

> If only the speech is clever, the actions and thoughts are still evil. As he [Duryodana] is clever with words, he can hide his thoughts and actions from others.

Somewhat earlier, Sangut also says: 'There are three things, *bayu-sabda-idep*: actions, speech and thoughts. These cannot be separated' (p. 154).

It is against this background that the educational value of the night *wayang* emerges. As already discussed, the iconography of the puppets is imbued with a symbolic meaning which is largely similar across the island. The features of a given figure, moreover, accord with the other dramatic elements in a play, i.e. the appearance of a character harmonizes with his thoughts, actions and generally, though not always – particularly in the case of the Korawas – speech. So the visual sense immediately unveils to the spectators the virtues or vices of an individual on the stage as well as indicating his motives and intentions. This aspect, moreover, carries special weight, as all the stories have a pronounced moral content. It is worth noting here that the shadow play is called *sesolahan*, as are the other genres of theatre, i.e. the dance-dramas. Initially the term simply refers to the fact that they all include dance and drama (acting). However, *sesolahan* has another meaning. In folk etymology it is derived from *solah*, or character, as this is said to be revealed by the visual in a play.

The value placed on sight also helps to account for the esteem accorded to *wayang kulit* in another way. While words in themselves are said to owe nothing to external reality, when they are written down they fix the tradition. At the same time they crystallize the essential ideas which permeate the intellectual life of the people. Irrespective of the fact that the *dalang* improvises in all plays – especially in the sub-plots – there is no dramatic genre which adheres so closely to the sacred classical literature as *wayang kulit*.

Learning through the shadow theatre

The value placed on sight lays the basis for discussing how the villagers are affected by the patterns of meaning conveyed by the various dramatic components when orchestrated together during a performance. A number of points then emerge to account for its didactic impact.

It is first relevant to recall that a night *wayang* primarily attracts adult men and boys of all ages. It rarely compels the interest or enthusiasm of females. This is in line with the complementary division of the sexes in Balinese society alluded to earlier. Although times are changing, men are ideally still considered responsible for the perpetuation of the cultural heritage. Particularly as they grow older, men become increasingly concerned with philosophical, religious and literary matters, and with acquiring verbal fluency. Men also hold the major roles in public affairs, whether this is in the village council, the irrigation association, orchestra or dance associations, and so on. In contrast, few intellectual demands were traditionally made on women. In the religious field they mainly had to know how to make the offerings required for rites and festivals. Their duties were primarily in the private sphere of the household.

As we have seen, the night *wayang* epitomizes the cultural tradition. Hence adults encourage children – especially boys – to watch plays, as it is common knowledge that cultural continuity depends on its adequate transmission from one generation to another. Since the arrival of the Dutch at the beginning of the twentieth century, schools have been established throughout the island which enable villagers to obtain at least four years of education, but the instruction is regularized and geared to equipping the individual with a training which is useful in life. The education which is imparted through *wayang*, on the other hand, is unsystematic and diffuse. Nonetheless adults recognize that it is on the stage that the core values, ideals and behaviour patterns of the society are made tangible. This implies that the spectators observe a variety of characters – most of whom are men – of different status and moral worth. Their roles are largely acted out in the public domain and the events pertaining to them revolve around a juxtaposition of opposing interests and attitudes. Thus the characters provide vivid examples which can be imitated (*ketulad*) in life. In fact the Balinese still draw attention to the importance of learning through imitation.

A few other reasons help to explain the process by which the values articulated in a performance are internalized by the people. These, though, are implicit as the Balinese are only marginally aware of them.

The night *wayang* is the most ubiquitous drama form. As it is performed in the most isolated of villages, the humblest of villagers are able to witness a play. But, as mentioned previously, the spectators' attention is not constant. Sometimes they may not even completely understand the story; this applies in particular to children. Yet the visual element in itself carries levels of meanings. Some of the axioms represented are immediately recognized by all alike. We need but think of the round, coarse eye in contra-distinction to the elongated eye (p. 99). The abstract concept of rank is also explicitly danced out on stage. Such symbols are repeatedly articulated as the stories unfold. Hence they enliven the memory and 'alert' the audience's attention to what is considered noble or base in the society (see Lewis, 1981, p. 19, on the alerting quality of ritual).

The full richness and complexity of the *wayang* story can generally only be grasped by the older members of the community. But again themes in the story are elaborated on and repeated. Much has been written about the quality of redundancy in art. Wollheim's approach is perhaps most pertinent to Balinese *wayang*. It is through repetition, elaboration and variation on a theme that an art work gains in unity, for as the scholar points out, 'our awareness of a pattern is coincident with a large number of our expectations being realized' (Wollheim, 1970, p. 150).

All the stories are also interspersed with humorous episodes. In fact the attention of the children, who always constitute the front rows of an audience, is riveted on the servants, who can act and tell blithe jokes. It can be suggested that the comic, spicy interludes may veil the ethical instructions implicit in the plays, and make them more palatable and accessible, particularly to the young.

The educational role of *wayang* is also recognized in everyday life. In order to illustrate the standards of proper behaviour villagers may compare men or older boys in the community to characters in *wayang*. The two princes Bima and Arjuna seem particularly often referred to, but references may also be made to ignoble characters. The following examples show this.

sekadi Bima: like Bima.
   The implication is that the person is like Bima, who is honest, brave and strong, though in Bali he is often said to drink too much.

sekadi Arjuna: like Arjuna.
   The implication is that the person is like Arjuna, who is refined and elegant, and easily attracts women.
sekadi Dursasana: like Dursasana.
   This prince exemplifies the worst qualities. The implication is that a person like him is bad-tempered, harsh and disdainful of others. 'He also enjoys publically to shame his friends' (*ida demen nyacad timpal*). These are all vices abhored by the villagers who value solidarity. This is threatened by anyone who seeks to better himself at the expense of others.

By making such pointed comparisons the villagers refer to qualities which they perceive in someone else and generally approve of and wish to encourage or, on the other hand, disapprove of or downright condemn.

At times villagers may also allude to *wayang* stories witnessed in order to elucidate moral axioms in the society. One such story is included here. It was dramatized by I Badra and said to be from the *Cantakaparwa* (see Chapter 4, note 8, p. 171).

Subadra in a flood of tears went to the monkey Hanuman to complain of the behaviour of her husband, Arjuna. He had a roving eye and was a philanderer. Moreover he had many wives, but no satisfactory arrangement had been made to ensure that they were all satisfied.

   Meanwhile Arjuna went to the tournament given by the king Suryaketu where he won the hand of his lovely daughter. On leaving the tournament grounds Hanuman and Subadra, in disguise as ogres, confronted Arjuna and demanded that he give them the newly obtained princess. Arjuna refused and fighting broke out. Although the prince stood out by his bravery, he and his supporters were defeated and his weapons removed.

   During the battle Arjuna's faithful servant, Merdah, ran off into the woods, crying bitterly. The god Ismaya (p. 55) descended and consoled him and told him that he could defeat the ogres by removing his clothes and lifting his arms above his head. Merdah returned to Arjuna and acted as suggested. The moment he was naked, Hanuman and Subadra were forced to emerge in their true shapes.

   Arjuna was abashed on seeing Hanuman and his wife, Subadra, and enquired their reason for making war. Hanuman explained that he was not treating his wives properly and that they were unhappy. He advised Arjuna to rotate on a fixed basis the nights he spent with each wife, so each one would have an equal amount of time with him. Arjuna agreed to mend his ways.

Although the *dalang* who narrated this story was known to depart considerably from a given text, the play was given in a small hamlet in

Gianyar at some distance from the sophisticated areas of the district, and most of the audience enjoyed it as they said it was dynamic and highly amusing. A number of references were made to it during the subsequent days. The villagers drew special attention to the story's admirable illustration of how a man should treat his wives. Men in Bali, especially if they belong to the high castes or are wealthy, may have a number of wives, although nowadays this does not usually exceed three. Recently the government has disapproved of this practice (but the play was dramatized in the 1970s). In order to have harmony in the home, it is important that, like Arjuna, a man learns to treat his wives equally.

It seems evident from the above that *wayang* is a unique vehicle of instruction which imperceptibly helps mould the individual to the traditional norms of the society. So it is an art form which is intrinsic to the process of socialization. Here it should also be mentioned that its iconographic principles are repeated in other art forms on the island whereby the message inherent in *wayang kulit* is reiterated in various ways. This is discussed in the next section.

Structuring and ordering experience

Wayang kulit is, however, more than a recognized medium of education. As a number of scholars (Belo, 1970, pp. 91–3 ; Mead, 1970, p. 200; and Holt and Bateson, 1970, pp. 91–3) have noted, the Balinese are acutely aware of the boundaries pertaining to the body, society and the environment. This implies an emphasis on body-self and space orientation in village life. It is in this context that the people draw on *wayang*. As described earlier, powerful classificatory schemes are articulated in each performance which categorize appearance, dress, expression, voice, movement, and behaviour. These schemes equip the villager with a conceptual map which enables him to structure and order new experiences. This is best seen by an example. In the course of my fieldwork, a large, hairy, pink-faced Australian came to my village. His movements were ungainly and he seemed to look down on others. One of a group of villagers who was passing by instantly applied the following epithet to him: *dageg Dèlem*, proud and pompous like Dèlem, the Korawa servant. So the villagers' experience of the foreigner was aired and pooled. As an unknown entity he also posed a threat which was neutralized once he was incorporated into a framework which all comprehended and shared.

The popular language abounds with pithy sayings and striking proverbs which refer to *wayang*. *Salé pesaudné*, for instance, is a phrase which often cropped up in my village; it is used within dialogue to indicate to the other person that his reply is ambiguous, possibly even devious. *Salé* is derived from the mythic prince Salya (p. 52), whose position in the great war is equivocal. The proverb *ngelanggung nyangut* (from Sangut), a rice implement which is sharp at both ends, has a similar implication. It is used to describe a person who follows both sides of an argument and refuses to commit himself. Sangut in *wayang* is known for his inability ever to commit himself fully to either camp – while drawn to the Pandawas as more virtuous, by rights he must serve the Korawas who are his masters. The Balinese in fact sympathize with the servant's dilemma. Comments and proverbs such as these enable the villagers to interact creatively with one another by exploring in mythic terms the underlying meanings of actual situations and roles.

The representation of meaning through the idiom of *wayang* takes another well-established and unique form in village life. This is in relation to *wang*, i.e. Chinese coins, *kèpèng*, with a picture of an agent in the middle. *Wang* are believed magically to confer attributes on a person which tally with the agent depicted. It is said that villagers find such coins by chance and regard them as gifts from the gods made available to upright people. Once found, these coins are rarely, if ever, shown to others. Different agents, including specific *wayang* charac-ters,[4] are depicted on the coins. The main ones are Kresna, Arjuna, Bima, Hanuman, Tualèn, Merdah and Sangut. In this context, *wang* Kresna primarily imparts intelligence and hence is sought after by men in administrative positions, such as the village headman (*klian désa*) or orators at village meetings. A man who possesses *wang* Kresna is believed to be shrewd, intelligent and clever, especially with words. The same, though to a somewhat lesser degree, is said of a villager who owns *wang* Sangut. This coin enables him to be a fluent talker and to instil compassion in his listeners. *Wang* Bima and *wang* Hanuman mainly impart strength and supernatural power to their owners. The finder of *wang* Arjuna is believed to be irresistibly attractive to women. *Wang* Malèn (Tualèn) exists, although rarely found. Indi-genous medical practitioners (*balian*) are eager to obtain such a coin for it endows them with great mystic power to combat negative forces, i.e. witchcraft. It seems evident that these coins enable villagers to order and crystallize their experiences, as well as communicate them to others. The different *wang* may even help to create the attributes they are said to confer. After all *wang* is a highly regarded, known medium through which the villagers can on certain occasions give public account of themselves.

As a final remark it is perhaps worth pointing out that by these frequent references to *wayang* in everyday life, irrespective of what form they take, the villagers are also redirecting their attention to higher or more sacred concerns. These, as we have seen, are exemplified by the actual performance.

The shadow theatre in relation to the other arts

As the *wayang kulit* is the most highly regarded and conservative art form, its rules link it to the other traditional arts. Of these it is considered the original form. It is with this in mind that Zoete and Spies wrote:

> [the] powerful shadow play is not only the first ancestor of the Balinese theatre, it is also the first school of style, accustoming the Balinese from babyhood to see reality in the symbol (1973, p. 163).

Bali is renowned for its flourishing artistic tradition. Large numbers of persons from all sectors of society are either musicians, dancers or actors. In this section, though, I will only consider the following dance-dramas: the masked dance, *topèng*, operetta, *arja*, and contemporary drama. They are of special interest as they all reach spectacular levels of display and, like the night *wayang*, they have great appeal to the community at large even today. Although the old-fashioned, majestic *gambuh* or *topèng pajegan*, with only one dancer who dances all the characters in rapid succession, are important forms of ritual dance, they are not dealt with here as they are now rarely performed and are less popular with the ordinary villagers. The dance-drama *Ramayana wong* is also now rarely performed. Apart from the above-mentioned genres of popular theatre, I will touch on the plastic and pictorial arts.

These different forms of art and theatre are of course each complex, rich fields of study which cannot be given their due credit here. My discussion will focus on how far they resemble or depart from the night *wayang*. As we shall see, the dramatic genres in particular assign elaborately patterned symbols to certain analogues in the experience of the Balinese. While these vary considerably, characteristics reminiscent of the night *wayang* are found in all the dance-dramas.

The pictorial and plastic arts

Traditional Balinese painting was linked principally to the courts and high castes. As in the past, it still plays an integral part in the ritual life of the people. The painting spans about 150 years and shows a distinct proximity to the *wayang* style which, too, involves painted flat representation. Since the 1930s modern art has developed on the island, initially under the impact of European artists, but it is hardly integrated into the indigenous culture and is not discussed here.

Although painters were generally Sudras, they formed special communities or wards, known as *sangging* (Ramseyer, 1977, p. 60), that were granted royal recognition by the kings of Gelgel and Klungkung up to the beginning of the twentieth century. These *sangging* supplied the courts with works of art. While a number of such wards still exist, only Banjar Sangging in Kamasam continues to produce paintings in the *wayang* style. Its best-known artist (with whom I worked) is probably Nyoman Mandara who, financed by the Department of Education and Culture, has set up a school to teach children how to paint (Plate 33). Their paintings are commissioned by courts, temple communities and wealthy Sudra families, as well as being sold to tourists.

The paintings were produced on cotton or barkcloth. Now only machine-made cloth or wood panels are used. The paintings are displayed temporarily, for the duration of a specific rite or ceremony, when they form an intrinsic part of the decoration of a pavilion or shrine in either a temple or a household. When not required, they are stored in baskets.

The paintings are best classified according to their use. *Ider-ider* are long narrative paintings which are hung under the eaves of pavilions in temples and palaces. The serial manner in which they tell stories is reminiscent of east Javanese reliefs or the Javanese scroll paintings, *wayang bèbèr*. Oblong paintings, *langsé*, are used as curtains to screen the bed where offerings are laid out or as wall hangings in the court. *Tabing*, roughly square in shape, may be set up at the back of a bed as a backdrop to offerings. They either depict a mythic scene or a calendar. The ceilings of pavilions may also be adorned with cloth paintings and flags or banners are evident in most ceremonies. Apart from these standard works of art, the *sangging* may illustrate such items as gourds, bamboo vessels or wooden altars.

Most of the mythic themes portrayed in the paintings like those in *wayang*, are derived from the classical literature. Gods, humans and

191

ogres, too, resemble the flat puppets: their shoulders are *en face*, while the legs and feet are turned to the side; yet, unlike the puppets, the faces are in three-quarter profile. The costumes, ornaments, facial features and skin colours also follow *wayang* conventions. So ogres have large, round eyes, sharp teeth and fangs, and often hairy, pink bodies. Noble characters, in contrast, have refined features. It is interesting, though, that the curvature of the elongated eye differs on males and females (Fig. 1).

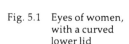

Fig. 5.1   Eyes of women,   Eyes of men,
              with a curved   with a curved
              lower lid   upper lid

As in *wayang* there are few characters who stand out as distinct individuals.

The night *wayang* has also left a strong imprint on the composition of the pictures. A marked duality is shown in them. Divine characters are on the left, while demonic, coarse ones are on the right, as they would be in the performance from the point of view of the spectators. A tree (parallel to the Kakayonan) or a rock takes the central position in most scenes which do not involve a battle. The parties then face each other. The postures of the characters tend, though, to be freer and more imaginative than those of puppets during a play. Paintings leave no open space. The motifs of clouds, flames or floral designs are often repeated in the background, thus achieving a recurrent rhythmic pattern. In *wayang* redundance is created by repeating the dramatic elements.

Nyoman Mandara's pupils build up their paintings rather as a craftsman makes new puppets. The figures are first outlined and then filled out with successive washes of colour. Traditional paints are generally used, as well as gold leaf. I Mandara also instructs his pupils by taking them to the old Court of Justice, Kreta Gosa in Klungkung, to inspect the magnificent paintings on wood panels lining the ceiling of

Plate 37 Galuh and her lady-in-waiting, *condong*, in *arja*

Plate 38 The younger servant, *wijil*, in *arja*

Plate 39 The servants in drama – chosen to resemble in looks Dèlem and Sangut

Plate 40 Tualèn in the night *wayang*

the building. The themes are in *wayang* style and include, among others, episodes from the *Mahabharata, Bima Swarga* and the Buddhist tale *Sutasoma* (Plate 34).

Kreta Gosa exemplifies what was probably the main purpose of traditional painting, which was to edify and teach. It was used by the supreme king (Dèwa Agung) of Klungkung as a court of justice before the conquest of the kingdom by the Dutch in 1908. Subsequently the Dutch took over the court. The paintings are indeed well suited to instructing the subjects of the kings. They show very graphically the punishments dealt out in hell to those who pursue a wayward path and are brought to justice (some of these are described in I Ewer's day *wayang* performance, p. 166–67, as well as illustrating in more serene terms celestial beings in heaven and the way men of virtue behave. The didactic function of the paintings also comes to the fore as the indigenous servants, although present, do not enliven the scenes with their witty, ribald verbal interchange, as is of course the case in a performance.

There is another barely surviving graphic tradition of illustration. This is the delicate illustration of palm leaf manuscripts, *lontars*. These were produced by educated members of the high castes and they are probably more closely linked to the Old Javanese court tradition than the paintings just described. The iconographic features of the characters resemble those of the *wayang* puppets. Irrespective of the contents of the text, the illustrations also portray Tualèn and the other servants. The compositions, though, are relatively unconstrained and perspective is introduced in the later illustrations.

The Balinese also excel in sculpture and carving. The craftsmen, unlike the *sangging*, do not live in special wards, but are scattered throughout the island. Craftsmen of repute are widely known. Most carvers are also architects who help to design public buildings. The most striking sculpture in *wayang* style is applied mainly to temples and palaces. As the material used is relatively soft, grey volcanic limestone (*paras*), the carving tends to be sumptuously ornate and has often to be renovated. Gateways in particular may abound with mythic creatures and humans or gods from the Hindu pantheon (Plate 35). The entrances are also often guarded by fierce ogres with staring, round eyes, holding clubs. As the formal sculptured and carved works of art adhere to *wayang* conventions, they mirror many of the values expressed by the puppets. Yet the plastic arts must be seen in their architectural context. Here they draw further attention to the special secular or religious significance of the building in question.

The popular genres of dance-drama

Before discussing each dance-drama, it is useful to lay out their different dramatic components (Table 1). The table also includes the type of stage used and the audience a given theatre genre tends to attract.

Although the night *wayang*, the masked dance, *topèng*, operetta, *arja*, and contemporary drama differ considerably, a few words should first be said about their common features. They all include narration, dance, acting and music. This applies even to contemporary drama, although the dancing is toned down and more like rhythmic walking. An interrelationship always exists between movement, music and the songs in *arja* which the Balinese refer to as *ngerereh angsel*, or harmonizing with the accents. This implies that movements contain both fluidity and rigidity which accord with the rhythmic structure of the music (cf. Zoete and Spies, 1973, pp. 26–8).

The visual features, especially those of the face, follow the same iconographic principle as the *wayang* puppets (see discussion of eyes, teeth and colour in particular in Chapter 3). Hence they are charged with essentially the same symbolic import.

All plays are characterized by an opposition between two groups on the stage, one of which is more virtuous than the other. Finally, after numerous adventures, the nobler side subdues the ignobler side. In *topèng, arja* and drama, each side is accompanied by a pair of male servants. The servants of each pair are described as 'real' or classificatory brothers, called in *topèng* and *arja* the *penasar* and *wijil* respectively.[5] In drama the servants are given names. It is of interest to note that often high castes enact the roles of the servants. This is said to be fitting as they are more fluent than the peasants and have greater ease in the use of the language levels to indicate status or familiarity. The servants in all theatre forms, moreover, have high repute. As in *wayang kulit*, they are outsiders to the main plot based on a specific text or folk tale on which they may comment extensively. The servants are further important in weaving together the dramatic elements so that a continuous, fluid action is created and the story coheres.

The main occasion for a play of any of these genres is in conjunction with the anniversary of a temple. *Topèng* is often performed in the outer court of a temple. *Arja* and drama may also be given spontaneously in the village community hall, *balè banjar*. In drama the scenery is drop-and-wing and the stage is illuminated by electric lights covered in red, blue, green and white cloths; microphones hang from the ceiling. Drama and *arja* are organized on a commercial basis,

Table 5.1   The dramatic components of the different dramatic genres and their settings

	Wayang peteng	Topèng	Arja	Derama gong
Actors	puppets (shadows)	humans (males) with masks	humans (males and females)	humans (males and females)
representing:	heavenly beings humans animals ogres	humans	humans	humans occasionally mythic beings e.g. celuluk
Costumes	traditional	traditional	traditional	daily wear
Language	kawi Balinese	Balinese some kawi	Balinese occasionally some kawi	Balinese some Indonesian
Music	gendèr	gamelan gong	nowadays gamelan gong with flutes, suling formerly gamelan arja	gamelan gong
Stories	mythic	historical	romantic	contemporary
derived from:	classical literature (see Chapter 2)	chronicles, babad	Javanese-Balinese Panji romances	folk tales
Stage	enclosed booth	pavilion in outer court of temple community hall, balé banjar	community hall, balé banjar	community hall, balé pavilion
Spectators	mainly adult men, boys	mainly adult men, boys	mainly middle-aged women and some men, children	mainly youth of both sexes

yet the cost of tickets for seats is minimal. All these theatrical genres are now serialized on television and, as the most isolated village has a television, even the humblest of villagers can watch plays.

I *TOPÈNG*: THE MASKED DANCE

Topèng, the Chronicle Play of Bali, was probably already performed for the king in the eleventh century (p. 22). The stories are recounted in chronicles, *babads*, most of which were composed by court scribes between the seventeenth and nineteenth centuries.[6] These *babads* tell the genealogical histories of high-caste families still present in Bali today who trace their descent from nobles in Majapahit. Although the repertoire provides the framework for endless variations upon a theme, one example of a story is given here, for it typifies the 'tokens' (p. 146) which stem from this theatre genre.

The conquest of the king of Nusa

The ruler of Bali died without leaving a successor to the throne. In consternation several prime ministers decide to go to Majapahit to ask advice from the Javanese king.

In Majapahit they discuss Bali's plight with the king's able prime minister, Gaja Mada. It is decided that a senior nobleman should go to Bali to become the king of Samplangan. This Satriya has three sons and one daughter. The daughter eventually returns to Java, where she marries into the royal house. The sons, though, remain in Bali and become the respective rulers of Samplangan, Tarukan and Gelgel.

The story now turns to tell of events pertaining to Nusa Penida and the descendants of the king of Gelgel. The king of Nusa is feared by his subjects as he is hard-hearted, grasping and haughty. The village headman (*bendésa*) sets off for Gelgel to ask assistance for his people. Humbly doing obeisance to the king, the headman begs him to kill the king of Nusa.

The king of Gelgel agrees to help and tells his prime minister, Gusti Jelantik, to go to Nusa. As requested, Jelantik departs to Nusa with his wife, who refuses to be left behind. In Nusa the king courteously requests the visitors to dine with him and then asks them why they have come. Jelantik explains his errand, and as a result fierce fighting breaks out between the men. Jelantik is, however, unable to kill the king as he is so powerful, *sakti*. Jelantik's wife then unobtrusively approaches her husband and gives him a weapon, consisting of the fangs of the demon-god Kala, which she secretly brought with her from Bali. With this magical weapon Jelantik kills the king of Nusa, who is then cremated in the style befitting a ruler.

Having accomplished his mission, Jelantik returns to Bali with the intention of bringing all the possessions of the king of Nusa to his master at

Gelgel. Yet he is unable to part with a golden bowl filled with glittering jewels which he hides on the beach. The bowl sends forth rays of light, and when Jelantick approaches the king of Gelgel, the latter asks him what the rays signifiy. Abashed, Jelantik fetches the golden bowl and presents it to the king.

(Narrated by the former *topèng* and *arja* dancer, Anak Agung Oka; cf. story in Zoete and Spies, 1973, pp. 301–2.)

In a standard performance all the actors are men, who generally come from the same area or even hamlet (*koban*). The training is extensive as the dance requires elegance and follows strict conventions. *Topèng* is said to be the theatre genre which most closely resembles the night *wayang* and hence it attracts a similar audience. The stories all revolve around political matters pertaining to male nobility. As in the night *wayang*, war and comedy are intrinsic to all plays. The visual element also clearly indicates the rank and status of the characters, as well as externalizing their type, i.e. whether refined, *alus, manis,* or coarse, *kasar.*

The king and prime ministers wear full masks. The senior king of the *manis* type wears an oval-shaped, cream-coloured mask with a serene expression. His eyes are elongated and narrow and his mouth is open in a faint smile. His adversary, in contrast, wears a reddish-brown mask. His eyes are wide open and his moustache and lips are thick. All aristocrats are attired in magnificent costumes of coloured brocades and woven materials decorated in gold leaf, which cover shoulders, arms and legs. Gold collars of hide encircle the necks. The headdresses, in particular, stand out. They are very elaborate and have gold leaves attached. The servants, on the other hand, wear half masks or hinged masks. There are other masks, comic in intent, which represent the common people (*bebondrèsan*). They have such facial defects as hare-lips, superfluous crooked teeth or lop-sided mouths.

The dance, too, emphasizes caste differences. The nobles move slowly with precise, small steps. Part of their costume may flow behind them like a copious cloak while a long cloth forms a swirling train on the ground. The servants move more freely with bold steps and unhampered gestures.

A striking feature of *topèng* is that the aristocrats remain silent throughout the play. It is left to the servants to interpret in words their miming gestures (Plate 36). This is reminiscent of the night *wayang.* Here the kings, too, are remote from actuality, but at least they speak, albeit in Old Javanese, a language which is inaccessible to most of the villagers.

The speeches made by the servants illustrate the special quality of *topèng*. They are stark, dry and direct, and primarily intended to give higher meaning to the realities of policy and monarchic rule. This is at variance with the poetic tone of the servants' speeches in the night *wayang*, which are replete with innuendos. In order to illustrate this, two extracts from dialogues are included here. They are taken from a performance that I witnessed in Tegallalang. These speeches are in Balinese, although Old Javanese words or phrases are sprinkled throughout.

The curtain has just opened and the servant, the *penasar*, introduces the play with these words.

Penasar   I am so happy that the king [called Cokorda Ketut Karang] is now staying in the palace of Padangtegal in Ubud. Forgive my stupidity, for I know nothing (showing respect to the audience). Now I shall tell of the king who left Sukawati as his relations with his family were strained. He first settled in Mambal [in Badung], but the prime ministers of Mengwi became suspicious of him, thinking he was an enemy. The king also became wary of him, and war broke out between them. The prime ministers hoped they would kill the king. Yet it was not his fate to die, and he fled to Padangtegal where he became the ruler. The supreme god, Sang Hyang Widi, took care of his needs, especially as the king brought peace to his kingdom.

Later on in the story, the servants, *wijil* and the *penasar*, eulogize on the loftiness of their king and master as follows:

Wijil   Elder brother, the king is following a religious path and strengthening the traditional rules and customs [*adat*] of his kingdom.

Penasar   That is true. He is also intelligent and so his subjects pay him obeisance. Were he to be foolish the kingdom would not prosper.

Wijil   He is a virtuous ruler and so he sets a good example [*contoh*] to his subjects. He also gives them all they need.

Penasar   Yes, he is following a virtuous path. He realizes that material wealth has no lasting value and cannot be taken with a person when he dies. The king desires that there is prosperity in the country, that the people of Padangtegal are united, that they grow in intelligence, and that their thoughts are in tune with *darma*, for then their descendants will be men of *darma*.

Wijil   When the god enters, his splendour is like that of the god of love, Semara.

In view of the orientation of *topèng*, it is hardly surprising that it appeals predominantly to men. Geertz (1970, p. 49) has stressed the aristocrat's role as patron of the arts in Bali which linked him to village aesthetic life. This applies more to *topèng* than to any other dramatic genre. The courts still today tend to be the centres of *topèng* productions and the costumes are often stored in the palace compounds. Men in general, and high castes in particular, appreciate the historical content of the stories which tell of their ancestors in Bali and Java. While the historical element is also present in the night *wayang*, it is more nebulous. Hence *topèng* is considered a basic mode of expression and validation of the high castes' exalted status and authority. As in the night *wayang*, stress is also laid on the effectiveness of *topèng* as a means of education. It does so by praising and creating heroic roles for the nobility which can be emulated by the villagers. But, unlike the night *wayang*, the actions unfold in a tangible world of pageantry, dance and gesture.

II *ARIA:* OPERETTA

Arja, which in style is derived from the spectacle Gambuh, is best translated as operetta or musical comedy (Zoete and Spies, 1973, p. 196) as it combines dance, singing, spoken lines and humorous interludes. Its theatrical devices all contribute to its lyrical, sentimental tone, which engenders a rarified and elevated (*singgih*, high, refined) analogue of emotive life. Thus, in an almost contemporary western sense, a performance is well adapted to sustaining aesthetic contemplation. The lyric spaciousness and graceful quality of *arja*, together with the stories which focus on the fate of women and the intimate circle of the family, initially veil its deeper parallels with the night *wayang*. Examination, though, shows that these do exist. The common features have only been modified to fit a theatre genre which mainly appeals to women.

The majority of stories in *arja* are based on the Javanese-Balinese romances (for a synopsis of stories, *ibid.*, pp. 311–22). They tell of the adventures of the prince Mantri *manis*, i.e. the prince of Koripan or Panji, and his gentle princess Galuh. The ugly, 'mad' *buduh* princess Liku, usually through the use of a magical tool, *guna* (Chapter 3, note 1, p. 123), given to her by her strong-minded mother or step-mother, Limbur, usurps the place of Galuh in Mantri *manis*'s affection. Other main characters are Galuh's servant *condong* (Plate 37) and two pairs of male servants described as *manis*, sweet, and *buduh*, mad, respectively (Plate 38). A corresponding character to Liku, who often enters plays, is the rich, foolish, mad prince Mantri *buduh*. He is a rival who may seek Galuh's attention. Although *arja* stories are for the most part derived from the Panji tales, each one is complete in itself, or a 'token' of the genre (cf. Robson in Zoetmulder, 1974, p. 427, who points out that all Panji tales have a similar 'nucleus' of plot).

Present-day *arja* groups are *bon-bonan* – implying that they comprise actors from different areas of Bali. Formerly some of the actors, who played the roles of such coarse or masculine characters as Liku or Limbur were burly men. Nowadays, apart from the male servants, all the characters are chosen for their attractive looks and pleasing, high voices. Stress is laid on the latter as the aesthetic appeal of *arja* is said to derive largely from the bright, vibrant songs. In these the hero or heroine often expresses sadness or reproaches himself or herself. This sentiment is especially marked in this genre of dance-drama. Two stanzas from a song are included here as an example. They are taken from the Chinese folk tale *Sampik* (for synopsis of story, see Zoete and Spies, 1973, pp. 322–3).

> I feel too embarrassed to let others see me.
> They would surely laugh at me.
> Each person who sees me
> Would smile unpleasantly.
> Their smiles would crush my heart.
> I feel like a tree with no leaves.
> So great is the heat of the sun.
>
> I am very thin.
> I cannot sleep day or night
> I am shrunken and yellow.
> I am so pale that I do not wish to be seen.
> I am like the moon
> When the demon Kala Rawu[7] swallowed it.
> I am sad and reproach myself (that I acted inconsiderately to my beloved one who left me).

For some years now the songs have been accompanied by a full-scale orchestra, *gamelan gong*, which includes bamboo flutes, *suling* (on the *gamelan arja* of the past, see McPhee, 1966, pp. 294–303). Their tunes, as they weave ornamental figurations around the songs, are clear, sweet and slightly reedy. A striking feature of *arja*, which bears distinct proximity to speech in *wayang kulit*, is that the songs of the high castes cannot be understood for the most part as the words when actually sung on the stage are long drawn-out and the syllables flow into one another to create fluid, melodic phrases. So each line of a stanza has to be translated by one of the servants.

Costumes in *arja* are unique to this genre. During a performance all the characters, even the servants, wear sumptuous clothes. Those of royalty are dazzling in their colour contrasts of rose, coral or purple with emerald green, or orange and dark or mid-blue. The dresses, sashes and stoles are often lavishly decorated in gold leaf. Aristocrats also wear gilded headdresses in which frangipani and red hibiscus flowers have been set.

Spectators and actors alike draw attention to the structural opposition in *arja* which subtly echoes that of the night *wayang*. In most plays the heroine, Galuh, is opposed to the mad Liku. Galuh, like Drupadi or Sita from the epics, is referred to as an incarnation of the rice goddess Sri, while her lover Mantri *manis* is an incarnation of Wisnu. After endless trials Galuh is finally reconciled to him.

All the dramatic components assist in creating the tension characteristic of this theatre genre. Each character dances according to his or her type. Thus Galuh, who is a slender, delicate girl with a pale, white face, dances slowly and gracefully, creating wide patterns through space. She often droops in lament while moving her hands in a precise, evocative manner, reminiscent of *mudras* (*ibid.*, p. 21). She may look sweetly from side to side, glance timidly, or gaze woefully with downcast eyes. Liku, on the other hand, is at present enacted by a robust girl. Her eyes are made up to appear round and her face has a pinkish tint. She may move her bushy eyebrows rapidly up and down alternately in an eccentric manner. Liku's demeanour and dance well express her specific state of 'madness', although this term does not necessarily imply illness. It can be used to describe a villager who feels no shame or restraint and hence transgresses social boundaries. In Liku's case she loves, to the point of folly, a man who has already given his affection to another. In passing, the Korawas are never called mad, as this is a quality which shows itself in the actions of real people; the Korawas, though, are mere representations (*gambar*) on the screen. So ungainly, mad Liku, in line with her haughty, uncontrolled nature, dances in a gawky and directionless fashion.

The servants reflect their masters in movement and speech. The pair serving the mad prince often parody the servants of the Korawas, Dèlem and Sangut in *wayang kulit*. The elder brother, *penasar buduh*, is stout, pompous and witless, while his younger brother, *wijil buduh*, like Sangut is thin, scraggy and a fluent talker. Tualèn and Merdah are never compared to the servants in other theatre genres; Tualèn is in any case too sacred to be compared to any mortal. The *condong*, the lady-in-waiting, in *arja*, too, has her counterpart in *wayang*, although the latter is frivolous in contrast to the dignity of the former.

The songs of Galuh and Liku intensify the opposition between them. Three short extracts from an *arja* play witnessed in Tegallalang are included as they illustrate the sentimental tone of *arja*, as well as the characters of the two princesses. The lines sung by Galuh and Liku are translated by their respective female servants. The language used is Balinese, although some words of Old Javanese are sprinkled throughout the songs and speeches.

Galuh	I am crying (as my husband has left me).
condong	Yes, princess, I am also distressed that you feel sad.
Galuh	I feel regret.
condong	Yes, princess, you are distressed and sad.
Galuh	Recalling my state, (I do) not feel happy.
condong	Yes, princess, it is true what you say. May you feel happier soon.
Galuh	(My) actions express sorrow.
condong	Yes, princess, it is true what you say. You are sad and acting in a distressed manner.
Galuh	Sang Hyang Widi [a higher truth] is not granting what I request.
condong	Yes, princess, perhaps Sang Hyang Widi is not granting to you what you request.
Galuh	Why live? I would prefer to die.
condong	Yes, may Sang Hyang Widi give you a quick release from your suffering.

Later in the play Liku boasts about her splendid looks to Madai Rai, her lady-in-waiting. Together they then go to the royal gardens where Liku meets the prince, Mantri *manis*, who falls under her spell and forgets his wife, Galuh, who is left lamenting at home.

Liku	(My) attractively coiled hair, (it) pleases the hearts (of men).

202

Madai Rai	Yes, it is true, princess, what you say about your hair. It is attractively coiled and has a dark, velvety sheen which will please men.
Liku	[My hair] resembles [the] clouds [of the] seventh month.
Madai Rai	Yes, it is true, princess, your hair resembles the clouds of the seventh month.
Liku	[These are] rain clouds.
Madai Rai	It is true, princess, the colour is like the dark rain clouds which conceal the sun.
Liku	[My] side curls [are] delicate.
Madai Rai	Yes, princess, men will find your side-curls delicate.
Liku	[Men will desire] to kiss [my] cheeks.
Madai Rai	Yes, princess, men will be attracted to you.

Liku invites Mantri *manis*, who is resting in the gardens as he is tired after hunting, to come with her to the palace. Liku is smitten with love for the handsome prince and hopes he will remain with her. The prince's servants view with sorrow the unvirtuous behaviour of their master, who forgets Galuh to follow ugly Liku.

Liku	(to the prince) You must be tired from hunting. Come and rest in my palace.
Mantri *manis*	Yes, I am happy to accompany you.
Penasar	Our master is now going with Diah Bedawati (Liku) to her palace. Yet his wife is pregnant!
Wijil	Elder brother, he is like Sang Arjuna, who though already married to Sumbadra, desired other women! Once when he went hunting for the heart of a white deer for Sumbadra, he too went off with another princess.[8]
Penasar	There is no sense in feeling remorse. Come, let us follow our prince.

Such references to *wayang* characters, as evident in the last dialogue, are fairly frequent in *arja*. In the same way, the mad prince may be compared to Duryodana in greed, and his evil prime minister to cunning Sakuni.

Arja in some ways almost presents a symbolic inversion of the night *wayang*. Most of the characters in *arja*, certainly the principal ones, are female, while *wayang* concentrates on male personages who are remote from actuality. In *arja*, in contrast to *wayang*, there is never violent warfare between the numerous men in the public arena. The conflict which is initiated between the princesses and their few select followers takes place in the private sphere and is subdued, distinguished by its pathos. The tone of the night *wayang* tends to be reflective, while that of *arja* is lyrical and romantic. In view of this it is hardly surprising that *arja* attracts mainly middle-aged women and the night *wayang* adult men.

Spectators explain that an excellent *arja* performance evokes a feeling of *ulangun*, or 'lingering enchantment'. This is associated with sadness and pity, *kangen*, for Galuh's suffering. Its educational role is also recognized, although this is more muted than in other forms of theatre. The audience's response to *arja* relates to daily life in the village. A husband may forget his wife (or senior wife if he has more than one), and even his children by her, if he becomes infatuated with another woman. She is generally thought to have ensnared him through the use of *guna* (see above). In fact the term *ngelikuang*, derived from Liku in *arja*, is commonly applied to such a man. On the other hand, an ideally marriageable woman may be compared to Galuh. She is sweet and 'cool' (p. 117–20), and brings harmony to the home. It is of course primarily the women in the audience who can empathize with Galuh's fate. Yet *arja*, as mentioned, has great aesthetic merit and thus it has wide appeal in the community, and men, too, may enjoy watching performances.

III CONTEMPORARY DRAMA: *DERAMA GONG*

Contemporary drama is still considered a new and immature theatre genre. It is still incorporating outside elements and so has not yet attained a stable form. Hence it rarely reaches the same standard of excellence as the other genres of dance-drama or its so-called counterpart in Java, *ludruk*, the proletarian drama. Correspondingly it attracts a very mixed audience which mainly consists of youths.

It seems first to have been established after the coup in 1965, in which thousands of people were killed on Java and Bali, when it was called *derama jangèr*. The term *jangèr* is derived from *jangeran* which has political connotations. It is a sickness which attacks chickens, when they act in a bewildered, even deranged manner. So *derama jangèr* mirrored the confused, disturbed period at that time. The stories (which have not been documented) centred on the discontent of the peasants vis-à-vis the high castes, which ended to the detriment of the latter.

The stories nowadays are light-hearted and romantic; adults may say they are banal. These stories are not derived from a fixed repertoire. They are often reminiscent of *arja* tales which tell of a refined prince (sometimes Wisnu incarnate) and princess who, after obstacles have been overcome which entail fighting, are happily united. One, or both Satriyas have mad (*buduh*) counterparts, while each side has its indispensable pair of male servants. The mad servants, as in *arja*, are often a take-off of Dèlem and Sangut in *wayang* (Plate 39). Mythic beings such as Celuluk who, with large sagging breasts, is a comic version of the witch Rangda, or wild creatures with mystic powers, may enter the plays; weapons, too, may have magic force. Names of old east Javanese kingdoms such as Daha (Kediri), Janggala or Singasari are mentioned regularly in the stories.

Present-day drama troupes are made up of members who come from various districts of Bali (*bon-bonan*).[9] Actors require very little training before going on the stage – three weeks is said to suffice. This contrasts with other genres of theatre where the actors have to learn the precise dance movements, and in *arja* where the songs must be learnt before the actor is permitted to give a performance. In drama the actors mainly need to be verbally fluent and feel no shyness in public.

Of all the theatre forms, contemporary drama is the furthest removed from the night *wayang*. Yet drama, too, takes place in a cosmological setting which entails complementary opposition between two sides, and a sacred aura still clings to the male servants. The dress of the characters in a play also reflects the *wayang*. For example, the kings wear headdresses and the servants are usually clad in short black and white checked *polèng*, loin cloths. Although the clothes are everyday ones, they are worn in a traditional style.

In the past the actors discussed the story on the way to the village where they were about to perform. For a few years now, the head of the troupe, the *sutradara* (who has been chosen by the troupe's members) sends each actor a short written outline of the story (*tes*) to be dramatized.

As the plot is often extremely flimsy, the servants ad lib a great deal. They are always the first characters to appear on stage when a play begins. It is their task to test the atmosphere of the audience by means of jokes, songs, skits and comic antics. This is referred to as *medal mancing*. The response of the audience enables the subsequent actors to attune themselves to the environment. Indeed, the servants in drama seem to have more individual freedom to play with ideas and fantasies, and to experiment, than in other genres of theatre which are strictly bound by traditional constraints. So drama performances may, on occasion, generate new symbolic worlds. Yet the actors must continually heed the spectators and adapt to their needs, for otherwise a play will not succeed in stimulating them.

While the main plots focus on the sphere of the court and are imaginary, entailing love and romance, the sub-plots refer to such contemporary issues as tourism, the introduction of films or television sets to villages, the growing traffic on the roads, the increase in the number of schools, and so forth. Balinese is spoken throughout, interspersed sometimes with Indonesian. The sub-plots primarily take place either in the vicinity of the court or away from it, in the village or forest. Three extracts of dialogues are included to show the orientation of the plays, which tends to be progressive, although many of the speeches seem trivial and commonplace. In the first example the two male servants, I Pangot and I Becol, converse about the kingdom of Candi Pura.

I Pangot	The kingdom of Candi Pura is well ruled. Everyone has work.
I Becol	Yes, the kingdom of Candi Pura is progressive [*maju*].
I Pangot	Yesterday, I went there to watch a film. The characters played skilfully. Many spectators were watching it.
I Becol	I never go to a film. I cannot afford to do so.
I Pangot	One of the characters in a film sang the Indonesian song *Aku Anak Désa* [I am a village child]:

> I am a village child, going to secondary school.
> I possess the desire to develop the country.
> Wearing a special shirt, I go to town
> in order to seek experience, apart from the diploma.
>
> Arriving in the city, I gain much experience.
> I almost cannot believe this is Indonesia.
> Cars and buses line the roads.
> I feel proud and do not wish to return home.
>
> I have only read the Koran.
> In the city there are many wicked people
> desiring to make much money.
> The corruption prevents development.

> I shall dedicate my services
> and promise that later
> I will develop my village in a noble manner.
> May the all-powerful god bless my intentions.

The second example of a dialogue is again between the servants, this time called I Lemuh and I Moleh.

I Lemuh	(to his brother) I am glad that we are servants in the kingdom of Janggala. It is good that the king is still young and has now chosen a wife.
I Moleh	Yes, that is true, elder brother. Also our country is progressive. Now our women can fetch water from the tap in the village and need no longer go to the stream. Formerly we had *setrongking* [oil lamps], but now the government has introduced electricity.
I Lemuh	Yes, schools too, have now been built where even the elderly who have never learnt to read can go in the evenings.
I Moleh	What schools are you referring to, elder brother?
I Lemuh	They are called *sekolah paket A* [introduced since 1984].
I Moleh	In my opinion, our king is as wise as the rulers of the past. Yet perhaps his aims [*tetujon pikayuné*] are different. Formerly the kings were above all concerned to be supernaturally powerful, for they had to be brave in war.

These two extracts of dialogue illustrate the process of modernization on the island. Schools called *sekolah paket A* have been established throughout Bali by the government since 1984 (just before my last trip there). Their aim is to ensure that there are no more illiterates. They are free, and adults of both sexes study there for at least six months, sometimes longer. The main language of instruction in these schools, as in others, is Indonesian. Electricity has been established in most hamlets, although it may break down. A central water tap has also been installed in many hamlets, so women no longer have to fetch water from a stream, often some distance away, and carry it back in a large vessel on their heads.

The last short extract of dialogue indicates how references may also be made to *wayang* characters. Such analogies seem to be frequent. In this example the refined prince Ambara Jaya from the kingdom of Janggala and the mad, greedy prince Angkara Pati have met in the woods and are exchanging a few words together. The latter is envious that Ambara Jaya has won the love of the enchanting princess, Diah Ratnaningsih, from the kingdom of Daha.

Angkara Pati   You have gone off with Diah Ratnaningsih! I am Angkara Pati from the kingdom of Metaum, and she was promised to me. If you refuse to give her up, prepare yourself to fight.

Ambara Jaya   You are speaking like the Korawa prince, Dursasana, who mistreated Drupadi. Fetch your weapon, for we will fight.

In line with the overall modern tone of the stories, the rules of etiquette relating to behaviour are laxer in the plays. In contrast to other genres of theatre, prince and princess may lightly caress each other. The servants should abide to traditional customs (*metata*) and lower themselves bodily when addressing royalty, while keeping a discrete distance from them. Yet on occasions the servants may dance around vulgarly or joke with the princess – although this is usually with the mad one. I have even seen a servant kick the head, the most sublime part of the body, of a prime minister.

The throngs of spectators at a drama performance mainly consist of young, single people of both sexes. When interviewed, they explained that the appeal of drama lies in the love scenes and the jokes with which a good show abounds. Even if a story is poorly composed, or banal, a play also offers an opportunity for members of the opposite sex to meet one another and 'play around' (*mecanda*). Such public flirtation was frowned on in the past. Respected elders in the community rarely watch plays, which they say are shallow and lacking in substance. Furthermore, they disapprove of the lack of constraint in etiquette which at times is displayed on stage, referred to as *kirang mewatas*, implying the 'decreasing awareness of boundaries'.

Peacock (1968) has eloquently argued of *ludruk*, the Javanese proletarian drama, that it helps the participants to shift their attitudes from conservative to progressive ones. It is difficult to estimate the impact of contemporary Balinese drama, as it is a relatively new form of theatre with as yet little repute. Peacock's argument does not, however, apply to this genre. It is more apt to say that it clarifies and crystallizes in the minds of the beholders the process of modernization. The main themes which seem to be articulated in drama are nationalism, individualism and universalism. As the short extracts from dialogues indicated, sub-plots are replete with allusions to issues relating to Indonesia as a nation and to the world beyond which is increasingly penetrating Bali in the form of tourism and modern consumer items. Above all, though, the plays lay stress on the individual's freedom and his growing self-mastery. This comes to the fore with the servants who are controlled by their own will and who act spontaneously, especially when away from the court. In their extensive improvisations they are mainly guided by the response of the audience whom they meet on essentially equal terms. Eventually this leads to the development of 'rational' man who justifies his actions by showing that they are an adequate means for achieving given ends, instead of claiming that they are traditional. Such a man is also inclined to judge a person according to his ability rather than on his caste origin.

The plays, however, in no way suggest the Weberian movement of 'the elimination of magic from the world' (1976, p. 105), for supernatural elements still pervade them. Further, the modern trends expressed in drama are always curtailed by its form and structure which adheres to tradition. Its lingering affinity to *wayang kulit* is also a constraining factor. It is here useful to draw attention to the Balinese view of theatre. The Balinese point out that in all genres of theatre, even the most contemporary ones, i.e. *derama gong*, the moral codes only gradually catch up with present-day behaviour' (*puniki susila sané alon-alon ngerereh laksana*).

Shifting views of reality

It seems apposite at the outset of this section to recall Bertrand Russell's words:

> What is valuable is the indication of some new way of feeling towards life and the world, some way of feeling by which our own existence can acquire more of the characteristics which we most deeply desire (1918, p. 109).

Crowds of spectators frequent the popular dance-drama. The audience, though, varies according to the genre performed. Mainly, adult men and boys watch the night *wayang* and *topèng*. Often they appear deeply absorbed in the story, which they may discuss animatedly the following day. Middle-aged villagers, consisting largely of women with their children, attend *arja*. They sit squashed together on rickety chairs set up for the occasion, savouring in particular the florid, melodic phrases in the songs. The attention of the youths at contemporary drama is sporadic. They easily slip in and out of the jostling crowds as often they are more intent in seeking out the opposite sex and flirting with them than in watching the show.

Dancing Shadows of Bali

The different genres of theatre, in line with the type of audience they attract, express abstractions from experience which convey varying views of reality. It is worth drawing attention here to Sangut's words to his older brother Dèlem in the performance given by I Berata, for they tersely summarize the shadow theatre's relationship to the other arts: 'That which appears as one has diverse elements. That which appears as diverse has an underlying unity' (p. 154). This statement also sheds light on *wayang kulit*'s wider significance in society.

Wayang kulit is the most revered and sophisticated genre of theatre on Bali. In order to account for the evocative power and sanctity of the night *wayang* in the eyes of the villagers, I have argued that it must be seen in conjunction with the day *wayang*. The former is then a metaphor for the time-bound universe while the latter is a rite, symbolizing the timeless heavenly abode of silence. When the night and day *wayang* are contrasted to one another within such a total system, each legitimizes and makes the other more valued. Against this background it is understandable that the night *wayang* is the main dramatic vehicle used to expound on the ethical and religious tenets of society.

So the night *wayang* appears initially to portray a stable universe which has cosmic dimensions. As such it represents an ideal version of the social structure, or, in Leach's words, provides the audience 'with an idealized model which states the "correct" status relations existing between groups within the total system and between the social persons who make up particular groups' (1977, p. 9). Such a view, however, is inadequate in regard to the night *wayang*, for it neglects the fact that we are dealing with drama which through its varied stimuli of light, form, movement and sound, creates or re-creates the categories through which men perceive reality – the axioms underpinning the structure of society and the laws of moral order. It is not simply the case of theatre on an idealized plane imitating life, but of social life being animated by theatre. This has been clearly recognized by Black, who argues that a metaphor can 'sometimes generate new knowledge and insight by changing relationships between the things designated (the principal and subsidiary subjects)', the implication being that some metaphors can be seen 'as ontologically creative' (1982, p. 37).

It is above all the servants in the night *wayang*, who are also the village philosophers, clowns and fools with sanctioned disrespect on stage, who negotiate and explore the meaning in the various dramatic components. Their particular creative role, moreover, has been taken over by the male servants in the other genres of theatre. The freedom of the servants is perhaps especially marked in contemporary drama, which lays stress on ideas of equality in contradistinction to those of hierarchy. The hierarchical principle is more pronounced in the night *wayang, topèng* and *arja*, than in contemporary drama, through the distinctive languages spoken (or sung) by the high castes and Sudras. Yet in plays of all genres the servants occasionally confuse the neat categories of order and rationality.

The servants should further be seen in conjunction with the audience, for theatre is never one-sided. In a spirit of 'communitas' (Turner, 1982, p. 47), spontaneity and immediacy, active interchange may occur between actors and spectators. Again this comes to the fore in contemporary drama, where the beholders may applaud, murmur agreement or loudly criticize the play. The audience's response primarily guides the servants, who are not bound, like the other characters, to the story. If they fail to add zest and colour to the plays the villagers simply go off to gossip at the stalls or return home.

Although the servants have similar roles in the dance-dramas, each genre selects, emphasizes and elaborates on different aspects of reality. The night *wayang* is the most conservative form of theatre. It articulates a cosmic conception of the world which has transcendental overtones. At the same time it highlights the traditional rules governing the moral order and organisational pattern of the universe. *Topèng* makes a powerful statement about authority and royalty, whereby the present is linked to the heroic ideals of the past and the ancestors. *Arja* evokes in poetic terms an intimate family circle, while conveying through its colour, lyricism and rhythms a sense of aesthetic dignity. Contemporary drama is the form of theatre least bound by specific rules. It crystallizes and clarifies in the minds of the participants a secular world affected by modern trends. In this, 'rational' man comes to the fore, one who is inclined to judge an act according to its use as a means towards some goal, which is generally a practical one. Here it is again relevant to stress that all the dance-dramas mentioned still have great popularity at the village level, and hence the villagers, depending on their preference, frequently watch plays of one genre or another.

So theatre provides the community with a set of mirrors or prisms of various shapes and sizes which not only present, but also probe, scrutinize and analyze in a dynamic way the axioms and assumptions of social life. Thereby it can be suggested that theatre helps the villager to develop his own selfhood or identity. Yet 'self', as Sapir insists, is 'gropingly discovered' (quoted in Turner, 1982, p. 64). This implies that the individual should not be conceived as a static entity but as 'a movement' through spheres, which involves transformation of self in relation to others (cf. Burridge, 1979, pp. 146–7). These spheres in Bali are vividly exemplified by the different genres of popular dance-dramas which allow the villager to shift his view of the world from a sacred, traditional one to a domestic one, or to a more modern view of the world where less emphasis is placed on polished, refined etiquette.

However, as repeatedly illustrated, it is above all the night *wayang* which provides symbols of permanence by articulating key values and orientations in society. These are then reflected to a greater or lesser degree in the other main genres of theatre, irrespective of whom the audience consists, as well as in the traditional pictorial and plastic arts. So *wayang kulit* helps to ensure a measure of continuity to the systems of social relationships, and as Fürer-Haimendorf (1967, pp. 208–10) has pointed out, a degree of permanence and continuity is an essential condition for any kind of regular social life. It is against this background that insight can be gained into the significance of *wayang kulit* in Balinese culture and society.

Conclusion

So the shadow play, *wayang kulit*, emerges as the most venerated and conservative form of theatre on Bali and one which has profoundly affected the other popular forms of dance-drama as well as the traditional plastic and pictorial arts. It is also an important organizing principle in the daily life of the people. The shadow play's significance must be seen in relation to the emphasis the islanders place on sight. In the hierarchy of the senses it is accorded the greatest value for comprehending the world of men. Yet each performance is ephemeral, a unique event, brought to life by a *dalang* for a particular audience. Through the pattern of lights, movements and sounds articulated during a play, beholders are provided ever afresh with an alternative or new way of looking at things.

Ultimately, however, the dancing shadows on the screen indicate the fact that the mind is fluid, that the lights and shadows which flicker through it have no distinct boundaries and no possibility of permanence. At this point it is worth recalling the words of the servant Tualèn (Plate 40) to his son Merdah in the play dramatized by I Ewer:

> If a jar is filled with clean water, the reflection of the moon will be clear. This also applies to mankind. If their thoughts are pure, a higher truth will be reflected within (p. 161).

It is no mere chance that this is said by Tualèn, the supreme mediator on stage, who exemplifies the status of the world as at once tangible, concrete and immaterial; always baffling, enticing and enigmatic. Though at times foolish, Tualèn is the wisest of the servants who on occasions provides insight into the essence of things. Yet truth is elusive and can only be glimpsed in moments of intuition.

It is, however, important to stress again that a fundamental part of Balinese dance-drama is entertainment. The servants add colour, charm and vitality to the stories by their general frivolity on stage and their spicy, bawdy jokes. Hence the plays allow the spectator freedom to muse and reflect on experience, and in so doing they inevitably help humanize the life of the villagers.

Notes

1 The theme of two (or three) brothers is found throughout much of Indonesia. The younger brother is generally more spiritually developed than the elder one. For accounts of examples describing the relationship of the brothers, see *Bubuksha* (Rassers, 1959, pp. 79–83), myths from Sumba (van Wouden, 1968, pp. 25–30), and the story of Grantang and Cupak on Bali (p. 40).

2 *Dalangs* related each of the senses to dominant traits perceived in the five brothers. Yudistira desires to hear no evil and thinks ill of no man. Bima is tempestuous. Arjuna enjoys looking at beautiful women. Nakula is fluent with words which require the use of the tongue. Sahadéwa is said to be an indigenous medico-ritual practitioner – one who smells many herbs as he requires these for his medicines. Ulbricht (1970, p. 26) in discussing the shadow theatre in Java, correlates the five senses somewhat differently: Yudistira represents smell, Bima hearing, Arjuna sight, Nakula feeling, and Sahadéwa taste.

3 It is interesting that Covarrubias (1965, pp. 281–2) infers a similar purpose to the ceremony *nyepi*, which is held once yearly, when the demons are expelled from the villages.

4 There are a few other *wang* like *wang kuda* (horse), *wang bulan* (moon) or *wang buta* (demon), but as they do not refer to specific characters in *wayang* they are not included here.

5   Zoete and Spies (1973, p. 73) call the two male servants in *arja* Poenta and *wijil*, and in *topèng*, *penasar* and Kartala (*ibid.*, p. 181). In my area they were always simply referred to as the *penasar* and *wijil*, the elder and younger brother respectively.

6   One of the main *babads* used is the *Usana Bali* which recounts the earliest period in Balinese history. The chronicle begins by telling how the holy hermit from Majapahit, Kulputih, founded the mother temple of Bali, Besakih. The legend also alludes to the fact that part of Mount Méru was transferred from India to Bali where it became the holy mountain, Gunung Agung (Swellengrebel, 1960, pp. 16–17).

7   In the legend of Kala Rawu it is told how this demon tried to drink the elixir of immortality. Wisnu caught him in the act and cut off his head. This continued to live as it had some elixir in its mouth. As revenge the demon now swallows up the moon and the sun which produces eclipses (Covarrubias, 1965, p. 299).

8   In the *Adiparwa* it is told how Arjuna violates the voluntary agreement between the five brothers concerning their intercourse with Drupadi. Hence he is forced to go into exile for twelve years (Zoetmulder, 1974, p. 71). It is during this time that he elopes with Sumbadra, Kresna's sister and makes amorous overtures to other women.

9   The best-known troupes in the early 1980s were Dewan Kesenian Denpasar (D.K.D.), Duta Bali and Panji Budaya.

Bibliography

Andersen, B. (1965) *Mythology and the Tolerance of the Javanese*, Ithaca, New York, Cornell University Press.

Bateson, G. and Mead, M. (1942) *Balinese Character: a Photographic Analysis*, New York, New York Academy of Science.

Becker, A. L. (1979) 'Text-building, epistemology, and aesthetic in Javanese Shadow Theatre', in A.L. Becker and Aram A. Yengoyan (ed.) *The Imagination of Reality: Essays in Southeast Asian Coherence Systems*, Norwood, New Jersey, Ablex, pp. 211–41.

Belo, J. (1960) *Trance in Bali*, New York, Columbia University Press.

Belo, J. (1970) 'The Balinese temper', in J. Belo (ed.), *Traditional Balinese Culture*, New York, Columbia University Press, pp. 85–110.

Black, M. (1982) 'More about Metaphor', in A. Ortony (ed.) *Metaphor and Thought*, Cambridge, Cambridge University Press, pp. 19-43.

Boon, J. A. (1977) *The Anthropological Romance of Bali 1597–1972: Dynamic Perspectives in Marriage and Caste, Politics and Religion*, Cambridge, Cambridge University Press.

Bosch, F. D. K. (1960) *The Golden Germ*, The Hague, Mouton.

Brandon, J. R. (1970) *On Thrones of Gold*, Cambridge, Harvard University Press.

Burridge, K. (1979) *Someone, No one: an Essay on Individuality*, Princeton University Press.

Chinkah, (1969) 'Statement of Chinkah on Bali', in *Indonesia*, vol. 7, Ithaca, New York, Cornell University Press, pp. 83–122.

Cohen, P. (1969) 'Theories of myth' in *Man*, New Series, 4, no. 3, pp. 337–53.

Conklin, H. (1955) 'Hanunoo colour terms', in *Southwestern Journal of Anthropology*, II, Albuquerque, University of New Mexico, pp. 339–43.

Covarrubias, M. (1965) *Island of Bali*, New York, Knoff.

Danziger, M. K. and Johnson, W. S. (1967) *An Introduction to Literary Criticism*, Boston, Heath and Company.

215

Douglas, M. (1980) *Purity and Danger*, London, Routledge & Kegan Paul.

Duff-Cooper, A. (1985) 'An account of the Balinese "person" from western Lombok', in *Bijdragen tot de Taal-, Landen Volkenkunde*, 141, Leiden, pp. 67–82.

Durkheim, E. (1976) *The Elementary Forms of the Religious Life*, London, Allen and Unwin.

Eck, R. van (1976) *Balineesch-Hollandsch Woordenboek*, Utrecht, Kemink.

Ehrenzweig, A. (1971) *The Hidden Order of Art*, Los Angeles, University of California Press.

Eliade, Mircea (1974) *Shamanism: Archaic Techniques of Ecstasy*, Bollingen Series LXXVI, London, Routledge & Kegan Paul.

Eliade, Mircea (1974) *The Myth of the Eternal Return*, Bollingen Series XLVI, Princeton University Press.

Ensink, J. (1961) 'Rekhacarmma: on the Indonesian play with special reference to the island of Bali', in *The Adyar Library Bulletin*, Jubilee vol., Madras, pp. 412–41.

Ensink, J. (1967) 'On the Old-Javanese Cantakaparwa and its tale of Sutasoma' in *Verhandelingen Koninklijk Instituut voor Taal-, Land- en Vokenkunde*, 54.

Forge, A. (1978) *Balinese Traditional Painting*, Sydney, The Australian Museum.

Friederich, R. (1959) *The Civilisation and Culture of Bali*. Calcutta, Gupta.

Fürer-Haimendorf, C. von (1967) *Morals and Merit*, London, Weidenfeld & Nicholson.

Geertz, C. (1960) *Religion of Java*, Illinois, The Free Press of Glencoe.

Geertz, C. (1970) *Peddlers and Princes*, Chicago, University of Chicago Press.

Geertz, C. (1973) 'Deep play: notes on the Balinese cockfight' in *The Interpretation of Cultures*, New York, Basic Books, pp. 412–53.

Geertz, C. and Geertz, H. (1975) *Kinship in Bali*, Chicago, University of Chicago Press.

Gennep, A. van (1960) *The Rites of Passage*, London, Routledge & Kegan Paul.

Gettens, R. and Stout, G. (1966) *Painting Materials: a Short Encyclopaedia*, New York, Dover Publications.

Goris, R. (1960) 'Holidays and holy days', in W. F. Wertheim et al. (ed.) *Bali: Studies in Life, Thought and Ritual*, The Hague, Van Hoeve, pp. 113–29.

Guthrie, W. K. C. (1980) *A History of Greek Philosophy*, vol. I, Cambridge, Cambridge University Press.

Hall, D. G. E. (1964) *A History of South East Asia*, London, Macmillan.

Hardjowirogo, (1968) *Sedjarah Wajang Purwa*, Djakarta, Balai Pustaka.

Harrison, J. (1912) *Themis: a Study of the Social Origins of Greek Religion*, Cambridge, Cambridge University Press.

Hazeu, G. A. J. (1897) *Bijdrage tot de Kennis van het Javaansche Tooneel*, Leiden, Brill.

Heine-Geldern, R. (1943) 'Conception of state and kingship in Southeast Asia' in *Far Eastern Quarterly*, New York, American Museum of Natural History, pp. 15–30.

Hidding, K. A. H. (1931) 'De beteekenis van de kekajon' in *Bijdgragen tot de Taal-, Land- en Volkenkunde*, 73, Leiden, pp. 623–62.

Hinzler, H. I. R. (1975) *Wayang op Bali*. The Hague, Nederlandse Vereniging voor het Poppenspel.

Hinzler, H. I. R. (1981) *Bima Swarga in Balinese Wayang*, Verhandelingen Koninklijk Instituut voor Taal-, Land- en Volkenkunde, vol. 90.

Hobart, A. (1983) 'Between things: the place of the Pandasar in Bali' in *Archipel*, 25, Paris, Centre National de la Recherche Scientifique et de L' Institut National des Langues et Civilisations Orientals, pp. 159–70.

Hobart, A. (to be published in 1986) *The Balinese Shadow Figures: their Ritual and Social Significance*, London, British Museum, Occasional Paper.

Hobart, M. (1979) *A Balinese Village and its Field of Social Relations* (unpublished thesis, London, School of Oriental and African Studies).

Holt, C. (1967) *Art in Indonesia: Continuities and Change*, Ithaca, New York, Cornell University Press.

Holt, C. and Bateson, G. (1970) 'Form and function of the dance in Bali' in J. Belo (ed.) *Traditional Balinese Culture*, New York, Columbia University Press, pp. 322–30.

Hooykaas, C. (1955) *The Old-Javanese Ramayana Kakawin*, The Hague, Nijhoff.

Hooykaas, C. (1966) *Surya-Sevana: the Way to God of a Balinese Priest*, Verhandelingen der Koninklijke Nederlandse Akademie van Wetenschappen, 3, Amsterdam, North-Holland.

Hooykaas, C. (1973a) *Religion of Bali*, Leiden, Brill.

Hooykaas, C. (1973b) *Kama and Kala: Materials for the Study of the Shadow Theatre in Bali*, Verhandelingen der Koninklijke Nederlandse Akademie van Wetenschappen, 79, Amsterdam.

Hooykaas, C. (1973c) *Balinese Bauddha Brahmans*, Verhandelingen der Koninklijke Nederlandse Akademie van Wetenschappen, 77, Amsterdam.

Hooykaas, C. (1974) *Cosmogony and Creation in Balinese Tradition*, The Hague, Nijhoff.

Hooykaas, C. (1975) 'Panca-Yajna-s in India and Bali', in *Adyar Library Bulletin*, 34, Madras, pp. 240–59.

Hooykaas, C. (1978) 'Review of: the art and culture of Bali', in *The Times Literary Supplement*, August 18, p. 937.

Hooykaas, J. H. (1955) 'A journey into the realm of death', in *Bijdragen Koninklijk Instituut voor Taal-, Land- en Volkenkunde*, 111, pp. 236–73.

Hooykaas, J. H. (1956) 'The Balinese realm of death' in *Bijdragen Koninklijk Instituut voor Taal-, Land- en Volkenkunde*, 112, pp. 74–87.

Hooykaas, J. H. (1961) *Ritual Purification of a Balinese Temple*, Verhandelingen der Koninklijke Nederlandse Akademie van Wetenschappen, 68, Amsterdam.

Juynboll, H. H. (1906) *Adiparwa, Oudjavaansch Prozageschrift*, The Hague, Martinus Nijhoff.

Kats, J. (1923) *Het Javaansche Tooneel*, Weltevreden.

Kempers, B. A. J. (1959) *Ancient Indonesian Art*, Amsterdam, Peet.

Kersten, P. J. (1970) *Tata Bahasa Bali*, Ende-Flores, Nusa Indal.

Langer, S. (1976) *Feeling and Form*, London, Routledge & Kegan Paul.

217

Leach, E. R. (1958) 'Magical Hair', in *Journal* of the Royal Anthropological Institute, 88, pp. 147–64.

Leach, E. R. (1977) *Political Systems of Highland Burma: a Study of Kachin Social Structure*, University of London, Athlone Press.

Lévi-Strauss, C. (1969) *The Elementary Structures of Kinship*, Boston, Beacon Press.

Lévi-Strauss, C. (1976) *The Savage Mind*, London, Weidenfeld and Nicolson.

Lewis, G. (1980) *Day of Shining Red*, Cambridge, Cambridge University Press.

Lewis, I. M. (1976) *Social Anthropology in Perspective*, Harmondsworth, Penguin Books.

Lienhardt, G. (1961) *Divinity and Experience*, Oxford, Oxford University Press.

Ma Huan (1970) *Ying-yai Sheng-lan, the Overall Survey of the Ocean's Shores* (1433), Cambridge, Cambridge University Press (for the Hakluyt Society).

Mangkunagara VII (1957) *On the Wayang Kulit, Purwa, and its Symbolic and Mystical Elements*, Ithaca, New York, Cornell University Press.

McPhee, C. (1966) *Music in Bali*, New Haven, Yale University Press.

McPhee, C. (1970) 'The Balinese wayang kulit and its music', in J. Belo (ed.) *Traditional Balinese Culture*, New York, Columbia University Press, pp. 146–97.

Mead, M. (1970) 'The arts in Bali', in J. Belo (ed.) *Traditional Balinese Culture*, New York, Columbia University Press, pp. 331–40.

Mellema, R. L. (1954) *Wayang Puppets; Carving, Colouring, Symbolism*, Amsterdam, Royal Tropical Institute.

O'Flaherty, W. D. (1984) *Dreams, Illusion, and Other Realities*, Chicago, Chicago University Press.

Plato (1981) *The Republic*, D. Lee (ed.), Harmondsworth, Penguin Books.

Pigeaud, Th. G. Th. (1929) 'Javaansche wichelarij en klassifikatie' in *Feestbundel Koninklijk Bataviaasch Genootschap*, 2, Weltevreden, pp. 273–90.

Pigeaud, Th. G. Th. (1938) *Javaanse Volksvertoningen: Bijdrage tot de Beschrijving van Land en Volk*, Batavia, Volkslectuur.

Pigeaud, Th. G. Th. (1967) *Literature of Java*, vol. 1, The Hague, Nijhoff.

Peacock, J. L. (1968) *Rites of Modernization: Symbolic and Social Aspects of Indonesian Proletarian Drama*, Chicago, University of Chicago Press.

Pink-Wilpert, C. B. (1975) 'Zur herstellung Balinesische schatten-figurinen', *Mit. aus dem Museum for Volkerkunde*, 5, Hamburg, pp. 47–62.

Pott, P. H. (1966) *Yoga and Yantra*, The Hague, Nijhoff.

Ramseyer, U. (1977) *The Art and Culture of Bali*, Oxford, Oxford University Press.

Rassers, W. H. (1959) *Panji, the Cultural Hero*, The Hague, Nijhoff.

Robson, S. O. (1972) 'The kawi classics in Bali', in *Bijdragen tot de Taal-, Land- en Volkenkunde*, 128, pp. 308–26.

Russell, B. (1918) 'Scientific method in philosophy', in *Mysticism and Logic*, London, Longmans pp. 97–109.

Schärer, H. (1963) *Ngaju Religion: the Conception of God among a South Borneo People*, The Hague, Nijhoff.

Schrieke, B. (1957) *Ruler and Realm in Early Java*, The Hague, Nijhoff.

Schulte Nordholt, H. G. (1971) *The Political System of the Atoni of Timor*, The Hague, Nijhoff.

Skorupski, J. (1976) *Symbol and Theory*, Cambridge, Cambridge University Press.

Soekawati, Tj. G. Raka (1926) 'Sartorial Bali', in *Inter-Ocean*, vol. 9, no. 9, Jakarta, pp. 526–32.

Sperber, dan (1979) *Rethinking Symbolism*, Cambridge, Cambridge University Press.

Steiner, G. (1975) 'Linguistics and poetics' in *Extraterritorial: Papers on Literature and the Language Revolution*, Harmondsworth, Penguin Books, pp. 135–62.

Stutterheim, W. F. (1935) *Indian Influences in Old Balinese Art*, London, India Society.

Stutterheim, W. F. (1956) 'An ancient Javanese Bima cult', in *Studies in Indonesian Archaeology*, The Hague, Nijhoff, pp. 107–42.

Sugriwa, I. Gusti Bagus (1963) *Ilmu Pedalangan/Pewajangan*, Denpasar, Balimas.

Swellengrebel, J. L. (1936) *Korawacrama: een Oud-Javaansch Prozaschrift Uitgegeven, Vertaald en Toegelicht*, Santpoort, Mees.

Swellengrebel, J. L. (1947) *Een Vorstenwijding op Bali naar Material door de Heer A J E F Schwartz*, Meded, Rijksmuseum, Volkenkunde, Leiden.

Swellengrebel, J. L. (1960) 'Introduction', in W. F. Wertheim et. al. (ed.) *Bali: Studies in Life, Thought and Ritual*, The Hague, Van Hoeve, pp. 3–76.

Tambiah, S. H. (1968) 'The magical power of words', in *Man*, vol. 3, no. 2, pp. 175–208.

Turner, V. (1969) *Chihamba: the White Spirit*, Manchester, Manchester University Press, Rhodes-Livingstone Paper, no. 33.

Turner, V. (1977) *The Forest of Symbols: Aspects of Ndembu Ritual*, Ithaca, Cornell University Press.

Turner, V. (1982) *From Ritual to Theatre: the Human Seriousness of Play*, New York, Performing Arts Journal Publications.

Tuuk, H. N. van der (1897–1912) *Kawi-Balineesch-Nederlandsch Woordenboek*, Batavia, Landsdrukkerij.

Uhlenbeck, E. M. (1964) *The Languages of Java and Madura*, The Hague, Nijhoff.

Ulbright, H. (1970) *Wayang Purwa*, Kuala Lumpur, Oxford University Press.

Ullman, S. (1963) 'Semantic Universals' in J. Greenberg (ed.) *Universals of Language*, Cambridge, Massachusetts, M.I.T. Press, pp. 172–201.

Weber, M. (1976) *The Protestant Ethic and the Spirit of Capitalism*, London, Allen and Unwin.

Weck, W. (1937) *Heilkunde und Vokstum auf Bali*, Stuttgart, Enke.

Werbner, R. (1984) 'World renewal: masking in a New Guinea festival', in *Man*, vol. 19, no. 2, pp. 267–89.

Widyatmanta, S. (1968) *Adiparwa*, vols. 1 & 2, Jogjakarta, U.P. Spring.

Wollheim, R. (1970) *Art and its Objects*, Harmondsworth, Penguin Books.

Worsley, P. J. (1972) *Babad Bulèlèng: a Balinese Dynastic Genealogy*, The Hague, Nijhoff.

Wouden, F. A. E. van (1968) *Types of Social Structure in Eastern Indonesia*, The Hague, Nijhoff.

Zoete, B. van and Spies, W. (1973) *Dance and Drama in Bali*, Oxford, Oxford University Press.

Zoetmulder, P. (1965) 'Die hochreligionen Indonesiens', in W. Stöhr & P. Zoetmulder, *Die Religionen Indonesiens*, Stuttgart, Kohlhammer, pp. 223–45.

Zoetmulder, P. (1974) *Kalangwan: a Survey of Old Javanese Literature*, The Hague, Nijhoff.

Index

Page numbers in *italics* refer to tables or diagrams;
postscript 'n' refers to notes and **bold** numbers are plates

Index

Index

www.ingramcontent.com/pod-product-compliance
Ingram Content Group UK Ltd.
Pitfield, Milton Keynes, MK11 3LW, UK
UKHW020356010325
455677UK00021B/482